PRA...

A SPIRITUAL WEAPON FOR PRAYER CHAMPIONS

"Remember the Lord, who is great and glorious, and fight
for your friends, your families, and your homes."
Nehemiah 4:14

365 DAYS OF UNIFIED PRAYER

"I urge you, first of all, to pray for all people. As you make your requests, plead for God's mercy upon them, and give thanks. Pray this way for kings and all others who are in authority, so that we can live in peace and quietness, in godliness and dignity. This is good and pleases God our Savior for He wants everyone to be saved and understand the Truth."

1 Timothy 2:1-4

HOW TO USE THIS BOOK

Knoxville is not different from other cities. The problems
are many; the solution is transformative. The battle in every
city is not against flesh and blood, but against Satan and his
demonic forces that use flesh and blood to oppose the Lord's
work; therefore, to win the battle and reclaim peace in our city
we must use the spiritual equipment that God has provided
(Ephesians 6:10-18; 2 Corinthians 10:1-6). You are holding in your
hand an additional piece of equipment. This book is designed to
mobilize the people of Knoxville and surrounding areas to pray
with a unified and sustained vision. God has enabled multiple
citizens of this community to share in this book of a time when
they sought the Lord during a period of personal transformation.
Each engaged in travailing prayer with a desperation that said,
"We will not let go until we hear from, You, God." Their stories,
scripture verses, and guides for prayer are offered to assist
you in your daily devotional prayer times. Join "together" with
other people in the Name of Jesus in a time of unified prayer
so that God will hear and answer (Matthew 18:20). Community
transformation, at every level, occurs when a culture is impacted
by God. God has called each of us to unleash His power on
Knoxville and make that transformation occur!

God is the God of destiny and we are a people of destiny;
therefore, focused and intentional prayer must become a priority
in our lives. Through the pages of this book we have the
opportunity to make prayer our offensive plan and use the
targeted prayers on each page to assist us in having a heart to
pray, an eye to see, and an ear to hear. Each page will also help
us:
• Strengthen our prayer lives.
• Direct our attention to the needs of the people in the
  community.
• Invite God into Knoxville and surrounding areas.
• Pray with clarity, authority, relevance, and in alignment
  with scripture.

There are 260 days of sequential weeks of prayer and devotions in this book. That is one daily time of focusing on God per week-day for fifty-two weeks. The daily format for each devotion is the same.

This means that you will accept the prayer challenge daily all week and stand in the gap for others in the community. However, Prayer Champions emulate Jesus seven days a week, so that leaves two days unscripted for our spiritual intake; therefore, we will not stop on FRIDAY and start again on MONDAY. Keep your PrayKnox Devotion Book nearby. We will use the weekend to expand our prayer lives and opportunities for spiritual growth, even though they are often busy times in family life. That expansion will include our family, others in our circle of influence, and new friends in our PrayKnox family. Consider using the following format.

Saturday: Family Day

• Revisit the MONDAY through FRIDAY guide just completed and join all family members together in prayer over the specific PRAYER TARGETs.

• Hold a family discussion about the devotions from the previous week and how you can apply them to your family and daily life.

• If no family members are available, be sure to connect with church members, friends or associates.

Sunday: Connection Day

• Connect with a new Prayer Champion outside your circle of influence, preferably someone within the PrayKnox movement.

Suggestions for reaching out:

1. Begin a new relationship with someone at the monthly prayer gathering.

2. Connect by phone or in person to follow the first two instructions under Family Day.

Note: If Saturday or Sunday absolutely cannot fit into your lifestyle, please be sure to select the day best for you and your prayer circle. While the above prayer schedule is strongly encouraged, the most important part is that you are praying with those closest to you and other PRAYKNOX Prayer Champions on a weekly basis.

An effective city-wide prayer ministry requires ongoing attention, spiritual alertness, and gratitude. Give your gratitude to the individual authors of the devotions when you see them. They are your friends and neighbors. Offer them a word of encouragement and praise. John Dawson in Taking Our Cities for God says, "Our cities are the keys to winning the world for Christ. They are encumbered by staggering problems and opposed by cosmic forces, yet these vast urban centers hold millions of people whom God loves." Pray for the people God loves, but remember that only God can make true and lasting change and He will do it through prayer. Your prayer! The transformative solution!

Live in a state of prayerful readiness. Enjoy the PRAYKNOX Devotional expereince.

"For I know the plans I have for you, declares the Lord, plans for welfare and not for evil, to give you a future and a hope."
Jeremiah 29:11

FORWARD

We are a world of people in need of a galaxsphere - like love. We are a people of many cultures, ethnicities, backgrounds, fundamentals, beliefs, all are which aren't always in cohesion. We come in all shapes, sizes, and colors. We disagree, misconstrue, and often misunderstand one another; but, yeah, despite all this, we have been chosen! We all have been chosen to share this beautiful earth, the one that God created and in which He intended for us all to reside until our expected end. Therefore, we are responsible for its maintenance and to uphold its beauty. How then can we value the lives of others if we fail to value the lives of ourselves? Your birth was a response to God's love, which means your being here has purpose. That purpose involves keeping His Commandments, continually seeking His Face, and praying without ceasing. John 14:15 tells it to us by saying, "If you love me then keep my Commandments." You may ask, how are we able to commune with God in an uninterrupted manner when we have work, kids playing, dogs barking, babies crying, our favorite television show running, Netflix available to binge watch, and social media buzzing with the latest gossip! How are we able to have time for God?

We find the excuse that making time for God is nearly impossible because of the frenzy of our lives. That is coupled with the problem of our perspective of prayer. Along the way we've become philosophically damaged. God has given us all the tools we need to pray every single day and to do so without ceasing. We can do this even with children and work, raising a family, and using Netflix. We have everything we need to pray without ceasing. Prayer is not a monologue, rather it is a dialogue between you and our Father.

Take a look at this book that you are holding. It will help you solve many problems of how to pray. Taking action on the prayer recommendations will be beneficial to help you increase your dialogue with God. It will even enable you to begin to follow His

Commandments – one of the biggest being to simply always communicate with Him! Through this book you may ask Him His thoughts, gain clarification on subjects and issues that you may face, and even request permission to have access to certain ventures you want to achieve in life. If you allow this book, along with your Bible, to become your social media, your Netflix, and your new healthy distraction, then not only will you see your life turn around but also your entire community. We don't need change, we need changers! This book gives you the opportunity to be that changer– to change lives, build a community, and start a commanded- movement. Be the change now by responding to the call. Read and pray!!

I pray you enjoy this book!

Chris Blue

"If my people, who are called by my name, will humble themselves and pray and seek my face and turn from their wicked ways, then I will hear from heaven, and I will forgive their sin and will heal their land."
2 Chronicles 7:14

OPENING PRAYERS

My prayer is for every brother and sister to experience a spirit of unity while reading this book and all division be eliminated from our city.

> Antoine Davis- Vols for Life Coordinator
> Former Football Player

I pray that God will open our hearts, minds, and souls to see the possibility of unity in our community.

> David B. Rausch – Police Chief,
> Knoxville Police Department

My prayer is that we will have an experience with God that causes us to pray like Jesus, love like Jesus and live as if we know the answer to everything is love.

> Hallerin Hilton Hill – Radio and TV Host

I pray we will experience the presence of the Lord with us and we receive the desire of our hearts to grow closer to Him.

> Jenny Bushkell – Christian Talk Radio Personality,
> Joy 620 WRJZ

My prayer is that we will be richly blessed and encouraged as we read these daily devotionals and grow more in love with our Savior. (Romans 8:37-39)

> Jim Vandersteeg – CEO of Covenant Health

God is the one who has drawn us together. He called us to make his name great and make his name known for his Kingdom. I pray we will become one and deepen our unity.

> Mi Jung Kang – International Ministry Leader,
> Providence Church

I pray we all become more dependent on prayer to solve our problems by allowing God to move us by His Holy Spirit and direct our steps.

Tim Harris – Owner of Knoxville Wholesale Furniture

As we kneel before our Father, may the Spirit of the Lord lift us up as one. I pray we possess the land God has promised us and souls be set free.

Theresa M. Gergis –Women's Ministry Leader Arabic

My prayer is that we would not act before we pray, but through committing to the action of prayer we would receive divine instruction.

Vrondelia (Ronni) Chandler – Executive Director, Project Grad

May we, your children, be found faithful to love you above all. Help us love and serve one another as well as pray for each other's needs in a way that honors you. Finally, empower us to be your ambassadors to those in the city who don't know you.

Yamil Gonzales – International Student Ministry Leader, Physical Therapist

PRAYKNOX IS A MULTIETHNIC, MULTIGENERATIONAL PRAYER MOVEMENT AIMED AT UNIFYING THE BODY OF CHRIST FOR THE SPREAD OF THE GOSPEL AND THE LOVE OF JESUS.

JEREMIAH 29:7 | JOHN 17:20-21

"Behold, how good and how pleasant it is for brethren to dwell together in unity! It is like the precious oil upon the head, running down on the beard, The beard of Aaron, running down on the edge of his garments. It is like the dew of Hermon, descending upon the mountains of Zion; For there the LORD commanded the blessing— Life forevermore."
Psalm 133

11

WEEK ONE: MONDAY

AUTHOR: SPENCER BARNARD
FAMILY STRUCTURE: WIFE AND 4 CHILDREN
OCCUPATION: ASSOCIATE/TEACHING PASTOR

COURAGEOUSLY WALKING OUT MY CALLING

"Have I not commanded you? Be strong and courageous. Do not be frightened, and do not be dismayed, for the Lord your God is with you wherever you go." Joshua 1:9

Since I was a kid one of my biggest internal struggles has been fear and anxiety. Fear is one of those things that stops me in my tracks. Fear also fragments my faith, and so often it keeps me from having God's best in my life.

A couple years ago my family and I felt God calling us to step out of a very successful, comfortable job and move to a new city. Fear and anxiety started to creep in. I was doing well financially, relationally, and building influence with-in my organization. Now I felt that God was calling me to something new. To step out would lead me down a road of uncertainty. For weeks, my wife and I prayed and asked God to make things extremely clear. The questions and fears began to creep in; *"What if financially I can't make it? What if the people there don't except me? What if this doesn't work out in the long run? What if God doesn't come through in the end?"*

It all came to a head one afternoon while I was parked in my truck behind my office building praying for an answer. I often would spend time alone with God there because I knew no one would disturb me. While I was praying, I had put my head down on the steering wheel and cried out to God concerning my fears. As I finished my prayer I lifted my head and saw that an eighteen- wheeler had gotten lost on its delivery and somehow found its way to a spot behind our office building. The truck had parked directly in front of me. On the driver's side door of the eighteen- wheeler was the name of the organization to which God had called our family. It was as if God was saying to me, *"Have I not commanded you? Be strong and courageous. Do not be frightened, and do not be dismayed, for the Lord your God is with you wherever you go."* I learned at that moment, and forward, that it is not as much about the destination to which God is calling me as it is about me trusting Him wherever He takes me. Pastor Charles Stanley once said, *"God takes full responsibility for the life wholly devoted to Him."* My job is to courageously walk out my calling; His job is the results that will glorify Him through me.

PRAYER TARGET:

For strength and courage in the face of wherever and whatever God is calling you to.

PERSONAL PRAYER FOR KNOXVILLE:

God, let us not live frightened or dismayed, but help each of us be strong and courageous in our gifts and our callings. We know, God, that You are with us wherever we go! We are trusting you, Jesus, for a God given vision through our obedience, and then we are trusting you, God, with the results of that calling in our lives.

WEEK ONE: TUESDAY

AUTHOR: CAROL HOUSER
FAMILY STRUCTURE: HUSBAND, ONE SON, THREE GRANDCHILDREN
OCCUPATION: RETIRED

CAN GOD USE ME

"Older women likewise are to be reverent in behavior, not slanderers or slaves to much wine. They are to teach what is good, and so train the young women to love their husbands and children, to be self-controlled, pure, working at home, kind, and submissive to their own husbands, that the word of God may not be reviled." Titus 2:3-5

I am a daughter, a sister, a wife, a mother, a grandmother, an aunt, and a friend. I have been very poor, somewhat poor, almost poor, and middle class. I have been a working wife and mother and a stay-at-home grandmother. I am a natural introvert but, in allowing God to use me as He sees fit, I have been changed into an extrovert. I say all this not to brag on myself in any way, but to emphasize the fact that God can use us at any stage of life, from any social strata, and in any financial position. He does not need me in any way, but He wants to use me to further His Kingdom. Do you know someone shy who just needs a friend? Do you have a friend who is headed toward disaster in her marriage or her job and needs someone to be lovingly honest with her? Do you know a young mom who is struggling and has no one with whom to just "rant without being judged?" Are you seeing a pattern here? Did you think God could not use you because you were too.......? You don't have to be able to speak in front of large groups, be dazzlingly beautiful, have money to give away, or be the best teacher anyone ever heard for God to use you in someone's life.

Just be available! Let God use you!

PRAYER TARGET:
Women struggling with insecurity and questioning God's use of them.

PERSONAL PRAYER FOR KNOXVILLE:
God, let each of us look for one person who needs an ability that each of us has to offer: one person who needs a special friend, one person who is hungry to study God's promises, or someone who just needs a friend like me to do this with her. This is what the scripture in Titus is telling us; we don't have to be a grandmother to be a mentor. We just need to make ourselves available. So, make us available, Lord, and let God lead us in what to do and say. May each woman in my city give God control of her life and give You glory in what You do in and through each person.

WEEK ONE: WEDNESDAY

AUTHOR: JEFF DEW
FAMILY STRUCTURE: WIFE AND 2 CHILDREN
OCCUPATION: PHYSICIAN PRACTICE MANAGER

DON'T MISS OUT ON WHAT GOD MEANS FOR GOOD

"As for you, you meant to harm me, but God intended it for a good purpose, so he could preserve the lives of many people, as you can see this day." Genesis 50:20

Many years ago, a trusted friend and fellow believer betrayed me to our mutual boss, and as the saying goes, "threw me under the bus." The incident caused me to go through some difficult and uncertain times in my job. This event happened at the same time when my wife and I had just built a house, were raising a young daughter, and had another child on the way. As I sat at home one night during this period, railing against the individual who aggrieved me and thinking on what had done to me, my wife stopped me in the middle of my tantrum and said very directly, *"You are bitter! This is not you. It is time for you to get with the Lord, find out what He is trying to tell you, and figure out what He wants to do in your life…in our lives."* As I started to pray with purpose, God opened a more rewarding position for me. The new offer was only three hours away and took my career trajectory to an entirely different level. During the following time of transition, God drew me into a dialog. It was during those conversations with Him that He shaped my theology of who He is, who I am, and how He works in the lives of believers. It shaped my theology of how sovereign He is in a world that is filled with sin and disappointment. It gave me fresh and tangible sense of just how much He loves me.

PRAYER TARGET:
Believers who have been wronged.

PERSONAL PRAYER FOR KNOXVILLE:
Dear God, let every believer in this city understand the ability that You as a sovereign God have to act for our benefits and betterment - even when we can't see the good. Father, I pray that we would look not at what is happening to us, but instead what You what want to do through us. May we not walk around in bitterness and defeat. Guide us in looking at our perceived disappointments and setbacks as road makers. Help us see where we are going and keep us on the path that You have chosen. Father, may I always look to see where You are working in my life and know that You are doing it so that I may be a blessing to others particularly, "the least of these".

WEEK ONE: THURSDAY

AUTHOR: SCOTT CAGLE
FAMILY STRUCTURE: WIFE, 2 CHILDREN, AND 1 GRANDSON
OCCUPATION: LEAD PASTOR

BEFORE YOU CALL

> **"Before they call I will answer; while they are still speaking I will hear." Isaiah 65:24**

Helen Roseveare was a medical missionary to the Country of Zaire in Central Africa. One night after helping deliver an extremely premature baby girl, she was fearful that the child would not live without the help of an incubator. The next day when sharing this prayer request with some small children at a close-by orphanage, a little 10-year-old girl named Ruth boldly prayed that God would send a rubber hot water bottle to keep the baby warm, and a little doll as well, to show her His love. The missionary gasped at the audacity of the prayer, knowing the only way it could happen was through a parcel from the States which she had never received in her four years of serving. Later that afternoon that very type parcel was unexpectedly dropped at her door. Stuffed with all kinds of supplies including a hot water bottle and a small baby doll sent by a little girls' Sunday School class, the package had been mailed from the states four months before! What a mighty God we serve!

I have been praying for spiritual awakening and revival to sweep through the city of Knoxville and the mountains of east Tennessee for the past 23 years. I feel, sense and see the birth pains of this all around us. I know that the Father has put people and resources in motion for several years in advance for us all to see this come to be – just as He made it possible for the hot water bottle to be sent to a foreign country that had a great need for it.

PRAYER TARGET:
Unified prayers of faith to be expectant of His great works!

PERSONAL PRAYER FOR KNOXVILLE:
Father, we believe that You desire spiritual awakening and revival in our city and region even more than we do. Continue, we pray, to send the people and resources for this move of your Spirit to our city from across the world. Lord Jesus, give us all a childlike faith to believe this movement will happen, even when we can't see it! Do this, Lord, in Your time and in Your ways. Do it in such a way that You get all the glory and that it increases our belief in this thing we call payer! We pray all these things in the powerful and precious name of Jesus! Amen.

WEEK ONE: FRIDAY

AUTHOR: HALLERIN HILL
FAMILY STRUCTURE: WIFE AND 2 CHILDREN
OCCUPATION: RADIO AND TV HOST

FROM TRYING TO TRUSTING

> "I will sprinkle clean water on you, and you shall be clean from all your uncleanness, and from all your idols I will cleanse you. And I will give you a new heart, and a new spirit I will put within you. And I will remove the heart of stone from your flesh and give you a heart of flesh. And I will put my Spirit within you, and cause you to walk in my statutes and be careful to obey my rules." Ezekiel 36:25-27

My brother, one of my greatest mentors, shared this verse with me. He was clear about God's love and grace and it was his immense joy to walk me deeper into the paths of the love of God. I think he saved my life with this verse.

One day I was frustrated with myself. I was tired of trying. I could feel Paul when he said, *"The good that I would…"* That's when my brother told me to stop trying and start trusting. He told me that God promised to do the work and said directly to me, *"Hallerin, let Him!"*

Look at the verse above. He says, *"I will, I will, I will, I will."* God promises to change your heart and your spirit. Moreover, He promises to give you His spirit and to "cause" you to walk His way. My brother told me there is a magnetic force that will draw you to Him if you get out of the way and give up the notion that He needs your help. Think of the Scripture, *"If I be lifted up I will draw all men unto me."*

"Therefore, Hallerin," He says, "Let Him 'cause' you."

PRAYER TARGET:

That the men of Knoxville would stop trying so hard and learn to trust in Him.

PERSONAL PRAYER FOR KNOXVILLE:

Father, I ask You to do the work You promised to do. First clean us up. Take down the idols that stand in the way of us loving You. And then get to work with the heart transplant. Hearts are hard. Many in the city are like stone. Stoney hearts don't beat. Please remove the stones and give us fleshy, receptive hearts. Change our spirit. Reset our desires. May we joyfully yearn for You. And then fill us with Your Spirit. Give us that promised latter rain. "Cause" us. Take us from trying to trusting. Pull us home with the magnetic force of your never- ending love. My prayer is that every man in this city would be filled with God's spirit and that he would go from trying to trusting. May every man feel the magnetic force of God's spirit pulling him, "causing" him to be all that God intends for him to be. And we claim this as done in the name of our Lord and Savior Jesus Christ. Amen.

AUTHOR: MELISSA LLOYD
FAMILY STRUCTURE: HUSBAND, 2 DAUGHTERS AND SONS-IN-LAW AND 4 GRANDCHILDREN
OCCUPATION: WRITER, COMPOSER, BIBLE STUDY TEACHER AND SPEAKER, AND OFFICE MANAGER

RAISE THE ROOF

> **"Jesus stepped into a boat, crossed over and came to his own town. Some men brought to Him a paralyzed man, lying on a mat. When Jesus saw their faith, He said to the man, "Take heart, son; your sins are forgiven."**
>
> **So He said to the paralyzed man, "Get up, take your mat and go home." Then the man got up and went home. When the crowd saw this, they were filled with awe; and they praised God, who had given such authority to man."**
> **Matthew 9:1-2, 6a-8**

Looking into his eyes, followed by a bitter season of emotional war, drained by heartbreak, staring, lifeless, numb, convinced any true feeling would prove lethal given his heart's fragility, made a pervasive sadness swept over me. Sadness quickly mingled with the aching realization that I couldn't fix it. His paralysis of soul, bound by weeks of crushing betrayal, left him stuck in the place where he'd given up.

Yet, in this story, even hopelessness doesn't hinder God's healing. This paralytic's only hope is the hope of his friends who carry the full weight of his hopelessness to the Only One who can take it away. Their reckless expectation raises the roof, revealing the Great I Am's invitation to be present, to remove the filters of past disappointments and future inevitabilities, as all possibilities become unpredictable when flung into hands that wield limitless power. Jesus bends, whispering, *"Take heart."*

It's a single word in the Greek, "tharseo," meaning "boldness." With one word, this God of right here, right now, reaches into the darkness where broken desires hide among the ruins, regenerating muscles long atrophied by disuse, muscles with no memory of believing, or even asking, to urge us, *"Be bold! Ask big! Believe!"*

PRAYER TARGET:
The brokenhearted in our city.

PERSONAL PRAYER FOR KNOXVILLE:
O God, we come to You carrying the full weight of those in our city who have lost all hope in the face of devastating hurt, abandonment or betrayal. We come today to ask big. We come to be bold in Your presence because we know You. We know Who You are, the Restorer of Souls, the Redeemer of all that's been wrecked and ravaged by sin, the One Who came to bind up the brokenhearted, that Place where we can begin again. Pull us from the ruins of the wounds of our past. Free us from the paralysis of our fears. Awaken hope in us. Defeat the onslaught of the enemy's attack on homes and families and relationships that You created to give us refuge. Make us brave. Empower us to forgive. Beckon us to believe that beauty can be found among these ashes because of You, Lord Jesus, because You love us too much to leave us where we are. Rewrite our stories to be all about what You did among us by Your extravagant grace. In the name of Jesus, we ask big, believing that You can, that You will, that You want to! Amen.

WEEK TWO: TUESDAY

AUTHOR: PHIL YOUNG
FAMILY STRUCTURE: WIFE, 3 CHILDREN, 2 SONS-IN-LAW, AND
2 GRANDCHILDREN
OCCUPATION: DIRECTOR OF MISSIONS

SO MUCH MORE, INDEED!

> **"They will rebuild the ancient ruins and restore the places long devastated; they will renew the ruined cities that have been devastated for generations." Isaiah 61:4**

Lord, there must be more to it than this!" These were the words that came out of my mouth in frustration. I was the pastor of a good church with good people and useful resources . . . yet it seemed that we had little impact on the lives of people in our city. In the days that followed, I was drawn into reflection by the words of the prophet Isaiah (61:1-4); the prophetic words which Jesus Himself fulfilled.

I began to realize that there was "more to it" than what I was seeing. It was about more than just making people comfortable and happy – it was about finding our complete healing in Jesus (61:1-2). It was about more than trying to make "bad people be good" – it was about making people who were "dead" in sin become "alive" in Christ (61:3). It was about more than making a name for ourselves as a "good church" – it was about extending our influence to make His name great (61:3). And it was about more than being a "good church with good people and useful resources" – it was about rebuilding, restoring, and renewing the city (lives) that had been devastated for generations (61:4).

There really is more to it than what we often see . . . so much more indeed!

PRAYER TARGET:

The Church-remembering the focus on His Glory.

PERSONAL PRAYER FOR KNOXVILLE:

Lord, I pray for the Church in our city. At times, we seem so focused upon our own desires and preferences that we fail to see the needs that paint the picture of lives that have been devastated for generations. Open our eyes, Lord, that we may see what you see. Open not just our eyes, but the "eyes of our hearts." May Your Church be filled with a passion to be more about healing than happiness; more about bringing life than being good; more about making Your Name glorious than making a name for ourselves; and more about being a church that rebuilds, restores, and renews our city . . . one life at a time. In the Name of Jesus we pray, Amen.

WEEK TWO: WEDNESDAY

AUTHOR: JASON HAYES
FAMILY STRUCTURE: WIFE AND 3 SONS
OCCUPATION: PASTOR

GOD ALWAYS REMAINS

In Colossians 1:17, Paul describes Jesus by saying, "He is before all things, and by Him all things hold together." We're reminded in Revelation 1:8 that God is "the One Who is, Who was, and Who is coming, the Almighty." In Jeremiah 10:10 proclaims, "The LORD is the true God; He is the living God and eternal King."

Scriptures like the ones above remind me that while the things of this world are fleeting, God always remains. Change is inevitable. My hunch is that many of you are experiencing some critical changes in your lives as well. Maybe you have a new baby in your home. Or maybe your baby is now grown up and moved away from home. Maybe a loved one is fighting illness. Or maybe you're fighting illness. It really could be anything – personal or professional.

Some of the things that once seemed most stable in your lives are now everything but that. My encouragement to you is to reflect upon the steady, faithful nature of God. Find your rest and hope in Him. He is very much aware of your circumstances and He remains very much in control of them all.

PRAYER TARGET:
The Church-remembering the focus on His Glory.

PERSONAL PRAYER FOR KNOXVILLE:
Father, I pray that you would bring peace to those who are in the midst of chaos. I pray that you would remind us of Your faithful,

steady hand despite the fleeting things of this world. May we all find our rest and hope in you. And may You be the center of our lives and the joy in our hearts. Amen!

WEEK TWO: THURSDAY

AUTHOR: ALICIA CHERRY
FAMILY STRUCTURE: HUSBAND, 2 DAUGHTERS, 2 SONS IN LAW, AND 5 GRANDCHILDREN
OCCUPATION: HOUSE WIFE

HE IS MY SPOTLIGHT

"I am the light of the world. Whoever follows me will not walk in darkness, but will have the light of life. John 8:12

The phrase dysfunctional family has nothing on me. There were loud, mean, ugly words, hitting, screaming, bloodshed, alcohol, craziness; all were common in our home when I was a little girl. I would hide in a room, or a closet, or outside and cover my ears to block out the noise because I was so afraid. I just wanted to get away from it all. I had no clue how to deal with my fear early on, but I would cry out to Jesus for help and He would protect me.

Later, as I went to middle school age, I realized Jesus too, had heard screaming. It was directed at Him. He was called bad names. He was beaten. He shed his blood and then He died for the sins of the people throughout the world. He didn't hide from it; He gave his life freely. As I became older I came to realize that Christ is in me and because of Him, I am free. I have only to call upon Him.

We all need to ask Him to shine His light on us and whatever we are going through. That may be done by calling on Him in prayer and reading His Word, the Bible. I'm here today; I was spared. I now know that He was always with me, and I live in the peace that He still is here. He placed His light on my situation and saw me through several sad situations. I am living testimony that He can place His light and peace on any event in your lives today just as He did me. He truly is our light in a dark world!

PRAYER TARGET:
People seeking the One that counts-the light in this dark world.

PERSONAL PRAYER FOR KNOXVILLE:
Father God, I'm thanking You for Your wonderful grace and mercy. My prayer is that every person in our area would realize that You are always with them, no matter where they are, or what they are going through. Each of us in Knoxville need to call out to You and seek Your face. Protect our marriages and families: protect them from the enemy, protect them from violence, evil, drugs, and harm. I ask that all seek your face Father, for you don't give us a spirit of fear, but of power, love, and a sound mind. Father God, protect and heal our hearts. Unify each of us with brotherly love. Father, help us turn our eyes upon you and look full in Your wonderful face, so the things of earth will grow strangely dim, in the light of Your glory and grace. Thank you right now for all You are going to do, in Your name, Jesus Christ. Amen.

WEEK TWO: FRIDAY

AUTHOR: MARINA DAGERMANDZHYAN FAMILY
FAMILY STRUCTURE: HUSBAND AND 3 CHILDREN
OCCUPATION: HOUSE WIFE

LET'S SPREAD THE JOY OF JESUS

"These things have I spoken into you, that my joy might remain in you, and that your joy might be full." John 15:11

I am a busy mom of 3 little kids. Sometimes I feel like life is going ahead and I am running behind it. However, we as Christians should always remember that we have people around us, and something as simple as a smiling face can have a positive impact on our families and the world.

Sometimes, amid the busyness of life here on earth, we may forfeit the joy that God intends for us to experience and share. Even on life's most difficult days, we may rest assured that God is in His heaven, and He still cares for us. Peace and joy are God's precious gifts, the intangible gifts offered to us and our families daily.

PRAYER TARGET:
Busy moms of the city.

PERSONAL PRAYER FOR KNOXVILLE:
Dear Father, let every busy mom in this city spread joy around generously. May every mom remember that a joyful family starts with joyful parents. Father, I ask You to help all moms redirect their thinking from negative to positive and to remember that we should always reflect God's joy in our lives through our daily behaviors with our families. In the name of Jesus. Amen.

WEEK THREE: MONDAY

AUTHOR: DENNIS SHARP
FAMILY STRUCTURE: WIFE, 2 CHILDREN AND 6 GRANDCHILDREN
OCCUPATION: PASTOR, AUTHOR, SERVANT LEADER

FIRST BE RECONCILED TO YOUR BROTHER

"Therefore, if you bring your gift to the altar, and there remember that your brother has something against you, leave your gift there before the altar, and go your way. First be reconciled to your brother, and then come and offer your gift." Matthew 5:23-24

A first century Jew hearing Jesus' words in this passage would have heard a deeper meaning than many of us would normally hear. For them bringing a gift to the altar was an act of worship. Jesus was saying, "Your worship is not authentic until you have been reconciled to your brother. You must go first and fix that relationship before you bring your worship to the Father." Why would Jesus put such a premium on reconciliation?

The night before Jesus was arrested, He spoke these words: *"By this everyone will know that you are my disciples, if you love one another." (John 13:35) Later He prayed this prayer: "I do not pray for these alone, but also for those who will believe in Me through their word; that they all may be one, as You, Father, are in Me, and I in You; that they also may be one in Us, that the world may believe that You sent Me."(John 17:20-21)* Reconciliation is so important because it is through our love that the world recognizes us as Jesus' disciples. Only when we are one in Him does the world recognize that it was the Father who sent Him.

PRAYER TARGET:
Leadership of the local gatherings in the Churches of Knoxville and surrounding areas.

PERSONAL PRAYER FOR KNOXVILLE:

Father, I ask that You answer this prayer for Jesus to come into the City of Knoxville and surrounding areas. Holy Spirit, come and make us one in Him. Grant to Your Church the grace of repentance. Lord, we have been competitive with one another instead of cooperative, and have, thereby, failed to impact our city for Christ the way that He deserves. May we put aside our differences in all disputable matters, and instead join forces for Christ around the Lordship of Jesus and the core essentials of the Gospel. Father, we ask for boldness to proclaim the Good News about Jesus the way that it should be proclaimed, and for Holy Spirit empowering in each of us to live out the truth of that same Gospel. Holy Spirit come and accompany the proclamation of the Gospel and a give us a unified Church with demonstrations of Your power.

WEEK THREE: TUESDAY

AUTHOR: KENZIE CARLSON
FAMILY STRUCTURE: DAD, MOM, BROTHER
OCCUPATION: STUDENT AT UT

HE HAS WON THE WAR

"Stop your fighting --- and know that I am God, exalted among the nations, exalted on the earth." Psalm 46:10.

The other day I was texting my friend and I said something about, *"What would happen if there were no guns or bombs or weapons in the world? What if we just talked things out? How much better would life be?"* The world today is filled with conflict. Republicans versus democrats versus liberals; pro-life versus pro-choice; black versus white; man versus woman; heterosexuals versus the LGBTQ community. The list is long and goes on.

Everyone has their opinions of what is right or wrong. Some people are more outspoken than others. In my opinion, it wouldn't be so bad for us to believe different things if we weren't so hateful when we say them. If someone voices their opinion in today's society it is typical for another person to start to degrade that opinion, all while exalting themselves. Pride overtakes the situation and then everyone is upset.

I've never been one to voice my opinions much, simply because I don't want anyone to get angry and I don't want to get in a fight with anyone - especially someone I consider a friend. I get uncomfortable, then things get awkward for me. Instead, I just sit back with my own opinions and know that God is bigger than all of it. It doesn't matter who the president is - God is King and He is sovereign. The best thing is that He knows what is going to happen. He knows the outcome of the world. He has complete control and He will never be surprised. The Bible assures me of this. As Christians, we shouldn't argue or hate. We should simply love. Let people have their opinions, and if you voice yours and they don't agree, it's okay. No one has to win. Let's all sit back and be fat and happy because we know our God, the Creator and Savior of the universe. He will be exalted in everything because He has already won.

PRAYER TARGET:
College students-being bold and unafraid to speak truth!

PERSONAL PRAYER FOR KNOXVILLE:
Father, as a college student at the University of Tennessee, I get things thrown in my face every day at school. There are presidential protests and pro-life movements and LGBTQ rallies. There are people who will come and try to talk about religion as I walk to classes. Father, I pray for the Christian students, that they can learn to love those who acknowledge everything except God. I pray for the unbelieving students, that they would open their hearts and their minds. Father, please open their ears to hear things about God and His greatness instead of the trivial things of this world. Help them learn that God has won a war against death. Father, thank You that the knowledge of this is a fact against which no one can argue.

WEEK THREE: WEDNESDAY

AUTHOR: STEVE HUMPHERYS
FAMILY STRUCTURE: WIFE AND 2 CHILDREN
OCCUPATION: NON-PROFIT EXECUTIVE DIRECTOR

GOD'S LAW - MY HEART

"This is the covenant I will make with the people of Israel after that time," declares the LORD. "I will put my law in their minds and write it on their hearts. I will be their God, and they will be my people. " Jeremiah 31:33

The year was 1997. I was struggling with God's purpose for my life. I had been a CPA for almost twenty years and suffered "major" depression. Now, I felt God calling me to full-time prison ministry, but I followed that feeling with a question: *"Would God really ask a man to give up a lucrative career to serve Him full time?"* I knew the answer to that because of a previous experience. Through study of the information in the Experiencing God class, God laid a relative on my heart. The person had been convicted of killing his mother and twelve-year-old brother, and I was being "asked" to visit him. I didn't want to go so I procrastinated until week nine of the class when the topic was on "obedience." The author's question in that chapter struck an impenetrable chord in my heart when he asked, *"Do you think God would give new assignments to a servant who had not obeyed what He previously commanded?"* I realized at that moment, that if I were to ever have God reveal any more of His will for my life, I had to be obedient to what He had already asked me to do.

I arranged to go to the prison for a first-time visit. I was scared but when I was taken into the visitation gallery, God showed me that these men were just like me except for a white stripe on their blue jeans that read TDOC. Many of them were being visited by spouses and children. As I watched their interchange

God did heart surgery on me - the uncompassionate Christian. He removed my stony heart and replaced it with a heart of flesh. That night I prayed about what I had experienced. God impressed on me the words above from Jeremiah. The Holy Spirit said, "Son, consider the laws of men. They may not change the men, but when I write My laws upon their hearts, they will be changed forever." I then felt directed by God to go and teach Experiencing God in prison to help the inmates learn about the incredible love God has for them. Looking back on my teaching of this class, I know that I began a long walk of faith that has given me, and others, a true purpose for, and an abundance in, life.

PRAYER TARGET:
Men struggling with "Purpose."

PERSONAL PRAYER FOR KNOXVILLE:
Father, I know there are men all over this city who are struggling with letting You be the number one priority in their lives. You have spoken Truth for men to hear that says, "Unless you love Me more than anything else in life, you cannot be My disciple." God, give them bold spirits to run after You regardless of the cost. Help them learn that You are the only thing worth giving their lives to this side of heaven. I pray that each would passionately pursue an intimate love relationship with You that will give their lives true meaning and purpose. I love You Father. Help us to be pleasing to You and bring honor to Your name today. Amen.

WEEK THREE: THURSDAY

AUTHOR: JANIE WEAVER
FAMILY STRUCTURE: SINGLE, PARENT, SIBLINGS, NIECE AND NEPHEW
OCCUPATION: HUMAN RESOURCES INFORMATION SYSTEMS SPECIALIST

OUR GOD IS WITH US

"For I know the thoughts that I think toward you, says the Lord, thoughts of peace and not of evil, to give you a future and a hope. Then you will call on Me and come and pray to Me, and I will listen to you. You will seek Me and find Me when you seek Me with all your heart." Jeremiah 29: 11-13

For most of my life I concentrated on Jeremiah 29:11, finding comfort in the knowledge that the Lord had plans for me, that He is not surprised by anything in life. Then one day I kept reading and discovered that, not only did God have plans, He planned on me seeking Him out. The Lord planned on me needing Him; but, just as importantly, He planned on answering! God did not intend for me to go through life alone! He gave us loved ones, yes, but He gave us so much more....Himself! When we are saved by grace, we find hope, peace and faithfulness for every day. God waits for us to realize we need Him, and He delights in answering us!

PRAYER TARGET:
All who seek hope, feeling hopeless.

PERSONAL PRAYER FOR KNOXVILLE:
Father, I pray for everyone who is hurting, confused, lonely or in need, no matter what. May they know that You, Lord Jesus, are not a distant and uninterested overseer. You are a loving Father who wants to live in close community with each. Father, walk through life with us every day. Help us not wait until we are in our darkest moments to lean on You, but learn to live each day

in Your presence. Help each of us to grow more like You, and become intimately acquainted with Your Truth and Your Spirit. Amen.

WEEK THREE: FRIDAY

AUTHOR: SHELBY MAXWELL
FAMILY STRUCTURE: MOTHER, FATHER, TWIN SISTER, YOUNGER SISTER
OCCUPATION: COLLEGE STUDENT

STRAYED BUT SUPPLIED

"God - He clothes me with strength and makes my way perfect. He makes my feet like the feet of a deer and sets me securely on the heights. He trains my hands for war; my arms can bend a bow of bronze. You have given me the shield of Your salvation; Your right hand upholds me, and Your humility exalts me. You widen a place beneath me for my steps, and my ankles do not give way." Psalm 18:32-36

*"How in the world did you get so far off track?"*I thought to myself, glancing at my windowsill and my succulent's new growth. Somehow (as if overnight), my little plant had sprouted a crazy, side-goggled stem that was sticking way out and leaning far from its designated space. This "wild hair" of my succulent was uncontrolled, unanticipated, and misunderstood. Still yet, it mirrored to me Christ's love and daily gift of grace.

Often, we find ourselves just like my plant, growing a wild, unplanned hair. It's as if our never-ending errands, weighty worries, and deep fears lead us far from the path planned for our lives. In a state of desperation, we feel lost, outcast, and unable to ever again hear God's voice. What encouragement exists for us in that situation?

In Psalm 18: 32-36, Jesus reminds us that even though we stray, He clothes us with strength and makes us perfect. In ALL TIMES, He widens a place for our steps and keeps our ankles from giving way. Though my plant's stem seems uncontrolled, it is still rooted in the ground and, therefore, protected and supplied with everything to meet its needs. That is an example for us. Though we stray, we must remember that Christ still holds, protects, and cares for us.

PRAYER TARGET:
Straying children of God-remembering His provision.

PERSONAL PRAYER FOR KNOXVILLE:
Dear Lord, may every child of God remember that he or she is never alone. In times of great struggles and much tribulation, You protect and shape us to be even more like You. You never leave us no matter how often we fail; but instead, You carry us on Your shoulders and pull us through life's battles. Oswald Chambers reminds us that "If we are going to be used by You, we are sometimes led down a road not meant for us at all. It's a road meant to make us useful in Your hands." Help us remember this today and find encouragement and purpose amidst our hardships. Yes, we often become tired, disappointed, and overwhelmed by our mediocrity and rebellion. Still, You love us. Strengthen our bones, Lord. Revive us, today. We want to bring You all the glory. Amen.

WEEK FOUR: MONDAY

AUTHOR: MARY GALE ROBERTS
FAMILY STRUCTURE: 2 GROWN DAUGHTERS
OCCUPATION: CO-DIRECTOR

WALKING IN YOUR AUTHORITY

"Behold, I give you power to tread on serpents and on scorpions and over all the power of the enemy; and nothing shall by any means hurt you." Luke 10:19

This scripture emboldened me as I began my walk many years ago with the Healing Rooms. Our clients came from different walks of life and from many parts of our country, even from foreign countries. Honestly, there were times I was fearful as their stories unfolded as they came forward for prayer. Many were confessing sinful activities in which they had willingly been involved - even murder. Now they were seeking freedom and sometimes forgiveness for their choices.

From the beginning, this Scripture stood out to me. As I reflected on it, I began to understand that I would see different and sometimes fearful things - like serpents and scorpions; BUT since "God has not given us a spirit of fear, but of power (there's that word again), love, and a sound mind" (II Timothy 1:7), I know that He will give me the power to tread or walk on all fearful things. He then will encourage me with the promise that nothing shall by any means hurt me.

My faith often leads me to rise in prayer for these individuals who want to be free. Through each incident, it is rewarding to me to know and be comforted by the fact that God gives all of us, that's me and YOU, the power to make the Glory of His Kingdom come here on earth. Praise His Name.
Amen.

PRAYER TARGET:

Intercessors of Knoxville that call on God's power for freedom for others.

PERSONAL PRAYER FOR KNOXVILLE:

I call out to You, Father, for God's chosen ones to recognize their calling and boldly come to the Throne of Grace. Let them find help and obtain mercy in time of need. (Hebrews 4:16) I also ask that they know God has prepared them for such a time as this through His power. Father, I call out for the intercessors to stand and take this authority from You into their prayer lives. Let them see God's Kingdom come. Now, Father, let Your people be set free and healed in Jesus' name. Amen

WEEK FOUR: TUESDAY

AUTHOR: LARRY KING
FAMILY STRUCTURE: WIFE, 4 CHILDREN AND 11 GRANDCHILDREN
OCCUPATION: CIVIL ENGINEER (RETIRED)

AN OFFENDED SPIRIT

> **"A brother offended is harder to be won than a strong city, and contentions are like the bars of a castle." Proverbs 18:19 "But if you do not forgive men, then your Father will not forgive your transgressions." Matthew 6:15**

All of us face times in our lives when we allow ourselves to be offended by a friend, a co-worker, or a family member. How we handle the offense is extremely important. If we fail to forgive, the unforgiveness may become like a festering sore that just does not heal, or it may feel like dragging a ball and chain around. Inevitably the lack of forgiveness will affect other relationships, especially our relationship to God.

Jesus taught numerous parables about the importance of forgiveness and He made a strong statement in Matthew 6:14-15 that the Father's forgiveness is conditional on our willingness to forgive our offender. We need to reflect on the possibility that we are being a "debt collector" (Matthew 18:21-35) of offenses that do not belong in our memory banks. To assist in thinking on this topic, let's ask ourselves these questions:

1.   Is there someone I resent, whom I have never let off the hook?
2.   Do I blame someone else for the mess I am in rather than me taking responsibility for my actions?
3.   Do I find myself reacting negatively to a person because he or she reminds me of someone else to which I hold offenses? Paul warned of this type of unforgiveness by saying that it is a trap or "a snare of the Devil, having been held captive by Him to

do His will." (2 Timothy 2:24-26) We need to release our offenses to the Lord and lay them at the foot of the cross.

PRAYER TARGET:
Those that are struggling with being offended.

PERSONAL PRAYER FOR KNOXVILLE:
Father, please draw all people in Knoxville to ask for mercy and forgiveness if they have an issue with someone who has offended them in the past. Guide them as they ask for release from their offended spirit. Enable each of us to have a clear conscience towards our offenders. I pray that my city will be known as a city which shows mercy and forgiveness within its borders and be a place where we are kind to all - being patient when wronged. May we become a city of refuge for those who need forgiveness and repentance from You. Amen.

WEEK FOUR: WEDNESDAY

AUTHOR: DANIEL OVERDORF
FAMILY STRUCTURE: WIFE AND THREE CHILDREN
OCCUPATION: TEACHER/PROFESSOR

TAKE DEAD AIM

> **"I do not run like someone running aimlessly; I do not fight like a boxer beating the air." I Corinthians 9:26**

The Professional Golfers' Association (PGA) of America honored Harvey Penick as their Teacher of the Year in 1989, recognizing his work with golf greats like Tom Kite and Ben Crenshaw. In 1992, three years before his death, Penick authored a small book of golf instruction titled Harvey Penick's Little Red Book. Propelled by Penick's amusing anecdotes and simple, easily understood instructions, the book remains the highest selling golf instruction book ever published.

Penick often said that the most important advice he could offer golfers was to "take dead aim." A golfer might swing the club with all the proper techniques—perfect balance, weight transfer, and flawless rotation of hips, shoulders, and arms—and hit the ball long and straight, but without proper aim the ball might fly long and straight into a lake.

Too many people muddle through unsatisfying, unproductive lives because they never consider their aim. Why did God plant me on this earth, in my city, and in this generation? To what can I devote my life that will outlast me? How can I make a difference eternally?

PRAYER TARGET:
Those struggling to find purpose in life and seeking to leave a legacy.

PERSONAL PRAYER FOR KNOXVILLE:

I pray that your Spirit will stir in the hearts of believers across the city to consider what you could do with our lives if we submitted them fully to you and your purposes. Please give us the strength and courage to lay aside selfish ambition, pride, and greed and to replace these with compassion, holiness, and a dogged commitment to live for your glory and your purposes. Teach us to aim our lives in the direction of your choosing. Amen.

WEEK FOUR: THURSDAY

AUTHOR: BILL MANCINI
FAMILY STRUCTURE: WIFE, 3 CHILDREN, AND 11 GRANDCHILDREN
OCCUPATION: COMPANY CHAIRMAN

TEACH THEM TO OBEY

"All authority has been given to Me in heaven and on earth. Go therefore and make disciples of all nations, baptizing them in the name of the Father and of the Son and of the Holy Spirit, teaching them to observe all things that I have commanded you; and lo, I am with you always, even to the end of the age." Matthew 28:18- 20

Jesus is speaking to His disciple just before he ascended into heaven and He gives them (and us) their marching orders! He first lets them know He has ALL authority to give them this command. This may be the most important thing Jesus has told them because it is His parting words. A commander to his soldiers; a Lord to His disciples!

I remember when I was young in the faith, I tried to teach others about the bible and give them facts about God. But Jesus is instructing us to teach them to observe or obey everything that He commanded them. This is not just teaching facts but teaching them to live according to the Word of God. This is life-on-life, one person pouring into another, sharing life according to the commands of God.

Everyone should have someone they are pouring into (a Timothy) and also someone who is helping them along the way (a Paul). If you pray and ask the Lord, He will send you a person you can disciple. That is His plan according to 2 Timothy 2:2. He will always give you all you need to do the work that He assigns to you!

PRAYER TARGET:
Men and women of Knoxville and surrounding areas, longing to be disciple makers.

PERSONAL PRAYER FOR KNOXVILLE:
Dear Lord, ignite a passion in the hearts of Your men and women in Knoxville for the great commission. Equip them and give them courage to teach others to obey everything that You have commanded them; to pour into them and disciple them, life-on-life. Help us, Lord, as Your local body of believers to focus on making disciples and we know that You will build your church!

WEEK FOUR: FRIDAY

AUTHOR: BILL PRESNELL
FAMILY STRUCTURE: WIFE, CHILDREN, RESCUE DOG
OCCUPATION: PRODUCTION MANAGER, ORDAINED CHAPLAIN

PRAYING WITH EXPECTATION

"Devote yourselves to prayer with an alert mind and a thankful heart." Colossians 4:2

According to the Scripture, prayer is something we all should do. Praying with expectation is critical. I have often heard people say, "I will pray for you," and they may, but with little or no expectation that God is going to move. If we are not going to expect God to give us what we are asking…why pray? Faith is believing that God is going to move. Never give up! Keep pressing in! It's time to see God move in our lives, in our families, and in our city!

PRAYER TARGET:
For all believers that they would pray expectantly with a desire to grow closer to Him.

PERSONAL PRAYER FOR KNOXVILLE:
Father, we come to You in the Name of Jesus, asking You to use us as never before. Give us a hunger that we will grow closer to You, that we will become obedient servants ready to do Your will. Use us, Father, in a mighty way, that souls will be saved, lives will be changed, and the sick will be healed. We pray that the men and women in our city will have a desire – unsatisfied by anything this world has to offer – to be the spark of revival in our city. We pray with expectation! May You be glorified! Amen.

WEEK FIVE: MONDAY

AUTHOR: JUDY J. GRAHAM
FAMILY STRUCTURE: HUSBAND, 2 CHILDREN, 2 STEP-CHILDREN,
2 GRANDDAUGHTERS, AND 1 GRANDSON
OCCUPATION: BUSINESS OWNER

FROM TRAGEDY TO TRUST

> **"Now to him who is able to do exceeding abundantly beyond all that we ask or think, according to the power that works within us, to Him be the glory in the church and in Christ Jesus to all generations forever and ever. Amen." Ephesians 3:20**

Every day since July 2015 I get to gaze into the face of a real live miracle. Eyes that open and close, a smile, and laughter from the lips that for weeks did not move or speak are a blessing. The arms, hands and feet that move today without the help of a therapist are actions that thrill. The lungs that inhaled and exhaled with the help of a respirator now take a breath without assistance. All the things that were once taken for granted, those unnoticed gifts both big and small, now have taken on a new meaning and importance. He wasn't expected to live. God had other plans.

My husband spent nine months in five hospital facilities, had twenty plus surgeries, and went through one and one-half years of therapies. With each new added gift, God helped us reach our new normal. God used the above scripture to help me get through each day. My husband was unaware of all he had gone through, but God used the little things - hiccups, coughs, or open eyes - to show me His glory.

I studied God's Word, prayed constantly and was reminded daily that God loved us and I could trust Him for the best outcome. I learned to have no fear because God was always with us.

Through each trial and triumph, we were blessed exceedingly, abundantly, beyond measure. I learned to Trust God…100%.

PRAYER TARGET:
Caregivers of the City.

PERSONAL PRAYER FOR KNOXVILLE:
Father, for every person in need, I pray that You draw their caregiver's heart to a 100% trust in You. Open eyes, Father, so they may see that You care about each tiny, minute detail of their lives. Give each a heart and life of surrender to You. Little by little, carve away, heal, and change those things that are an injury to their lives. Let all know the fullness of Your love and plans. Help each surrender the adversity, the pain, and the suffering. Let each use the groans deep in their souls as a surrendered gift to You. Father, caregivers go through the pain and suffering, too. Help each learn to serve and care with a dependence on You. Open eyes to see You one day at a time, so that nothing is taken for granted. Keep our hope and focus above. Help us understand that Your ability goes way beyond anything we can conceive in our minds. At all times, show us how to best care for those You have entrusted to us in their time of need. Amen.

WEEK FIVE: TUESDAY

AUTHOR: TERESA SLADE
FAMILY STRUCTURE: SINGLE
OCCUPATION: GRADUATE STUDENT

ABIDING IN HIM

> "Remain in me, as I also remain in you. No branch can bear fruit by itself; it must remain in the vine. Neither can you bear fruit unless you remain in me. I am the vine; you are the branches. If you remain in me and I in you, you will bear much fruit; apart from me you can do nothing."
> John 15:4-5

Abiding in Christ daily is no small task. To abide means "to act in accordance with," so the Scripture above tells us that the only way we can bear spiritual fruit is to live in faith-filled submission and obedience.

This hit me as I was doing the dishes one night. Stubborn as ever, I wanted to fit one last cup in the dishwasher, but it absolutely wouldn't fit unless I rearranged every other dish. I felt the Lord speak to me as I tried, in vain, to fit this cup on the top rack. Metaphorically, my life had been the dishwasher, and the Lord's will in my life was the cup. I often try to fit the Lord and His purposes into my own life, on my own terms, instead of submitting my heart to the Lord. The metaphor should be flipped—we are called to surrender our hearts (the cup) to the Lord (the dishwasher).

Thinking about my schoolwork, my future career, and my family, I often struggle in giving those things to the Lord. But He is the best guide and knows exactly what is needed. Surrendering our lives is how we give Him the most glory—and bear the most fruit. In what areas of your life are you holding back from God?

PRAYER TARGET:
Students of the City that are relying on their own terms.

PERSONAL PRAYER FOR KNOXVILLE:
God, we are in desperate need of You. May You fall upon our hearts and give us the desire to surrender to Your will. As we look to the future, change our majors, start new jobs, work long hours, and wonder what life has in store, let us give You all of ourselves. May every dream and every task we undertake glorify You. Let us not meet roadblocks with fear or despair, but let us praise You in faith, believing that You know best. Give us community and fellowship with others who will keep us accountable and be a part of our faith family.
Strengthen us as we share Your light around Knoxville, and although we are young, help us set examples in our faith, in our life, and in our purity. We can only do this through our Lord and Savior King, Jesus Christ. We love you. Amen.

WEEK FIVE: WEDNESDAY

AUTHOR: BARBARA M. LEE
FAMILY STRUCTURE: MYSELF AND TWO DAUGHTERS
OCCUPATION: PUBLISHER

THE ANCIENT PATH

> **"This is what the Lord says: Stand at the crossroads and look; ask for the ancient path, ask where the good way is and walk in it, and you will find rest for your souls. Jeremiah 6:16**

Ancient in Hebrew came from the word that means eternal, everlasting. So, this is the path that always was true – always will be true. It is God's way, the covenant way, as opposed to the current way, the trendy way, the cultural way. God led Abram out of the land of Ur to get him out of the cultural way which was idolatry and to show him the ancient path; the way that was eternally true. Jesus is "the way, the truth, the life." His light shines in the darkness. Evidence of this ancient path shows up all through the Bible to lead us in the straight way. God had this book written so we and our children would not be lost. So, as we are pulled on by today's culture and have so many different choices of directions that we can go, especially as single parents without a mate that we can counsel with, there is a path that God has established for us and we can know that we are on the right track, with God Himself backing us up.

PRAYER TARGET:
The single parents of the city, seeking confidence in their decisions for their families.

PERSONAL PRAYER FOR KNOXVILLE:
I pray that every single parent in this city and county will turn their face to God Almighty, the Creator of the universe, the

Redeemer of mankind, the Lover of our souls, and ask Him for His light to guide them through the darkness of this time in history, so they can have encouragement and direction for themselves and for their children. God, You said You would give strength to Your people and that You would bless them with peace (Psalm 29:11). I'm asking You to give Your strength, Your peace and Your light to every single parent in this city, that they will not be discouraged and go off track where there is no light or provision. Jesus, You are our King. Lead us in Your straight path. Be glorified in our lives and let us see Your presence and Your order all around us. May our children be firmly planted on Your ancient path all the days of their lives, in Jesus holy name. Amen.

WEEK FIVE: THURSDAY

NAME: AARON SMALL
FAMILY STRUCTURE: WIFE AND 2 CHILDREN
OCCUPATION: YOUTH DIRECTOR

TRUST

> **"Trust in The Lord with all thine heart and lean not on your own understanding. In all thy ways acknowledge Him, and He shall direct thy paths." Proverbs 3:5-6**

In 2005, I was ready to walk away from professional baseball after 17 seasons. The reason was pride and selfishness. I didn't like what I'd become. I gave my life to Christ as an eight-year old boy, but during this season of my life I began to trust myself more than God. I came to a breaking point! I lost it on the baseball field one afternoon in early July of 2005. I SNAPPED! At that moment, in my heart, I was done with the game. I was quitting! However, God had other plans. It was at that time the two verses above, found in Proverbs became very real to me.

Four days after that incident on the field, I confessed to God and told Him that I was sorry for my attitude. That same afternoon, I walked into the locker room where the manager greeted me with, *"Come to my office. I need to talk with you."* My heart sunk. I thought I was getting released or fired because my season was not going well to that point. My record was 1-4 with a 4.96 ERA. After the manager shut his office door, he sat down across from me at his desk and told me that I was getting promoted to the Big Leagues. I was going to be the starting pitcher for the Yankees in six days, playing against the Texas Rangers. Through God's grace, I went on to compile a 10-0 record for the Yankees in the second half of that season.

Trust Him, not yourself! He has a plan.

PRAYER TARGET:
All males struggling with a defensive and protective spirit.

PERSONAL PRAYER FOR KNOXVILLE:
God, please help the people of Knoxville submit to You and trust You with all their being. You have an amazing plan for our lives. Let us seek You, Lord, and all Your ways. Help each of us remember to call on You when making plans for our lives. Your thoughts are much higher than our thoughts and Your ways are much higher than our ways. You know best, Father. Hear this prayer and guide us to trust You. Amen.

WEEK FIVE: FRIDAY

NAME: STEVEN N. WALLER
FAMILY STRUCTURE: WIFE AND FOUR CHILDREN
OCCUPATION: UNIVERSITY PROFESSOR AND ASSOCIATE PASTOR

GREAT THINGS LIE AHEAD

"This is God's Message, the God who made earth, made it livable and lasting, known everywhere as God: 'Call to me and I will answer you. I'll tell you marvelous and wondrous things that you could never figure out on your own.'" Jeremiah 33:2-3

At one point in my Christian journey, I found myself spending an inordinate amount of time trying to figure out the complexities of life and asking several questions. More importantly, one of the questions was how should I live as a Believer in a fallen the world? Others included, why does God allow natural disasters to occur? What does the current war mean relative to Jesus' return? Where is God taking me on my personal journey? What will become of my children in a society where race matters?

Of course, I would search the Bible and would read secular and faith-oriented books in search of answers to this barrage of questions. I would get pieces of answers to some of my questions from the teaching and preaching that took place at the churches I attended along the way. One day, as I was sitting at our kitchen table having a cup of coffee and engaging in my early morning devotion, the answer came as I was reading an entry by author/pastor/theologian Max Lucado! Simply ask God in specific terms and wait for the revelation, which will come through the Holy Spirit. He will show you and tell you what you need to know!

Verse 33:3 makes it clear, *"Call to me and I will answer you. I'll tell you marvelous and wondrous things that you could never figure out on your own."* Simply put, ask Me, I will not only tell you, but will show you the incredible answers to your questions. The things that perplex you I will make plain!

PRAYER TARGET:
People of faith in the city, with questions and doubts.

PERSONAL PRAYER FOR KNOXVILLE:
Dear God, show all in the city what they need to know about family, community, faith, and life in general and then help them wait for You to show them. You promise that not only will You answer, but You will reveal it to us in a way that is specific to You. The 'icing on the cake' here, God, is that You have promised to show us the marvelous and incredible things You have in store for us - things that we cannot begin to imagine! So, we ask YOU, trust YOU, and wait on YOU to respond! In the name of our Lord, Savior, King and soon returning Judge, I offer this prayer. Amen, Amen, Amen.

WEEK SIX: MONDAY

AUTHOR: JENNIFER DICKSON
FAMILY STRUCTURE: HUSBAND AND 3 CHILDREN
OCCUPATION: AUTHOR, SPEAKER, BLOGGER, DIRECTOR, HOMESCHOOL MOM

BE A WATCHMAN

> **"On your walls, O Jerusalem, I have set watchmen; all the day and all the night they shall never be silent. You who put the LORD in remembrance, take no rest, and give him no rest until he establishes Jerusalem and makes it a praise in the earth." Isaiah 62:6-7**

The term "watchmen" has lost significance to us in modern times, but in Biblical times it was literally the guardians of the city. They sat on the highest points to watch for the enemy coming and alert the armies to prepare for battle. They were vital to the protection of the city. In Isaiah 62:6, God refers those who intercede for the city as spiritual watchmen, or guardians. They were to not only intercede, but be looking for the fulfillment of God's promises. As the body of Christ in Knoxville, we should be confident and bold in our position as watchmen for our city. Praying for God's promises to be fulfilled and anticipating the fulfillment of them. Can you imagine if we were all asking God to move and actively watching for Him to show off in Knoxville? God has never failed to show up and show off in my relationship with Him, especially when I am actively watching for Him. He delights in blessing His people, and our culture notices when someone is being blessed or favored.

What better way to introduce others to Christ, than because they took notice you were being blessed beyond measure and they want what you have? There is spiritual blessing awaiting us as we fulfill our callings as watchmen on the walls of Knoxville, because we will get a front row seat to God moving in our communities, churches, and homes. The second half of verse 6 instructs us to not take rest when petitioning a move of the Lord. This doesn't mean don't take physical rest, but rather be like a two-year old who wants a treat! Be persistent and bold in your asking God to move, asking with full faith that He will move! Let's link spiritual arms in prayer as we boldly go before our Lord and ask Him to move in Knoxville.

PRAYER TARGET:
Christians within Knoxville to remain persistent and watchful for His works.

PERSONAL PRAYER FOR KNOXVILLE:
Dear God, we have seen You move throughout the pages of scripture and also in our own lives. We ask You to open our eyes to what You are doing in Knoxville, but also to what we need to be interceding for. Show us where the enemy is approaching, help us seek Your mighty right arm to defend our city, and let us not grow tired in asking You to move. We join together with a spirit of expectation as we ask You to show up and show off in Knoxville. Ephesians 3:20 our prayers, Lord. Thank you for Your faithfulness in all You do. Amen.

WEEK SIX: TUESDAY

AUTHOR: WESLEY MILLS
FAMILY STRUCTURE: MARRIED
OCCUPATION: MISSIONS MOBILIZER

INFORMATION VS. TRANSFORMATION

> **"Go therefore and make disciples of all nations, baptizing them in the name of the Father, of the Son, of the Holy Spirit, teaching them to observe all that I commanded you." Matthew 28:19:20**

Recently, I was reading a book on neighboring – what does it mean to be a good neighbor? It had some helpful insights and practical applications that made me think. All in all, it was a solid read. Once I finished, almost instinctively, I put the book away and began to research the topic more. And then the Lord stopped me, made me reflect, and then in a gentle nudge I felt, "Wesley, you don't need more teaching. You need to do it."

We in the American Church – and specifically in the Bible belt – have so much teaching. We may have more teaching than any time in the history of the world. We have more podcasts and articles and books than we know what to do with. We know a little about a lot of things.

But when we listen to Jesus, we see how he defines teaching: *"teach them to observe all that I have commanded you."* Our lives – as much as we like to think this – are not about accumulating information. It's about growing in transformation. It's little about turn-a-phrase or an insightful thought, and more about asking ourselves, *"Are we obeying what Jesus says?"*

PRAYER TARGET:
Young adults (20s-30s) seeking information instead of transformation.

PERSONAL PRAYER FOR KNOXVILLE:

Lord, please stir our hearts to do more, not just know more. Lord, help us be good neighbors, humble spouses, gentle friends, integrity-filled co-workers and passionate disciple-makers. Help us restore the city's brokenness, not merely talk about it. Give us the courage and tenacity to kill sin within us, not just confess it. And provide us opportunities to be witnesses of Your love to our peers. May the grace that has been granted to us be poured out from us as grace unto others. And may we desire transformation over information; praying that the kingdom of God would come in us first so that it may come through us. Amen.

WEEK SIX: WEDNESDAY

AUTHOR: CLAUDIA HOOD
FAMILY STRUCTURE: HUSBAND AND 2 GROWN SONS
OCCUPATION: PASTOR'S WIFE, MISSIONARY, TEACHER, COUNSELOR

PRAYING WITH EXPECTATION

> **"Then they cried to the LORD in their trouble and He brought them out of their distresses." Psalm 107:28**

Often, we pray for days, months, years and yet there is "no answer" to the desire of our prayerful heart. Does "no answer" mean God does not hear, or listen, or answer or ever intend to answer? Our enemy, Satan, with his sneaky spirit, whispers, "Did God really say?" For 20 years I have cried to God for change in our son's lifestyle. I have prayed thousands of words and phrases and also desperate one-word pleas, "HELP," because I know nothing more to pray.

Often, I feel in a vacuum, all alone, feeling pain and needing prayer for me to keep up the vigil. God's nudging prompted my focus on other grieving parents and a prayer group, Praying for Our Prodigals, formed. God answers the prayer of just one person but our ears at times need to hear others call our name and need in vocalized prayer. It simply encourages us as we hear intensity of prayer for us. It encourages us to know we are not alone in a vacuum as together we rest in the God Who has proven Himself Faithful in the past and we wait for His change of our prodigal sons and daughters.

PRAYER TARGET:
Parents of prodigal children.

PERSONAL PRAYER FOR KNOXVILLE:
Father, we know children are a gift from the Lord and that You,

are the One Who created each person in the mother's womb. Thank You for giving us the privilege to be a parent. While our parenting skills were not always perfect, our love for our children is deep and abiding. Our heart's desire has been for our sons and daughters to love You, walk in Your ways, and be close to Your heart and purpose. We are crying out to You, the Most High God, to move in the lives of prodigal and wayward children throughout our city and give them a hunger for You and allow You to bring them into the close relationship You desire with them. Give them the wisdom, strength, and desire to align their lives with Your Word. We know You hear and answer prayer and we will be faithful to persevere in a vigil of prayer. Guide us to join with others in prayer whose hearts are deeply grieved over the lifestyle of their dear child as we wait to behold Your work in their lives. Amen.

WEEK SIX: THURSDAY

AUTHOR: ALAN BRADFORD
FAMILY STRUCTURE: WIFE AND 3 DAUGHTERS
OCCUPATION: PASTOR

MAY GOD GREET YOU

> "I pray that the eyes of your heart may be enlightened in order that you may know the hope to which he has called you, the riches of his glorious inheritance in his holy people, and his incomparably great power for us who believe." Ephesians 1:18-19a

From the age of four until age fourteen I had the privilege of living in Heidelberg Germany. It was a good- sized city in the southwest part of the country. While I never fully became fluent in German, I would sometimes hear a phrase that intrigued me. Southern Germans will sometimes greet (and to a lesser extent say farewell) with the phrase "Grüß Got" (Gruss Gott). The phrase is a shortened version of "Grüße dich Gott" which means "May God Greet You."

May God greet you…

To have our eyes and hearts open to the fact that where ever we go, God is there to greet us. There is no place where God is not. Even when it seems God is far away, He is always there.

My prayer for our community is that we constantly remember God is at work where ever we are. No matter where you are… God was there before us. He is there to greet us into the work that He has been doing.

May God greet you…in your home, your work, your classroom…
May God greet you…in your fears and your joys…
May God greet you…in your hopes…in your dreams…

in your failures…
May God greet you…in the extraordinary parts of your day…and in the humdrum dullness of your life…

PRAYER TARGET:
All citizens of Knoxville and surrounding areas to recognize all the ways and places God greets us.

PERSONAL PRAYER FOR KNOXVILLE:
God, may each follower of Jesus be sensitive to the movement of the Holy Spirit in our families, neighborhoods, and communities. May You, the God of all creation, quicken our hearts, spirits and minds to the work that the Holy Spirit is doing all around us and may we join You in the good work You are doing in Knoxville and surrounding areas. Amen.

WEEK SIX: FRIDAY

AUTHOR: GAYLA LEMONS
FAMILY STRUCTURE: MOTHER OF ADULT CHILDREN
OCCUPATION: ADMINISTRATOR/COORDINATOR

"R" YOU READY?

> **"Wherefore come out from among them, and be ye separate, saith the Lord, and touch not the unclean thing; and I will receive you. And will be a Father unto you, and ye shall be my sons and daughters, saith the Lord Almighty. Having therefore these promises, dearly beloved, let us cleanse ourselves from all filthiness of the flesh and spirit, perfecting holiness in the fear of God." 2 Corinthians 6:17-7:1**

Annually, in the fall leading up to The Day of Atonement, I spend forty days in a Season of Teshuvah (repentance), soul searching, introspection, and realigning. Teshuvah includes the Biblical month of Elul and the first ten days of Tishri. I have come to appreciate these annual times of focus and intentionality in my walk with the Lord. This is the format: Recognize, Responsibility, Repent, Renounce, Remove, Rub, Resist, Rejoice, and Restore. Prayer is the key to unlocking each layer of the process.

James 4:4, 6b-10 says, *"Do you not know that friendship with the world is enmity with God?"* He also says: *"God resists the proud, but gives grace to the humble."* Therefore, submit to God. Resist the Devil and He will flee from you. Draw near to God and He will draw near to you. Cleanse your hands, you sinners; and purify your hearts, you double-minded. Lament and mourn and weep! Let your laughter be turned to mourning and your joy to gloom. Humble yourselves in the sight of the Lord, and He will lift you up." The goal of repentance is RESTORATION... Restoration between you and God. Restoration between you and others.

PRAYER TARGET:
Personal introspection and repentance that brings restoration.

PERSONAL PRAYER FOR KNOXVILLE:
Heavenly Father, illuminate our lives in the Light of Your holiness. Allow us to see areas where we need to take responsibility for our lives instead of blaming others or circumstances. Show us where we need to repent and return to Your ways. Empower us by Your grace to renounce ungodly alliances and to remove that which is hindering us from representing You well. Help us to rub out – dash against - The Rock Christ Jesus, the things that cause us to stumble. Draw us to humility so that we can resist the enemy of our soul. We desire to rejoice in Your presence in intimacy! Please bring full restoration in our lives! We want to be known for our love for our brothers and sisters and seen walking in unity for the sake of Your Kingdom! May we all bow at the feet of the King of Kings and Lord of Lords! In His name, the name above all names, Jesus, we pray! Amen!

WEEK SEVEN: MONDAY

AUTHOR: DAVID A. MCDANIEL
FAMILY STRUCTURE: WIFE, 2 DAUGHTERS, 1 SON, 1 DAUGHTER-IN-LAW, AND 1 GRANDSON
OCCUPATION: WORSHIP PASTOR

MAKE US ONE

"I do not pray for these alone, but also for those who will believe in Me through their word; that they all may be one, as You, Father, are in Me, and I in You; that they also may be one in Us, that the world may believe that You sent Me. And the glory which You gave Me I have given them, that they may be one just as We are one." John 17:20-22

There should be unity in the Body of Christ. Jesus prayed that His followers would be "one" or unified. For we Christians to be one doesn't mean that we're all the same. We're not all alike. What if our hands had 10 thumbs? What if we had two left feet?

To be unified or "one" speaks of a shared purpose. All parts are different, but share a common vision, purpose, and goal. My hands can't see. My eyes can't grasp. My feet can't chew food. My mouth can't walk. All the parts of my body have distinct functions, but when they're properly assembled they make a very unique and functional being. They make ME.

We, as members of His body, when properly connected and assembled, in a very real sense make Him. We cannot even survive, much less function, as He designed us, unless we are "one" or properly assembled. And when the world sees us live in unity as we were designed to live, it bears witness to the truth that God Himself created, loved, and sent us into the world to represent, or "re-present," Him.

PRAYER TARGET:
Members of the body of Christ-to identify their uniqueness and design.

PERSONAL PRAYER FOR KNOXVILLE:
Father God, I come to You in the Name of Jesus. I'm absolutely convinced that if there was ever a prayer that You would be delighted to answer, this would be it. So, I simply come into agreement with the prayer that Jesus prayed as He made His way to the Garden of Gethsemane. I pray that You, O Holy Father, would make us one, as You and Your Son are one, so that all would know that You sent Him into the world. And just as You sent Him into the world, in like manner He will send us. Father, He said that the works that He did we would do also, and even greater works than these we would do because He returned to His Father. So, make us one, Heavenly Father, so that we might bear witness to the reality of Your power and presence, the lovingkindness that You demonstrate to all humankind, and Your ability to save to the uttermost those who come to You through Him.

My prayer is that You, Heavenly Father, would answer the prayer of Your only begotten Son, Jesus Christ. Make us one, Father. In Jesus' Name, Amen.

WEEK SEVEN: TUESDAY

AUTHOR: KIM JAGGERS
FAMILY STRUCTURE: HUSBAND AND 3 ADULT CHILDREN
OCCUPATION: LOCAL BUSINESS OWNER, CHRISTIAN AUTHOR, AND SPEAKER

DO NOT LOSE HEART

> "Therefore, since we have received this ministry, as we have received mercy, we do not lose heart. But we have renounced the hidden things of shame, not walking in craftiness nor handling the word of God deceitfully, but by manifestation of the truth commending ourselves to every man's conscience in the sight of God."
> 2 Corinthians 4:1-2

I am blessed to travel the country speaking at women's events, usually sponsored by local churches. Often, I get to know the pastors, pastor's wives and ministry leaders as the event is planned.

Over and over, I see the same thing - pastors and ministry leaders are tired. The battle is fierce as they are fighting on the front lines. Their job is difficult and their accolades fewer and fewer in a world where "right is wrong and wrong is right."

These unsung heroes have a target on their backs. Many are leaving the ministry exhausted while others are being taken down as they fall into the enemy's traps - giving into sin. I will soon speak at a church where one of the pastors took his life after having an affair.

We need our pastors and ministry leaders to be strong more than ever. Yes, the battle is fierce; but we are not asleep to the tactics of the enemy, and we are not ignorant of his devices.

Let us be a people who care for our shepherds and their families. May we hold them up in prayer and serve them in practical ways. May God use us to strengthen them with our love, encouragement, and support.

PRAYER TARGET:
Weary Pastors, ministry leaders and their families.

PERSONAL PRAYER FOR KNOXVILLE:
Father God, no matter how difficult or how great the opposition, may our pastors, families and ministry leaders not lose heart but keep their eye on the prize who is Christ Jesus. Father, we ask You to strengthen Your shepherds. Though hard-pressed on every side, they are not crushed; though they are perplexed, they not remain in despair; though persecuted, they will remember they are not forsaken; though struck down they will not be destroyed. May they find strength as they are always continuing to share in the death of Jesus Christ through their suffering. I pray that the LIFE of Jesus also may be manifested in their body so others may find the freedom that is You, Christ Jesus. (2 Cor 4:8-10). God, may we be relentless in remembering to cover these soldiers in our prayers and lavishly love them so they may be strengthened in the battle. Amen.

WEEK SEVEN: WEDNESDAY

AUTHOR: HEATHER PETERS
FAMILY STRUCTURE: HUSBAND AND TWO CHILDREN
OCCUPATION: PRODUCER, WRITER & COMMUNICATIONS CONSULTANT

FINDING CONTENTMENT

> **"But godliness with contentment is great gain, for we brought nothing into the world, and we cannot take anything out of the world. As for the rich in this present age, charge them not to be haughty, nor to set their hopes on the uncertainty of riches, but on God, who richly provides us with everything to enjoy. They are to do good, to be rich in good works, to be generous and ready to share, thus storing up treasure for themselves as a good foundation for the future, so that they may take hold of that which is truly life." I Timothy 6:6-7, 17-19**

By the world's standards, most of us are rich. We have food and clothing; reliable transportation; shelter; freedom; and much more. So, why is it that we often crave what we don't have? Why do we look at people and things in this world and convince ourselves that we need more?

Paul taught Timothy that there is great gain in godliness with contentment. He urged Timothy to the fight the good fight of faith and take hold of the eternal life to which we are called. *What encouragement!* My heart sings because this is my desire. But, Paul didn't stop there. He said, *"Do good, be rich in good works, be generous and ready to share."* I feel challenged by these words and pray you do, too.

In my overseas travels, I've witnessed brothers and sisters in Christ be content with so much less than what many of us enjoy daily. Let's invite God to create this heart of contentment in us. Imagine what our city, our nation, our world would look like with content people who strive toward taking hold of "that which is truly life."

PRAYER TARGET:
People desiring contentment in what they have been given.

PERSONAL PRAYER FOR KNOXVILLE:
Father in Heaven, thank you that You are King of Kings and Lord of Lords. Praise YOU from whom all blessings flow. God, help us to be content with the blessings we've been given. Help us every day to realize the abundance and provision in our daily lives. Change our hearts, minds, and actions where we are sinful, greedy, and selfish. Give us a spirit of contentment, and fill us with goodness and generosity. We are grateful for Your unconditional love, mercy, and sovereignty. In Jesus' Precious & Holy Name, Amen.

WEEK SEVEN: THURSDAY

AUTHOR: SHARON BARBER
FAMILY STRUCTURE: HUSBAND, 2 SONS, 2 DAUGHTERS IN LAW, AND 2 GRANDCHILDREN
OCCUPATION: HOMEMAKER

GOD IS ALWAYS FAITHFUL

"Delight yourself in the Lord and He will give you the desires of your heart." Psalm 37:4

Nearly twenty years ago I was invited to go on a prayer walk to China. I believed God was asking something else of me, but I began praying about it, fully expecting God to close the door. The day came when I realized that I, a fifty-five-year-old grandmother with rheumatoid arthritis, was going to prayer walk in China. "God must have a sense of humor," I thought.

I explained to God that I did not like the Chinese, I did not like Chinese food, and I did not like the way the Chinese dressed. God responded in my spirit by saying, "This trip has nothing to do with you, but everything to do with your children and grandchildren."

My response to that prompting from God was to say, "God, I will be on the plane."

My husband and I followed God's call again when He later sent us to serve in East Asia for many years. Through my experiences I have found that I love the Chinese and like some Chinese food.

In His time, God even fulfilled His promise of my prayer walking as being an influence on my children. He called one of my sons and precious daughters-in-law to serve in Germany at Black Forest Academy. They now are helping keep other missionaries on the field by providing a safe place and quality instructional program for the missionary's children. I continue to wait and see what God will do in the life of my grandchildren. It is important to follow His leading. Following God is following the example of Jesus and being willing to sacrifice selfish desires. Through those obedient actions we learn that our God is always faithful. That begs the question, however, are we always faithful to Him?

PRAYER TARGET:
Those waiting for God to answer.

PERSONAL PRAYER FOR KNOXVILLE:
God, you know where we are in Knoxville, TN. You have heard many prayers from people desiring their loved ones and others to invite Jesus into their life. I want them to love You deeply, to live for You daily, and to want to be in Your Word. I wait, knowing You have heard my prayer for my grandchildren and look forward to the day when they will delight themselves in You. Should I no longer be living when that time comes, I trust You, Father, with the future generations of my family and Knoxville. May Knoxville lead the way in choosing and honoring You. Amen.

WEEK SEVEN: FRIDAY

AUTHOR: ANDREW SELVARAJAN
FAMILY STRUCTURE: WIFE AND 2 CHILDREN
OCCUPATION: MISSIONARY, AUTHOR, COMMUNITY CHAPLAIN

CHILDREN OF LIGHT

> **"You are the light of the world. A city set on a hill cannot be hidden." Matthew 5:14**

The greatest privilege of being a Christian is that we are the light of the community. That is because Jesus is the 'Light of the world.' Since He is our Lord and Savior, we belong to Him, and we reflect His light through the radiance of His grace and power endowed within us. Consider phosphorus. It radiates light only after being energized. In some way, all chemicals have varying degrees of brightness, color, and length of time they glow after being energized. Contrary to this, the truth and the power of the gospel stand in that, once ignited in us, they transform us into the children of light which will never vary or diminish. We do not reflect the light! Rather, we are the producer of the light through Jesus.

Our speech, action, modesty, integrity, and lifestyle will radiant like a diamond, which attracts and impresses the world of darkness to draw towards the light of Truth. This is the greatest concept ever told in history by any of the philosophers! By our Teacher, the LORD Jesus, His sermon still lives, speaks, and acts through us. According to the verse in Matthew 5:16, we have our charge: *"In the same way, let your light shine before others, so that they may see your good works and give glory to your Father who is in heaven."*

PRAYER TARGET:

For community members longing to live in unity and make a difference.

PERSONAL PRAYER FOR KNOXVILLE:

Dear God, make me an instrument of light and a bearer of faith, hope, trust, love, mercy, and compassion. Help all in Christians our city be a source of help to the needy, broken hearted, and sick. Father, bring all those who are captivated by the darkness into the light of Your love. In Jesus name. Amen.

WEEK EIGHT: MONDAY

AUTHOR: DEBRA SPARKS
FAMILY STRUCTURE: BLENDED FAMILY OF 6 AND 3 GRANDCHILDREN
OCCUPATION: MINISTRY, MISSIONS

THERE HE IS

> **"Be joyful always; pray continually; give thanks in all circumstances, for this is God's will in Christ Jesus." 1 Thessalonians 5:16-18**

Being joyful always isn't always easy, is it? What is so amazing to me is that our heavenly Father can see so far beyond our daily lives and heart-breaking circumstances. It's like He is saying, *"Oh, if you only knew my child, what I am doing behind the scenes, and what I have planned for you and your loved ones in the future, you would be amazed."*

Being a mother brings so much joy into my life, but along with being in awe of watching their personal journeys unfold, I'm also consistently brought to my knees in prayer for them. It is during those times of prayer that God's calming presence overrides all the struggles in the family. Through His help I stay in His will. That alone fills me with the sense of His sovereignty over my life and the life of each person in my family.

There are days when situations look hopeless, but when I call on Him, there He is. Amid the fog when the enemy wants to engulf me, there He is. He is always faithful; always merciful; and always ready to pour out His perfect love, grace and peace. I am learning to embrace this season of shaping me into a completely dependent soul who is slowly but persistently learning to shift my flawed flesh into an in-tune spirit. I am learning to keep my head up, have my eyes fixed on Jesus, and continually pray   and give my Abba Daddy thanks for another day of grace.

PRAYER TARGET:
Mothers and grandmothers seeking joy in their daily lives.

PERSONAL PRAYER FOR KNOXVILLE:
Father, I thank You and praise You for Your love, power and authority over our lives. I acknowledge that without You our marriages, families, and city would not flourish. Lord, help us join in persistent prayer and petition. Have Your way in this city. I also pray for our beautiful state and nation. Make it shine brighter and stronger than it ever has in history. Help us, Lord, to stay bold as Christians for Your kingdom; to rebuild faith that's been lost; and to make a difference as mothers who will affect generations to come. Lead each of us as we teach the children in our families of Your goodness. In the name of Jesus. Amen.

WEEK EIGHT: TUESDAY

AUTHOR: JESSICA BOCANGEL
FAMILY STRUCTURE: HUSBAND AND 2 CHILDREN
OCCUPATION: NONPROFIT PROGRAM DIRECTOR

IMMIGRANTS ARE A BLESSING

> "Consequently, you are no longer foreigners and strangers, but fellow citizens with God's people and also members of his household, built on the foundation of the apostles and prophets, with Christ Jesus himself as the chief cornerstone. In him the whole building is joined together and rises to become a holy temple in the Lord. And in him you too are being built together to become a dwelling in which God lives by his Spirit." Ephesians 2:19-22

Ephesians says all of God's people are members of God's household. I look at my own household: my husband is a naturalized American and our children are American-born. With extended family in South American and Europe, I often imagine how different our lives would be if we lived in Knoxville as unauthorized immigrants.

Children of undocumented immigrants arrive in Knoxville with their families seeking a brighter future. These children grow into young adults who have ambition, talent, and drive to pursue a future as a physician's assistant, a CPA, or an electrical engineer, only to name a few options. They may graduate in the top ten percent of their class, yet they face the harsh reality that their college options are severely limited and financially out of reach.

The loss of potential within each young person leaves me with a crushing sense of hopelessness. I cannot fix our nation's broken immigration system, nor can I construct avenues for these students to access higher education. Let's work together to make God the cornerstone in the lives of these children and youth, and let us point them to our source of hope as members of God's "household."

PRAYER TARGET:
Undocumented youth.

PERSONAL PRAYER FOR KNOXVILLE:
Lord, You teach us in the Scriptures that You can send strangers as a gift; an angel may be disguised as a stranger, or a stranger could be the very presence of Christ Himself (Matthew 25). I pray that Knoxville's immigrant population will experience an overwhelming sense of belonging. Lord, help each of us strike the language we use that says, "They're not from around here." Help us humbly replace it with, "I wonder how God worked to bring this person, this family, to Knoxville." Lord, we have learned that hostile reception breeds alienation. Soften our hearts and let us look for the hopes and dreams in the eyes of our immigrant neighbors. Show us ways to welcome them. Reveal to us when You would have us support the pursuit of the dreams You've given them. Allow us to receive the blessing of immigrants in our city through their music, food, and traditions. God, nurture in our hearts a genuine curiosity to learn about the cultures that built our immigrant neighbors before they arrived in Knoxville.

Give us courage to affirm their presence, and allow us to see every stranger and foreigner as a member of a household where Christ is the Cornerstone. Amen

WEEK EIGHT: WEDNESDAY

AUTHOR: LARRY F. BOYLES
FAMILY STRUCTURE: MARRIED, 2 SONS, AND 3 GRANDCHILDREN
OCCUPATION: RETIRED MINISTER

A WORD FITLY SPOKEN

"A word fitly spoken is like apples of gold in a setting of silver." Proverbs 25:11

Our English language has some very interesting words. We don't always think about the words we use and how we communicate. It would likely be a major challenge for someone trying to learn English to be able to interpret our language. Consider these as a few examples:

- Why do doctors call what they do a "practice?"
- Why is the person that helps you manage your investments called a "broker?"
- Why do they call multifamily housing buildings "apartments" when they are all together?
- Why do we drive on "parkways" and park on "driveways?"
- Why is it that when you transport something by car or truck it is called a "shipment" but when you send it by boat it is called "cargo?"

These are just a few examples of how we can easily miscommunicate our meaning. Our words are very important. The average person speaks enough words in one year to fill 66 books, 800 pages long. We speak approximately 20,000 words a day.
Solomon had much to say about our words. There are over 120 verses in the book of Proverbs related to different things about our speech. We can summarize Solomon's teachings in these three statements:

1-Think before you Speak. Proverbs 16:23 says, *"A wise man's heart guides his mouth and his lips promote instruction."*

An old friend once said, "Silence can never be repeated."

2-Always speak the truth. Proverbs 24: 26 says, *"An honest answer is like a kiss on the lips."* When we speak truth, there is no need to "spin" a situation to make it better.

3-Speak the truth in love. Proverbs 12: 17-19 says, *"A truthful witness gives honest testimony but a false witness tells lies. Reckless words pierce like a sword but the tongue of the wise brings healing. Truthful lips endure forever but a lying tongue lasts only a moment."*

PRAYER TARGET:
Leaders and workers from all areas of our city that are seeking wisdom.

PERSONAL PRAYER FOR KNOXVILLE:
Father, help us learn from Solomon that our words do matter. We have the choice in every situation to treat others with respect as we speak the truth in love. May it be so, Jesus. Amen

WEEK EIGHT: THURSDAY

AUTHOR: VAL DAGERMANDZHYAN
FAMILY STRUCTURE: HUSBAND AND 3 CHILDREN
OCCUPATION: NURSE

WE ARE GOD'S FELLOW WORKERS

> **"And he who reaps receives wages, and gathers fruit for eternal life, that both he who sows and he who reaps may rejoice together. For in this the saying is true: 'One sows and another reaps.' I sent you to reap that for which you have not labored; others have labored, and you have entered into their labors." John 4:36-38**

Many of us have a friend or relative who is not saved yet. Of course, as Christians we want them to come to know the Lord because we love them. We share the gospel, we invite them to church, we pray for them and often don't see results. There may be times you wanted to give up! I want to tell you: there is a possibility you may never see result; but, it doesn't mean that your work was in vain. God may let somebody else reap what you sowed. God may let you reap that for which you have not labored; others have labored, and you may enter into their labor.

Why does it work this way? Because God is the One who gives increase and He will not give His glory to another. So, nobody can boast. Moses brought children of Israel out of Egypt, but could not bring them to the Promised land. He himself could not even enter it. Joshua lead the same people into the land God gave them, but Joshua was not the one who saved them from Egypt.

Each one of us may witness only part of the complete story. However, Jesus Himself promised that there will be the day when both he who sows and he who reaps may rejoice together.

PRAYER TARGET:

People praying for the salvation of family members or friends.

PERSONAL PRAYER FOR KNOXVILLE:

Dear Father, You know the people in our city who don't yet know You, but are precious to us. We try to do what we can, but without You we can't do anything. Please help us to be faithful until the end. Help us to remember that even though we may never witness results we may know that You are faithful and keep Your promises. Father, we are the like a poor widow begging You. Not because we deserve for You to answer, but because of Your sovereignty. Hear my prayer. In the name of Jesus. Amen.

WEEK EIGHT: FRIDAY

AUTHOR: MARK MCKEEHAN
FAMILY STRUCTURE: WIFE, 4 BIOLOGICAL CHILDREN, AND 1 SON ADOPTED FROM ETHIOPIA
OCCUPATION: LEAD PASTOR

LET'S PRAY BIGGER!

> **"But Jesus looked at them and said to them, with men this is impossible, but with God all things are possible." Matthew 19:26**

Honestly, many of our prayers sound more like "Now I lay me down to sleep…" than they do if we say something like, *"God make the sun stand still."* (Joshua 10:12-13) Can you imagine asking the Lord to stop the sun from setting…and Him saying yes? Verse fourteen says, *"There has been no day like that… that the Lord heeded the voice of a man; for the Lord fought for Israel."*

What are you praying for right now that only God can do? Many times, as we pray we ask God to do things He was already going to do, such as, *"God, please be with my wife today."* Guess what? He is always with her if she is in Christ! Actually, He is in her!

The Scripture says, *"With men this is impossible but with God all things are possible."* What if we asked God for our city? What if we all came together and asked for a Holy Spirit takeover to happen within our churches that would spill out into our city? We may think that is impossible but that impossibility opens the door for God to work and get all the glory! He has healed the sick, opened the eyes of the blind, and even raised the dead! He can do it! Will we ask? James writes that, *"We have not because we ask not."* (James 4:3) Let's ask Him to give us our city right now!

PRAYER TARGET:

People in the city of Knoxville-longing for more of Gods blessings for our city.

PERSONAL PRAYER FOR KNOXVILLE:

Jesus, You are good and You are God! Like David cried out in 2 Samuel, we echo, "How great are You, O sovereign Lord! There is no one like You. There is no other God. We have never even heard of another God like You." You alone are the God who makes the impossible a possibility. So, like Caleb asked during the conquest for You to give him the mountain we are asking you, Jesus, to give us the city of Knoxville for Your glory! Holy Spirit, sweep through our churches and crush our cultural Christianity. Heal what is broken, mend what needs to be fixed, and bring alive those who are dead in worldliness and religion. Awaken us, God, to Your leading. Unite us, call us out in power from our comfortable pews and lead us as grace warriors into our city. May we engage Knoxville with the love, grace, and mercy that comes from You, Jesus! Holy Spirit, fall on us and make what seems to be impossible a reality! Amen.

WEEK NINE: MONDAY

AUTHOR: DAVID R. COLLINS
FAMILY STRUCTURE: WIFE, 3 ADULT CHILDREN, AND 1 GRAND-DAUGHTER.
OCCUPATION: ASSOCIATE PASTOR OF CONGREGATIONAL CARE

HOW CAN THEY DO THAT?

> **"Let every person be subject to the governing authorities. … Would you have no fear of the one who is in authority? Then do what is good, and you will receive his approval, for he is God's servant for your good. But if you do wrong, be afraid, for he does not bear the sword in vain. For he is the servant of God, an avenger who carries out God's wrath on the wrongdoer. Therefore, one must be in subjection, not only to avoid God's wrath but also for the sake of conscience." Romans 13:1, 3-5**

Have you ever been driving down the road a "little" to fast when you catch the glimpse of a police officer and your first response is OH, NO? Obviously, you, like me, immediately recognize that you are at fault and your conscience lets you know that you are guilty.

One Sunday afternoon, while serving as a Pastor in a rural county, a sheriff's deputy asked dispatch to contact me and have me come to a parishioner's home. The situation needed a minister. The son- in-law in the family had just hurt his step daughter, then murdered his wife, and completed the tragedy by committing suicide. A short time after ministering to the family that traumatic day I began to look at law enforcement personnel differently. Officers experience the darkness of the world and depravity of mankind daily. Each episode happens quickly and then are dispatched to the next call to deal with something totally different. Yet they remain a peacemaker. HOW CAN THEY DO THAT? It is by God's GRACE! (Rom. 8:31)

Each time you pass an area where blue lights are flashing on the cars of law enforcement officers breathe a prayer for the officers who are doing what God has called them to do. They are serving as servants of the LORD!

PRAYER TARGET:
Law enforcement officers.

PERSONAL PRAYER FOR KNOXVILLE:
Lord Jesus, thank You for bringing us to the reality that Law Enforcement Officers are Your servants, used by You to execute the laws of our governing authorities. Thank You that they desire to be peacemakers in a place of confusion. Father, instead of following the behaviors of people who only spew contempt and hatred for the men and women in BLUE, help us be peacemakers through falling to our knees to talk to You. Because there are those who are guided by Satan to throw insults, punches, rocks, and shoot bullets at the officers, let us be found daily lifting our officers to You in prayer, asking You to protect them and keep them safe. Remind us daily to meet these officers with words of encouragement for the service they do continually. In Your Name, Jesus, Amen.

AUTHOR: WILLIAM B. STOKELY, III
FAMILY STRUCTURE: WIFE, 4 CHILDREN, AND 13 GRANDCHILDREN
OCCUPATION: OWNER, EAST TENNESSEE BASED COMPANIES

SURRENDER IS A GOOD THING!

"Purify me from my sins, and I will be clean: Wash me, and I will be whiter than snow. Oh, give me back my joy again: You have broken me – now let me rejoice. Don't keep looking at my sins. Remove the stain of my guilt. Create in me a clean heart, O God. Renew a loyal spirit within me. Do not banish me from your presence, And don't take your Holy Spirit from me. Restore to me the joy of your salvation, And make me willing to obey you. Then I will teach your ways to rebels, And they will return to you." Psalm 51:7-13 (The Psalm that directed me when I first gave my life to Christ.)

"Show me the right path, O Lord; Point out the road to follow. Lead me by your truth and teach me, For you are the God who saves me. All day long I put my hopes in you. Remember, O Lord, your compassion and unfailing love, which you have shown from ages past. Do not remember the rebellious sins of my youth. Remember me in the light of your unfailing Love, for you are merciful, O Lord." Psalm 25:4-7 (The Psalm that directs my daily walk with God.)

After many years of being what I would term a "cafeteria" Christian, I became acutely aware of my incomplete relationship with God. There was a gulf or separation between what He wanted for me and a "real" relationship with Him. I needed to surrender my humanness, that ten percent or so of my life that I had not turned over completely to God. I did surrender in faith, to all those impediments and questions, and gave my life fully to Christ and His Father, God. It was like a veil had been lifted from my eyes and a weight off my heart. I developed a love and desire to immerse myself in the Word. That action brought a new understanding to me.

My heart was changed upon repentance of my many sins and my outlook towards life and other people was changed forever. I regret that this change come after too many wasted years but it was my running away and His patience that finally crossed paths. It is my deep honor now to mentor others along their walk with the Lord in the wonderful study of the Gospel. I try to let others see Christ in me as I pass through this life. Praise God!

PRAYER TARGET:
The men of the city who are walking in darkness but believe they are walking in light.

PERSONAL PRAYER FOR KNOXVILLE:
Heavenly Father, I pray that others will read these devotions and find the spark that triggers them to examine themselves carefully. Guide them in searching their hearts and lead them to determine if their walk is real or just going through the motions without any real relationship with You, Jesus. If they want to come closer, Father, draw them to "surrender" themselves to the Holy Spirit and let the heart change begin in their lives. I pray in the Name of Jesus and God that their hearts will be stirred in a real way. Bring each man in Knoxville closer to the path that You have planned for them. This prayer is prayed in Your Name, Jesus. Amen.

WEEK NINE: WEDNESDAY

AUTHOR: JERRY R. JOHNSON
FAMILY STRUCTURE: WIFE, 3 CHILDREN, AND 9 GRANDCHILDREN
OCCUPATION: RETIRED PHYSICIAN

OUR WALK

"Therefore, be careful how you walk, not as unwise men but as wise." Ephesians 5:15

The Christian life is a "walk," not a sprint. Our walk is enabled by the Holy Spirit filling us and ordering our steps. In the Psalms we are told, *"How blessed is the man who does not walk in the counsel of the wicked, Nor stand in the path of sinners, Nor sit in the seat of scoffers! But his delight is in the law of the LORD, and in His law, he meditates day and night. He will be like a tree firmly planted by streams of water, which yields its fruit in its season and its leaf does not wither; and in whatever he does, he prospers."*(Psalm 1:1-3)

To walk with God means we choose to glorify Him in every way we can, regardless of personal cost. We must choose the "narrow road" over the broad way to destruction.

PRAYER TARGET:
Followers of Christ who "walk" in our community daily.

PERSONAL PRAYER FOR KNOXVILLE:
Father, we are tempted by the evil one to walk in a way that is pleasing to the world. Convict us by Your Spirit, to walk our daily lives as You have instructed. You, Father, have also empowered us by your Spirit to lead non- believers to Jesus. Help us present You to them so they will be drawn to You. Lead us to use our God-given power in a mighty way. Help us to be the salt and

light that You made is to be in the midst of a wicked and perverse generation. Send us forth, Father, to do as You command. Amen.

WEEK NINE: THURSDAY

AUTHOR: ALISHA BALLENGER
FAMILY STRUCTURE: HUSBAND AND 2 CHILDREN
OCCUPATION: ELEMENTARY MINISTRY COORDINATOR

REDEEM MY FAMILY TREE

> **"Here it is in a nutshell: Just as one person did it wrong and got us in all this trouble with sin and death, another person did it right and got us out of it. But more than just getting us out of trouble, he got us into life! But sin didn't, and doesn't, have a chance in competition with the aggressive forgiveness we call grace. When it's sin versus grace, grace wins hands down." Romans 5:18-19, 21**

Holidays are often for the gathering of family members. I have to admit that sometimes I have a sense of dread when it comes to seeing certain family members. If everyone is honest we all have at least one person that we dread seeing. They often stir up a lot of drama and harsh feelings. Some have addiction issues that they don't try to hide. If we examine our family tree it's often full of brokenness, sin and pain. Yet, we see in scripture that God can redeem even those that are the farthest away from Him.

Recently I've been working my way through the gospels and observed that Jesus had a messy family tree too. Abraham tried to fulfill the promise for a son with his own plans by taking a concubine. Jacob was a liar and a manipulator. Tamar had an inappropriate relationship with her father in law in order to have a son. Ruth was a despised foreigner. David was an adulterer and a murderer. Amidst the brokenness of the people in Jesus' family tree, God was at work in their lives. He was at work pouring out His grace. They were part of His ultimate plan to redeem humanity. As I reflect on these stories it gives me hope that God can redeem those who are lost in my family. His grace is truly greater than all our sin.

PRAYER TARGET:
Family members who need to be transformed by the Gospel.

PERSONAL PRAYER FOR KNOXVILLE:
God, every person in Knoxville has members of their family who are lost without You. First, I pray for our own families and specifically for those who don't know You and are far from You. Thank You God, that You pursue us even when we are far from You in sin. I pray that you would help us show grace and the love of Christ to these family members. Finally Father, I pray for all those who are lost without You in Knoxville. Help each of us to be willing to share our faith with those around us. Lead everyone to have a desire to be a part of your family God. Amen.

WEEK NINE: FRIDAY

AUTHOR: KATE HENDRIX
FAMILY STRUCTURE: AN ADULT DAUGHTER
OCCUPATION: ORGANIZATIONAL VOLUNTEER

KNOXVILLE - A PLACE OF WORLD REACHING BLESSING!

"In him all the nations of the earth will be blessed." Genesis 18:18

Knoxville is peppered with a plethora of places of worship; our airways are filled with broadcasts of the good news; and several bookstores supply us with faith building resources. We have many blessings to share! Our institutions of education and industries attract people from all over the world, and since 1982 Knoxville has been a City of Refuge.

Some of our international neighbors may be from countries where the gospel is restricted. There have relatively few mentors in the Christian faith and limited opportunity for fellowship in the Spirit. We have an abundance to share!

Internationals who receive life in Christ here are superbly equipped to share this new life with their families and communities, extending the blessing both here and abroad! As God's people, let's have a prayer-full priority to bless our international neighbors with His love and truth, to see our neighbors enter the Kingdom of righteousness and peace, and to experience the joy of salvation!

PRAYER TARGET:
International neighbors.

PERSONAL PRAYER FOR KNOXVILLE:
Lord, may we love You, the Maker of every nation, with our

whole heart. May we love our international neighbors as we love ourselves. May we make the most of every opportunity to share Your abundant blessings. God, we desire the blessing of worshipping together with every tribe and tongue that You have brought to Knoxville. We pray all this in the name of our Lord Jesus Christ for the sake of Your Kingdom coming on earth and Your glory covering the earth! Amen.

WEEK TEN: MONDAY

AUTHOR: CHUCK MORRIS
FAMILY STRUCTURE: WIFE AND 2 CHILDREN
OCCUPATION: MINISTER, PROFESSOR

PLANTED BY THE SOURCE

> **"Thus, says the Lord: 'Cursed is the man who trusts in man and makes flesh his strength, whose heart departs from the Lord. For he shall be like a shrub in the desert, and shall not see when good comes, but shall inhabit the parched places in the wilderness, in a salt land which is not inhabited. Blessed is the man who trusts in the Lord. For he shall be like a tree planted by the waters, which spreads out its roots by the river, and will not fear when heat comes; but its leaf will be green, and will not be anxious in the year of drought, nor will cease from yielding fruit.'" Jeremiah 17: 5-8**

Here, we see a contrast between two "men," one who relies upon his own strength and the other who places his trust in God. The prophet Jeremiah paints a dramatic picture that shows how, based upon where we place our trust, our lives will either show curse or blessing. If we desire to succeed in God's eyes, we need to be planted very near our Source of strength and nourishment. The one who is far from the Source will experience a blindness to the good things of God, shall live in a place of desolation and loneliness, and will eventually wither. On the other hand, the one who plants himself by the waters will enjoy constant access to the Spirit, including not being afraid when the drought comes (and it will). Additionally, this "tree" will have green leaves, offering shade to others and be a visible testimony, giving credit for his leaves to the One who nourishes him.

Finally, this blessed man will not "cease from yielding fruit." His life will bear both the fruits of the Spirt as well as the fruits of salvation seen in evangelism. Truly, the one planted by the waters will be able to fulfill the call that God has placed upon his life.

PRAYER TARGET:
Believers in the City longing to be firmly planted in Him.

PERSONAL PRAYER FOR KNOXVILLE:
Father, I pray that every Christian in Knoxville would come to understand the importance of knowing where they are planted. Relying upon our own strength, whether as people, denominations, or other divisions, will leave us unprepared to do what You, God, have called us to do. So, plant us close to You and the Spirit, and assist us as we fully function in Your will. Keep us with You, the Source, even in the face of tough times. Lead us to always desire to have Your leading in our lives.
May we be so planted! Amen.

WEEK TEN: TUESDAY

AUTHOR: LARRY ANDERSON
FAMILY STRUCTURE: WIFE, 5 CHILDREN, AND 5 GRANDCHILDREN
OCCUPATION: PASTOR, BUSINESSMAN, CONTRACTOR

CLEANSING WATERS

> "Now there is in Jerusalem by the Sheep Gate a pool, which is called in Hebrew, Bethesda having five porches. In these lay a great multitude of sick people, blind, lame, paralyzed, waiting for the moving of the water. For an angel went down at a certain time into the pool and stirred up the water; then whoever stepped in first, after the stirring of the water, was made well of whatever disease he had. Now a certain man was there who had an infirmity thirty-eight years." John 5:2-5

In life, we all have times of despair. We feel alone and unseen. The world is in the same place as the lame man at the Sheep Gate found himself at the pool known as Bethesda (translated house of mercy in Hebrew). He was frightened…isolated…in need…and helpless.

The real point for us in this teaching is not the healing…for God heals; nor the angel…for God sends the angels; nor the water…for water is only figurative of cleansing. The point for us is twofold;

    1. *The man had the patience to wait upon the Lord so his delay of healing was not his doing.*

    2. *The people that passed him were guilty of a) demanding God to do something by sending an angel or b) being indifferent to the plight of someone they saw daily.*

As we pray, let us be mindful that God (Jesus) chooses to work in, of, by, and through His people…the Church. Prayer is where the action is because God releases the blessings in response to the fervent prayers of His people. Once prayed down, the *blessings* are ours and those blessings demand that we be available and faithful to deliver to others in need by God's grace.

The man at the pool had faith. He was there every day. Are we?

PRAYER TARGET:
The people that are seen daily—but that Christians may step over unknowingly.

PERSONAL PRAYER FOR KNOXVILLE:
Father, help us stop trying to appear to be the righteousness of Christ and become the righteousness of Christ. We know that the Holy Spirit heals the afflicted, feeds the hungry, and draws the lost to salvation. Help us be as Spirit-filled as we appear. May we act daily in a manner that people will want to walk as we walk. Lord, lead us to be a shadow that falls over those in need just as Peter was when he served You in his caring ministry in Jerusalem. Make us worthy to be called Christians. (Acts 5:12-16) Now, as we seek to fulfill Your call to the compassionate ministry of Christ, may the evidence of the Holy Spirit be so magnified in our walk in the world that people are amazed as needs are met with our assistance. Father, lead us to walk in love and peace so we too can be a Bethesda (House of Mercy) in our communities. Open the eyes of our hearts Lord!!! Amen.

WEEK TEN: WEDNESDAY

AUTHOR: ASHLEY SHEPHERD
FAMILY STRUCTURE: HUSBAND AND 2 BOYS
OCCUPATION: AUTHOR, BUSINESS FOUNDER

PRAYING WITH EXPECTATION

> **"You have turned for me my mourning into dancing; you have loosed my sackcloth and clothed me with gladness, that my glory may sing your praise and not be silent.**
> **O LORD my God, I will give thanks to you forever!"**
> **Psalm 30:11-12**

As a work-from-home mom of two very energetic boys there are many nights I go to bed just wanting to stare at a blank wall. My to do list is pulling me in eighty-seven different directions and I crave to be that "present" mom I read about in all of those "feel good" mom blogs.

One night as I was trying to shut my brain off to rest the Lord told me to open my Bible. When I did I landed on Psalm 30. Immediately the stress of my messy house, dirty dishes, laundry left in the dryer, and dirty kids turned into a HOPE that in the morning I could let the God of the Universe clothe me with gladness. It would be a great opportunity to give Him thanks for all of my blessings.

As a woman, it's easy to focus on things I don't do perfectly, but if I listen to God I find that He wants me to focus on the things that matter. He beautifully designed me for a purpose, so I'm now planning to enjoy my beautiful mess and focus on the HOPE that each morning brings in Him.

PRAYER TARGET:
The women of the city with young children.

PERSONAL PRAYER FOR KNOXVILLE:

Father God, I want to pray over every woman as they wake up in the mornings. I pray they know their significance comes from You and that perfection does not exist. I pray that every mother can rest their identity in You, the One who beautifully designed them. I pray they stop and enjoy the small moments and not focus on getting to the next "stage" or "day." Father, there is no beginning and end with God. He wants us to soak up every minute we have with our beautiful children, be they young or old. I pray that each woman can close their eyes at the end of each day and REST in your Peace. Help them nightly to get ready to rise and cling to YOUR joy when they wake in the morning. Amen.

WEEK TEN: THURSDAY

AUTHOR: ERIN SANFORD
FAMILY STRUCTURE: HUSBAND AND 2 CHILDREN
OCCUPATION: NURSE

AN UNREPENTANT HEART

"So, when you, a mere human being, pass judgment on them and yet do the same things, do you think you will escape God's judgment? Or do you show contempt for the riches of his kindness, forbearance and patience, not realizing that God's kindness is intended to lead you to repentance?" Romans 2:3-4

"If we deliberately keep on sinning after we have received the knowledge of the truth, no sacrifice for sins is left, but only a fearful expectation of judgment and of raging fire that will consume the enemies of God. Anyone who rejected the law of Moses died without mercy on the testimony of two or three witnesses. How much more severely do you think someone deserves to be punished who has trampled the Son of God underfoot, who has treated as an unholy thing the blood of the covenant that sanctified them, and who has insulted the Spirit of grace? For we know him who said, "It is mine to avenge; I will repay, "and again, "The Lord will judge his people." It is a dreadful thing to fall into the hands of the living God." Hebrews 10:26-31

If we truly knew who we were sinning against would our actions continue? There was a time in my life I had an unrepentant heart and simply did not care that there was sin in my life. The Lord showed me multiple scriptures that helped me understand how holy, powerful, and set apart that He is. Sin has no place anywhere near such a holy God. My sin didn't just ruin me, but I was sinning against a God who is holy. He owes me nothing, yet

gives me everything. I had all this sin in my life but would take advantage of the love and kindness of my Savior.
I don't know it can be really called a relationship if all I did was take advantage of His love for me. What a pitiful relationship! I would tell myself, "I know that He will forgive me…surely He understands this life we live is just so hard," and allow that to justify my actions.

That is not the intention of His kindness and grace. He revealed to me that my sin is against a holy God who is to be feared and respected, and sin puts a barrier between us. His grace and mercy towards us does not show a lack of intent to judge sin and is not meant to be taken advantage of. Only by His grace is He so kind and loving to give me the opportunity to be called "His." This transformed my response to the sin in my life and in the lives of others. I no longer respond with complacency in my own life but with grief and repentance, realizing the weight of my sin. I also no longer condemn or judge the sins of others but respond with a God-given love, with sorrow and sympathy, and a longing for others to experience the fullness of life Christ has to offer.

PRAYER TARGET:
Unrepentant hearts.

PERSONAL PRAYER FOR KNOXVILLE:
Lord, break our hearts and help us understand how sin separates us from You and prevents us from having a relationship with You. You are holy and set apart. Sin has no place anywhere near You yet You gave Your son for us because you love us so dearly. Thank You for sacrificing Your son so that we may be able to have a relationship with You, Father. I pray that we understand the gravity of our sin and the extent of pain Christ had to endure to save us. May that soften our hearts and compel us to love You with everything we have and live a life worthy of our calling. May we show others truth and love in hopes that they may also experience the fullness of life that You offer. In Your holy, worthy, precious name we pray. Amen.

WEEK TEN: FRIDAY

AUTHOR: TERRY BLALOCK
FAMILY STRUCTURE: WIFE AND 2 ADULT CHILDREN
OCCUPATION: BUSINESS DEVELOPMENT MANAGER

FAITH OR FEAR

"For if you remain silent at this time, relief and deliverance for the Jews will arise from another place, but you and your father's family will perish. And who knows but that you have come to your royal position for such a time as this?" Esther 4:14

"I am the vine; you are the branches. If you remain in me and I in you, you will bear much fruit; apart from me you can do nothing." John 15:5

Today, to make a stand for Christ opens us up to criticism, insults, rejection and accusations. Many believers feel under attack in public and the workplace. But followers of Christ must share our faith unashamedly, boldly and in love, not only in our words but also our actions.

What drives you? What drives me? Faith or Fear? For me it depends on the day, but when I read the verses above and ask God for courage, guidance, and His love, my dilemma changes. The Holy Spirit makes clear that I face a choice – Faith or Fear. These difficult and sometimes scary situations are not new to God nor His people. God used people, like Esther, to glorify Himself and to encourage us. The same example is appropriate for all today. God knows our situations because He allows us to endure them – and maybe this circumstance is the very reason we were born. God will not allow us to walk through this valley alone. He is with us.

If I act as Christ leads, I will bear much fruit. Therefore, why don't I always choose to stand for Christ? Because sometimes fear rules my life. But not today. I cannot speak for tomorrow, but today Faith rules.

PRAYER TARGET:
Believers facing rejection for their faith.

PERSONAL PRAYER FOR KNOXVILLE:
Father, lead all in this city to choose to live by faith daily. Help us, please, to rely on the Holy Spirit to identify our choices and learn how He wants us to respond. It is our desire, Father, to make decisions that glorify You. Magnify our trust in Christ and allow us through that trust to bear fruit through our lives. I pray that we will see others as Christ sees them and act in boldness and love. For the times that we have stayed silent, withheld our help, and rushed past many key opportunities, we ask forgiveness. God, today slow us down. Give us courage to choose faith and love to rule in our lives. Let us have no fear today. I ask this as Your child and in Jesus' name. Amen.

WEEK ELEVEN: MONDAY

AUTHOR: BO SANFORD
FAMILY STRUCTURE: WIFE AND 2 DAUGHTERS
OCCUPATION: LAWYER

THE BELIEVER'S FREEDOM

> **"Everything is permissible, but not everything is beneficial. Everything is permissible, but not everything is constructive. Nobody should seek his own good, but the good of others." I Corinthians 10:23-24**

In response to a recent desire to improve my physical health, I decided to subject myself to the "paleo" diet. I then began 'googling' different foods that I liked to eat to determine whether they were, in fact, "paleo". Not surprisingly, my focus quickly shifted from improving my physical health to satisfying the technical rules of this new diet.

We must not make the same mistake in our pursuit of Jesus. Paul notes in his letter to the Corinthians that "everything is permissible, but not everything is beneficial". This is important because, through Jesus, we are set free from the bondage of sin. Moreover, we are free to shift our focus from what we can and cannot do, to what Jesus has done and what He is calling us to do.

Such freedom, though, is not to be exercised selfishly. When presented with the opportunity to exercise our freedom, our concern should not be "can I justify this?" or "is this a sin?", but rather, "will this glorify God or further His Kingdom?"

PRAYER TARGET:
All believers seeking freedom from bondage of this world.

PERSONAL PRAYER FOR KNOXVILLE:
Father, I pray that the Holy Spirit would give us the confidence and discretion to go out into the world and see both the lost and one another as Jesus sees us; that we would instinctively act and move in accordance with Your will, Father. May we not abuse the freedom that Jesus won for us, but live in uninhibited pursuit and furtherance of Your kingdom. Amen

WEEK ELEVEN: TUESDAY

AUTHOR: MELISSA CAGLE
FAMILY STRUCTURE: HUSBAND AND 2 ADULT CHILDREN

EVERYTHING WE NEED

**"His divine power has given us everything we need for life and godliness through our knowledge of him who called us by his own glory and goodness. Through these he has given us his very great and precious promises."
2 Peter 1:2-4a**

In Revelation, Satan is called the "accuser of the brethren" and in the book of John, Jesus calls him "a liar and the father of lies." As a Christ follower, if I choose to listen to the lies and accusations of Satan, I will spend most of my time either regretting the mistakes of my past or living in fear and anxiety for my future. And when I am paralyzed by fear or regret, I am totally ineffective for the kingdom work that God has called me to today.

But as one who has trusted Christ to do for me what I could not do, I can forget what is behind and trust Christ for what is ahead. I don't have to waste my life regretting what He has already forgiven. I can lay down my fears for tomorrow and trust that He will take care of me, my family and my future. I can understand that my obedience today is the only thing I have to give Him.

PRAYER TARGET:
Christians bound by fear and regret.

PERSONAL PRAYER FOR KNOXVILLE:
God, may we walk in the knowledge that You have given us everything we need for life and godliness. May we show You that we believe Your promise of forgiveness by laying down the sins of our past that You have already forgiven and not taking them

up again. May we show You that we believe Your promises to care for us by laying down our worries about tomorrow. Help us to choose not to manipulate our circumstances or the people around us to fit our own agendas, but to trust Your plan for our best. And when our hearts and minds are free from these distractions, help us to hear Your voice and get busy obeying the call You have given us for today. Amen.

AUTHOR: HAILEY ROSE VIARS
FAMILY STRUCTURE: PARENTS AND ME
OCCUPATION: COLLEGE STUDENT

FINDING PURPOSE IN THE PAIN

"For if you remain silent at this time, relief and deliverance for the Jews will arise from another place, but you and your father's family will perish. And who knows but that you have come to your royal position for such a time as this?" Esther 4:14

My favorite part of this verse is the last line. Mordecai is telling Esther: *"Perhaps this is the moment for which you have been created."* At the time Esther could not see God's hand in her life. All she could see was the pain and suffering she and her people were facing. But God had a plan. God had a purpose for their suffering. Because in the end, God got the victory.

I often find myself in the same position as Esther. I wonder and worry about the outcome of something and focus on the pain of the situation rather than focusing on God's purpose for my pain. At times like this, I forget just how big my God is. Because the truth is, as cliché as it sounds, everything truly does happen for a reason, and He works all things for our good. After all, God is the artist and our lives are His masterpieces. Though we can only see a small section at a time, He sees the entirety of His painting and the entirety of our lives. He sees the purpose in our pain.

Someone wise once said: *"You have been given this mountain to show others that it can be moved."* God uses our struggles. He uses our faithfulness. He uses His masterpieces to be a light unto the world. He knows what struggles we will face, but He is not worried. Why worry when He knows, that in the end, we will be victorious.

PRAYER TARGET:
The doubtful.

PERSONAL PRAYER FOR KNOXVILLE:
God, how great and how wonderful You are. You are all-knowing and all-powerful. As we walk through these valleys let us never forget that You are walking with us. That You have led us through these storms for a reason. That You have the victory! God, You have created each and every one of us to lift Your name and to glorify You in all that we do. I pray for guidance as we go through our daily lives that we would seek Your face, Your will, and Your purpose. I pray that You would heal our broken hearts and would take away our pain. But God, if that is not Your will, then I pray that You would ease our suffering. Surround us with Your peace that passes all understanding. I thank You, God, for Your unfailing love. In Your name, I pray these things. Amen.

WEEK ELEVEN: THURSDAY

AUTHOR: GREG TREVATHAN
FAMILY STRUCTURE: WIFE AND 3 CHILDREN
OCCUPATION: PASTOR

DO NOT HOLD BACK

> "Enlarge the place of your tent, and let the curtains of your habitations be stretched out; do not hold back; lengthen your cords and strengthen your stakes. For you will spread abroad to the right and to the left, and your offspring will possess the nations and will people the desolate cities."
> Isaiah 54:2-3

Death compels honesty. The dying have no reason to hold back; the purpose of life is in sharp relief. There is no reason any longer for pretense or guile or guise. We should listen to what people with nothing to lose have to say. Most of them say they wish they hadn't held back. More than not making more money, not accomplishing greater feats, or not being more well-known, a dying person regrets not having really lived life.

Jesus told us in John 10 that He came to give abundant life. This above passage in Isaiah shows this about the Father's heart as well. God wants to increase in our lives. He desires to enlarge us, stretch us, lengthen us, and strengthen us. Why? So that our lives might be a refuge for others.

We're told how to have a life with just that kind of impact; Do not hold back. Today live with the courage to be completely who the Father made you to be in His image. Do not be who others tell you to be or even believe you to be. Sons and daughters, do not hold back!

PRAYER TARGET:
Those desiring a wholehearted life-holding nothing back.

PERSONAL PRAYER FOR KNOXVILLE:

Father, thank You for holding nothing back. I rejoice that You gave the greatest gift you could, Your one and only Son, Jesus Christ! May I know who I am in Christ today. Let confidence in Your love for me override every fear. Help me today to not hold back. I want to live wholeheartedly for You, as You lived wholeheartedly for me. I want to partner with Your Holy Spirit today to live without fear. Thank You, Father, that what You think about me, say about me, feel about me, and have done for me matters above all else. Today help me to not hold back my love for You, my forgiveness of others, the truths I need to speak, or the love I need to show. Help me to live this day wholeheartedly. Father, I ask You to show me now one way I've been holding back and one thing I can do today to respond in obedient love. In Jesus' name, Amen.

WEEK ELEVEN: FRIDAY

AUTHOR: RAFAEL RODRIGUEZ
FAMILY STRUCTURE: WIFE AND 2 CHILDREN
OCCUPATION: PROFESSOR OF NEW TESTAMENT

LET THERE BE PEACE

> **"One of the winged creatures flew to me, holding a glowing coal that he had taken from the altar with tongs. He touched my mouth and said, 'See, this has touched your lips. Your guilt has departed, and your sin is removed.' Then I heard the Lord's voice saying, 'Whom should I send, and who will go for us?' I said, 'I'm here; send me."**
> **Isaiah 6:6-8**

When God speaks, things happen. In the Bible's opening chapter, God speaks into the darkness, "Let there be light" (Gen 1:3). Prior to that moment, light had never been. God spoke the impossible, and at His command creation contorted itself in obedience to His word. *"And there was light."* Paul has this in mind when he says God "Calls into existence the things that do not exist." (Rom 4:17) When God speaks, things happen.

If only God would speak more. Consider the broken state of our city, our state, our country, and our world. In Turkey, a two-year old boy washes ashore, drowned trying to escape his war-torn homeland. In a Minneapolis, Minnesota suburb, a mosque explodes just before FRIDAY prayers. In Chattanooga, a school bus crashes and six children's voices fall silent. In Knoxville, a fifteen- year old is killed shielding his friends from danger. And we strain our ears to hear God speaking.

Today, the voice of God echoes through the words and deeds of His people, the Church. Today, He sends us, who are called by His name, to feed the hungry, welcome the stranger, and care for the sick. If we would see God create anew what was good—even very good—let us be His word to our city: *"Let there be peace."*

PRAYER TARGET:
The Church that they may see God in His people who are called by Him.

PERSONAL PRAYER FOR KNOXVILLE:
Father, this world is the work of Your hands, and as such it bears Your goodness and we bear Your image. In a city wearing the scars of brokenness, marked by sin, give us the faith, the courage, and the grace to provide strength for those who stumble, peace for the restless, and compassion for the estranged. Work Your healing in us. Then, send us to work Your healing in others. May we see Your kingdom spread throughout our city, in all its neighborhoods, among all its peoples. And may Your Church heed Your Spirit in order to do Your work in this, our home. In Jesus' name. Amen.

WEEK TWELVE: MONDAY

AUTHOR: MARTY THOMPSON
FAMILY STRUCTURE: WIFE, 2 CHILDREN, AND 14 GRANDCHILDREN
OCCUPATION: EXECUTIVE DIRECTOR

A SERVANT'S GAZE

> "To you I lift up my eyes, O you who are enthroned in the heavens! Behold, as the eyes of servants look to the hand of their master, as the eyes of a maidservant to the hand of her mistress, so our eyes look to the Lord our God, till he has mercy upon us." Psalm 123:1-2

In the midst of my busy schedule I don't often reflect how much I need the Lord. However, when I stop to remember how needy I am, it helps me look at God differently; especially when I pray.

This passage in Psalms compares my relationship to God to that of a servant and his master, a maidservant to her mistress. And because of Christ, I have become a bondservant of God (Romans 1:1); utterly in need of His provision. Therefore, realizing I am a needy servant, dependent upon God's mercy and grace, points me to the importance of prayer. Prayer that is not a duty, nor an obligation. When I remind myself who I am and who God is, prayer becomes my spiritual life's breath; a way for me to acknowledge my God and Savior as the One who provides me with everything I need for life.

With this perspective, I can remove prayer from our list of things to do and place it back where it belongs – a vital part of my walk with God. Life-changing prayer rests on the foundation of acknowledging my need for God – in other words, it begins by having the attitude of a dependent servant.

PRAYER TARGET:
The men and women of the city longing to be dependent

PERSONAL PRAYER FOR KNOXVILLE:

Father, I praise You for Your lovingkindness, Your mercy and grace. You alone are worthy of my praise. The men and women of our city are fruitful, hardworking and accomplish much for the good of people and our city. However, many find it difficult to slow down enough to remember who we are in Christ. Through your Holy Spirit Lord, help us all find spiritual eyes that gaze upon You and beseech You as a servant. Humble each of us and help us become people who rely not on the works of our hands, but on you Father, our Sovereign God. Amen.

WEEK TWELVE: TUESDAY

AUTHOR: JOSH SMITH
FAMILY STRUCTURE: WIFE AND 4 CHILDREN
OCCUPATION: BUSINESS OWNER

DON'T CHASE MORE "STUFF"

"But all too quickly the message is crowded out by the worries of this life, the lure of wealth, and the desire for other things, so no fruit is produced." Mark 4:19

I grew up in a financially challenged, single mother household. I always looked at other people with money and thought that "Happiness" was something that I could have if I attained "a lot" of money. My search began, and I pursued this "a lot" of money, working very hard and waiting for the feeling of happiness to come as I reached various levels of success. I watched others buy things they couldn't afford with money they didn't have, working tough jobs that left them stressed out and keeping them from family and fellowship. All this was happening while pursuing this "happiness," but like me not truly finding it.

The scripture above talks about the message of God being crowded out by the worries of life, the lure of wealth, and the desire for other things. It's so easy to lose our kingdom perspective when we are chasing things that one day will mean nothing in the light of eternity. This is SO HARD, for both those who have little as well as for those who have a lot, but are continuing to pursue more. 1 Timothy 6:6-12 we read, *"Yet true godliness with contentment is itself great wealth. After all, we brought nothing with us when we came into the world, and we can't take anything with us when we leave it. So if we have enough food and clothing, let us be content. But people who long to be rich fall into temptation and are trapped by many foolish and harmful desires that plunge them into ruin and destruction. For the love of money is the root of all kinds of evil.*

122

And some people, craving money, have wandered from the true faith and pierced themselves with many sorrows.

What should our focus be on? What should drive us? What can we be involved with that will help us keep an eternal perspective?
These are excellent questions for all of us to ponder.

PRAYER TARGET:
All those that are seeking happiness.

PERSONAL PRAYER FOR KNOXVILLE:
Father, let us be cravers of You God, and not just stuff. Help us be givers into Your work and kingdom, with both our time, our talents, and our resources. Bring us together, lead us, and walk with us as we do what You called us to do. Forgive us, God, for getting so caught up in the junk of this world and putting our worldly desires before You. You are so good to us. Help us honor Your goodness with everything we have. We owe you everything Lord!!! Have your way in us, which will allow You to have Your way in our city and in our communities! Bring us together as a body in unity, to impact those who don't know You. Lead us as we testify to Your goodness. Give our leaders in the community the wisdom to develop ideas that can impact generations to come in a way that builds the kingdom! Thank You, Lord, for letting us be a small part in Your big, glorious plan! We love You, Lord!!!! We owe you everything, and are nothing without You!!! Have your way in us, God! Amen.

AUTHOR: BRAD MAYNARD
FAMILY STRUCTURE: WIFE AND 4 CHILDREN
OCCUPATION: CEO

GETTING REAL

"For it is God who is at work in you, both to will and to work for His good pleasure." Ephesians 3:21

I will put My Spirit within you and cause you to walk in My statutes, and you will be careful to observe My ordinances." Ezekiel 36:27

Christianity is not, as "conservatives" presuppose, a moral code. Nor is it, as "liberals" insist, an ideology. Christianity is a relationship with the living Father God. It's God's answer to the deepest longing in a man's heart.

It's time to press on beyond the Law to the fullness of what Jesus died to give men--namely, Sonship. Herein lies the ultimate "men's movement," fueled by this central, New Covenant truth: Jesus did not come to tell us what to do but, rather, to do once and for all what we could not. We're not saved by our promises, but by God's promises.

Jesus' saving work in men is prompted, therefore, not by the shame which makes us strive to do right, but by the grace which allows us to be real. It's sustained not by trying to measure up but only by confessing that we can't. It proceeds not from a determination to do the right thing, but from a longing to know the true Father.

This ultimate "men's movement" is today stirring in the hearts of men everywhere. But it has yet to break forth, largely because we men haven't discovered that self-discipline is a fruit of the Spirit-- not a natural product of our own efforts, but a supernatural product of the Father s grace (Gal. 5:22-23). A real man is a man who's real. And only real men can lead us into this New Covenant manhood--men who have dared to cry out their own inadequacy and surrendered it to Jesus for Him alone to bear.

PRAYER TARGET:
Men seeking to understand what a real man is.

PERSONAL PRAYER FOR KNOXVILLE:
Father, I pray that each man would know that they don't have to have all the answers or all the discipline because You, God, have provided that. Do not allow men to fall for the deception that it's all about our own efforts. Help them know, Father, that men will not be saved by our promises to one another but by Your promises. Dear God, You are the true Promise Keeper. Thank You for that! Father, help men cease their anxious, striving mentality. Change it to having an awareness that they are a son of The Heavenly Father, and that makes them free indeed. Lead men to embrace a peace that is opposite from fear and simply learn to cry out to You, Father. In Your Precious Name. Amen.

WEEK TWELVE: THURSDAY

AUTHOR: ANGELIA BLALOCK
FAMILY STRUCTURE: HUSBAND, 2 DAUGHTERS AND A SON-IN-LAW
OCCUPATIONS: PRISON MINISTRY

FROM FEAR TO FOLLOWING

"When I am afraid, I will trust in you. In God, whose word I praise, in God I trust; I will not be afraid. What can mortal man do to me?" Psalm 56:3-4

An acrostic for fear is: FALSE EVIDENCE APPEARING REAL. Growing up, I not only had a spirit of fear, but lived the first half of my Christian journey walking in fear. I was raised fearing almost everything and that grew into fearing almost everyone different than me. My fear led to a life of 'sitting on the sidelines' and missing many 'God opportunities.' Twenty-five years ago, God began dealing with my fears by calling me to evangelism, then later to multi-cultural ministry. He placed diverse cultures in my life and gave me a heart and love for them. He gave me the ability to learn languages to communicate on a greater level. What a delight it was and still is to spend time and learn from others who are different from me.

Many years ago, Psalm 56:3-4 became one of my favorite verses. The Lord taught me how to confront my fears by trusting, obeying and following Him wherever He leads.

The Bible uses the phrase "FEAR NOT" over 365 times. The Lord does not want us to fear but to follow Him, knowing He is always with us. "FEAR NOT, for I *am* with you;…" (Isaiah 41:10)

PRAYER TARGET:
People fearful to minister to other cultures.

PERSONAL PRAYER FOR KNOXVILLE:

Lord, I'm praying for those who are fearful to minister to other cultures. You are the One True God who loves everyone and calls us to make disciples of all nations. I ask that You remove the chains of fear and empower Your people in Jesus' name. Please make Your presence so evident and irresistible in the lives of those who are walking in fear, as I was. May they look to You, The Author and Perfecter of their faith, to move them out of their comfort zones, off the sidelines, and into the adventurous journey of following Christ. Father, cause them to seek Your will and to set aside prejudices. May we be a people that seeks to be unified with You and each other. May we be diligent in allowing Your Word to wash us, so that we can follow and know You on a deeper level. Help us not to expect prayer to change things, but expect You to change us through prayer. Holy Father, give us Your heart, love for other cultures and the desire to follow You wherever You lead. In the powerful name of Jesus Christ, I pray, Amen.

WEEK TWELVE: FRIDAY

AUTHOR: MALLORY DENNING
FAMILY STRUCTURE: PARENTS AND 2 SIBLINGS
OCCUPATION: FULL TIME STUDENT, PART TIME BARISTA

FLESH VS SPIRIT

> **"…And by this we will know that we belong to the truth, and will assure our hearts in His presence: If our hearts condemn us, God is greater than our hearts, and He knows all things." 1 John 3:19-20**

A Poem for the Faint of Heart

There is no glory in feeding an environment of uncertainty.
Curiosity, unbalance, and a fickle heart are a recipe for an empty heart.
Those ingredients provoke a fleeting flame, leaving you ready for the next match to strike.

The world encourages you to remain flighty, and justify carelessness
Do not be numbed to the reality that your choices reciprocate heavy scars.
Not just for yourself,
But also for those destined to a covenant with you amidst the wake of your previous storms.

To think today's mindset will not predict tomorrow's platform is ignorant.
And dear soul, tomorrow's platform is too precious to be scorned by today's loneliness.

PRAYER TARGET:
Those in the city who face the constant battle between flesh and Spirit.

PERSONAL PRAYER FOR KNOXVILLE:

Jesus, thank You for writing the end of our victorious stories. The confidence of knowing You are the author rather than ourselves may be one of the greatest gifts You have bestowed upon us. Thank You for the grace You provide as we battle with that reality every day. Be ever near as Knoxville faces constant distractions eager to satiate us. Create in us an unsatisfied spirit, unable to be satiated with anything less than Your truth. Be constant in stirring up in us conviction, courage, and commitment to what You desire for us. To Your glory may we find failure and victory as we near the closing chapters of Your redemptive story. Amen.

WEEK THIRTEEN: MONDAY

AUTHOR: KENNANIAH MOORE
FAMILY STRUCTURE: WIFE AND 2 CHILDREN (ONE IN HEAVEN)
OCCUPATION: WORSHIP LEADER

INADEQUATELY CALLED

> "Before I formed thee in the belly I knew thee; and before thou camest forth out of the womb I sanctified thee, and I ordained thee a prophet unto the nations. Then said I, Ah, Lord GOD! behold, I cannot speak: for I am a child. But the LORD said unto me, Say not, I am a child: for thou shalt go to all that I shall send thee, and whatsoever I command thee thou shalt speak. Be not afraid of their faces: for I am with thee to deliver thee, saith the LORD. Then the LORD put forth his hand, and touched my mouth. And the LORD said unto me, Behold, I have put my words in thy mouth."
> **Jeremiah 1:5-9**

I grew up fatherless on the South-Side of Chicago and struggled my entire life with my identity as a man. Never sexually, just who I was and who God was calling me to be. About a year ago I searched for my father and found him on the prisoner website of the Cook County, Illinois. I felt so embarrassed and ashamed. I wondered why I was not good enough for him to have loved.

I was scheduled that same week to lead a group of men in worship from various churches across Knoxville. I felt insecure and thought that maybe I should seek out a substitute leader for them. I was going to make up some excuse why I couldn't lead because I didn't want anyone to know the truth. How could I stand and lead when I felt so inadequate?

We all have moments of deficiency. He knows your story and that is precisely why God wants to use you. The Bible is filled with stories of flawed men doing wonderful things for God's

Kingdom. There is a purpose for your life regardless of your back story. God works best in us when we are at our worst.

PRAYER TARGET:
Every leader in our city who feels inadequate.

PERSONAL PRAYER FOR KNOXVILLE:
Father, I pray for every leader of our city. Whether religious, political, or community leaders, we believe that all authority is instituted by You. We lift them up and ask that Your grace would cover them. Strengthen them and place those around them that will hold up their arms when they're weak. Give them the wisdom to lead. Give them the courage to stand up for that which is right, even when it may not be popular. Let Your will be done in our communities and Your saving work be done in the hearts of men. Lead them to the path of righteousness so that You may be glorified in this great city. We love and thank You that it is done, in Jesus' mighty Name. Amen.

WEEK THIRTEEN: TUESDAY

AUTHOR: JEFF BEMESDERFER
FAMILY STRUCTURE: WIFE, 2 CHILDREN, AND 2 GRANDCHILDREN
OCCUPATION: CHAPLAIN

WHEN DID WE?

> **"I was naked and you clothed me, I was sick and you visited me, I was in prison and you came to me." Matthew 25:36**

Think on this illustration: Pussycat, Pussycat, where have you been? I have been to see the queen. Were you in the throne room? Yes. What did the queen look like? I don't know. I thought you said you were there. I was. Well what did you see? I saw the biggest mouse I have ever seen under her throne.

What we are determines what we see. I ask myself frequently – What do you see? A person of love sees need. I am challenged every day not to see inmates as offenders but as men. Many who need to find the love of Christ. They have a stripe on their leg. There does not need to be a stripe on their heart.

When did I? When I clothed the naked, visited the sick, ministered to the incarcerated. God help me do for others…

PRAYER TARGET:
Church people who need new eyes to see.

PERSONAL PRAYER FOR KNOXVILLE:
Father, help us to be people who share Your love with those in real need so that we can meet those needs. People who are homeless, sick, those who are incarcerated or those who are returning citizens to the free world need re- acclamation to the free society. They badly need our love. Help us to be Your hands

and feet in a hurting world and give freely of ourselves. In Your Name, Jesus. Amen.

WEEK THIRTEEN: WEDNESDAY

AUTHOR: AMY CRAWFORD
FAMILY STRUCTURE: HUSBAND, 4 CHILDREN, 1 SON-IN-LAW, AND
1 GRANDDAUGHTER
OCCUPATION: MIDDLE SCHOOL TEACHER, ORGANIZATIONAL FOUNDER

FEARFULLY AND WONDERFULLY MADE

"I praise you because I am fearfully and wonderfully made; your works are wonderful, I know that full well." Psalm 139:14

Several years ago, I found myself questioning my calling to teach. It seemed the focus of education was shifting toward assessments & accountability and away from what had drawn me to the profession – students.

One spring afternoon, just after my students had left for the day, I was grading papers at my desk when I came across a poem written by a young man who was failing my class.

On this particular day, however, the words he wrote were blurry and hard to read through the tears that streamed down my face. "I'm the piece that never fits," he wrote. "The world is the cheese, and I am the mouse… I am the piece that never fits." How was it possible for this child to spend time in my classroom every day, and not know that he "fits"?

Today, I make it my first order of business to create a climate of acceptance in my classroom. How can we possibly teach students rigorous content and encourage them to achieve at high academic levels without first building a foundation of trust and mutual respect? Our schools should be a place where all students "fit." Each one has something to teach us, if only we'll take the time to learn.

PRAYER TARGET:
Teachers and those who serve in our schools.

PERSONAL PRAYER FOR KNOXVILLE:
Dear Lord, I praise You for the holy calling You've placed on our lives to serve You as teachers. I thank You for providing resources and strength in order face the challenges each day brings. My prayer is for every child who walks through the doors of our schools to know, without a doubt, that someone in the building loves him or her. I pray for those who serve selflessly behind the scenes and pour their hearts, minds, and resources into the lives of children who may not say thank you, or even remember the sacrifices that were made so they might succeed. I pray for supernatural patience and divine discernment for the many times when we must decide whether we should do things right, or do the right things. May You, Lord, grant us Your eyes to see the least of these, Your ears to hear what children may not say aloud, and Your heart to love without conditions, simply because You first loved us. Amen.

WEEK THIRTEEN: THURSDAY

AUTHOR: ANGIE SIZEMORE
FAMILY STRUCTURE: HUSBAND AND 2 ADULT CHILDREN
OCCUPATION: EDUCATIONAL ASSISTANT

JESUS, THE TRUE SHEPHERD

"I will seek the lost, and I will bring back the strayed, and I will bind up the injured, and I will strengthen the weak..." Ezekiel 34:16

I was reminded of the Lord's faithfulness to His Word from Ezekiel 34:16 as I cried out for the soul of a wayward loved one to return to Him. The answer to my prayers came years later when she was convicted by the Holy Spirit, bringing her to brokenness over sin; she repented and was reconciled to Jesus.

Pray for those who need Him in your circle of friends and acquaintances. Ask Jesus to draw them to Him.

PRAYER TARGET:
The lost, strayed, injured, and the sick.

PERSONAL PRAYER FOR KNOXVILLE:
Father, our hearts' cry is for the lost, strayed, broken and the sick in our city to be found, restored, and healed in Jesus Name. I pray for those "held captive, that they may come to their senses and escape the snare of the devil..." (2 Timothy 2:26). May they turn and be restored to You, the Shepherd and Guardian of their souls (1 Peter 2:25).

WEEK THIRTEEN: FRIDAY

AUTHOR: SUZANNE STELLING
FAMILY STRUCTURE: HUSBAND AND 2 ADULT DAUGHTERS
OCCUPATION: DIRECTOR OF WOMEN'S MINISTRIES

THE WEIGHT OF LEADERSHIP

"The rabble with them began to crave other food, and again the Israelites started wailing and said, "If only we had meat to eat! We remember the fish we ate in Egypt at no cost—also the cucumbers, melons, leeks, onions and garlic. But now we have lost our appetite; we never see anything but this manna! ...Moses heard the people of every family wailing at the entrance to their tents. The Lord became exceedingly angry, and Moses was troubled. He asked the Lord, "Why have you brought this trouble on your servant? What have I done to displease you that you put the burden of all these people on me? Where can I get meat for all these people? They keep wailing to me, 'Give us meat to eat!' I cannot carry all these people by myself; the burden is too heavy for me. If this is how you are going to treat me, please go ahead and kill me—if I have found favor in your eyes—and do not let me face my own ruin."
Numbers 11:4-6, 10,11,13-15

Leadership can crush a person. Have you got some "rabble" around you like Moses did? "Rabble" are typically characterized by an unreasonable discontent; a rebellious, surly attitude; and foolishness. There are two lessons here. First, discontentment is contagious, and moves from tent to tent, house to house, person to person, computer to computer, and media to media like a virus. Secondly, the discontentment of today produces the consequences of tomorrow.

Moses got fed up with the rabble-induced wailing, complaining, and whining and turned to the Lord. We would do well to do the same. Moses poured out his heart to the Lord, saying, *"The burden is too heavy for me."* What is too heavy for you right now?

God saw Moses' fatigue and intervened. He had a leadership lesson for Moses: *healthy leaders delegate.* God didn't add just one or five or even ten men to help Moses; He added seventy! If your load is heavy, delegate some of your responsibilities to capable, trainable, and faithful people of effectiveness and integrity. Ask God to help you identify them.

PRAYER TARGET:
Our city's leaders, civic and spiritual who feel the weight on their shoulders.

PERSONAL PRAYER FOR KNOXVILLE:
Father, we lift our leaders to You -- those who bear the weight of leading our city and our churches. God, bless them! Encourage them! Strengthen them! Help them cry out to You, delegate, and train others. Thank You, Lord, Leader of all. We love You! Amen.

WEEK FOURTEEN: MONDAY

AUTHOR: JACK KING
FAMILY STRUCTURE: WIFE AND 2 CHILDREN
OCCUPATION: PASTOR

PRAYING SCRIPTURE IN THE DARKNESS

"In you, O Lord, do I take refuge; let me never be put to shame; in your righteousness deliver me!
Incline your ear to me; rescue me speedily!
Be a rock of refuge for me, a strong fortress to save me!
For you are my rock and my fortress; and for your name's sake you lead me and guide me; you take me out of the net they have hidden for me, for you are my refuge.
Into your hand I commit my spirit; you have redeemed me, O Lord, faithful God." Psalm 31:1-5

In my life as a pastor, I'm frequently walking with people who are seeking to pray when they don't have words to pray. How do I pray when I feel powerless, helpless, when there's nothing I can control? When I don't know how to pray, I look at the example of Jesus in His hour of distress when He looked to the Psalms. From the cross, He prayed Psalm 31.5: *"Into your hand I commit my spirit."*

When I bear my own cross, I offer this prayer to the Lord when there is nothing else I can do. I might substitute "my spirit" with the name of a person, a situation, or a circumstance that lies heavy on my heart. In the prayer of weakness, I learn anew the truth of the prayer—I am a servant, not a savior. Into the capable hands of the Lord, I entrust all that exceeds my wisdom, understanding, and power. And when I pray in that way, I'm praying in the same way our Lord did in his hour of great suffering.

PRAYER TARGET:
Broken family relationships.

PERSONAL PRAYER FOR KNOXVILLE:
Almighty God, our Heavenly Father, who sets the solitary in families. We commend to Your continual care the homes in which Your people dwell. Put far from them, we beseech You, every root of bitterness, the desire of vainglory, and the pride of life. Fill them with faith, virtue, knowledge, temperance, patience, and godliness. Knit together in constant affection those who, in holy wedlock, have been made one flesh. Turn the hearts of the parents to the children, and the hearts of the children to the parents; and so enkindle fervent charity among us all, that we may evermore be kindly affectional one to another; through Jesus Christ our Lord. Amen. (The Book of Common Prayer)

WEEK FOURTEEN: TUESDAY

AUTHOR: MARK NELSON
FAMILY STRUCTURE: WIFE AND 3 CHILDREN
OCCUPATION: LEAD PASTOR

ALLOWING GOD TO GET LOUDER

> "Leave this cave, and go stand on the mountainside in My presence. The Eternal passed by him. The mighty wind separated the mountains and crumbled every stone before the Eternal. This was not a divine wind, for the Eternal was not within this wind. After the wind passed through, an earthquake shook the earth. This was not a divine quake, for the Eternal was not withinthis earthquake. After the earthquake was over, there was a fire. This was not a divine fire, for the Eternal was not within this fire. After the fire died out, there was nothing but the sound of a calm breeze. And through this breeze a gentle, quiet voice entered into Elijah's ears." 1 Kings 19:11-13

As we read I Kings 19 we enter into the story of Elijah on the run. Shortly after Mount Carmel, Jezebel had threatened this prophet of God. Exhausted and fearful in the desert he found himself wishing he were dead.

But God showed Himself as the Good Father and provided Elijah with water, food and shelter. After walking another 40 days to Mount Horeb, God again made Himself known, but Elijah complained that he has been working hard, but the people had abandoned God.

Elijah was told to go and stand on the mountain and God would pass by. Elijah did as God directed…and a hurricane wind ripped through the mountains and shattered the rocks (but God wasn't found there) …, then an earthquake (again, not God)…, and finally a raging fire (God still hadn't shown Himself). At this point, the Scriptures tell us, it was in the sound of the calm, gentle, quiet breeze that Elijah encountered the Divine.

PRAYER TARGET:
Every person working hard to see God put this world back together.

PERSONAL PRAYER FOR KNOXVILLE:
Father, may we make the space in each of our lives to hear the gentle, quiet voice that comes in the breeze of the Holy Spirit or the gentle whisper that comes to us during the times of trying to "do so much for You, God."
May we allow the voice that speaks directly into our hearts to be heard; the voice that lets us know we are loved and taken care of by You, a God who adores His sons and daughters.
May we allow You, God to get louder in our lives and in our city as You bring restoration to all things through the grace of Jesus. Amen.

WEEK FOURTEEN: WEDNESDAY

AUTHOR: EARLE SEGREST
OCCUPATION: INDUSTRY PRESIDENT

SIGNS AND WONDERS; HEALINGS AND MIRACLES

> **"And as you go, preach saying, 'The kingdom of heaven is at hand. Heal the sick, raise the dead, cleanse leapers, cast out demons; freely you have received, freely give.'"**
> **Matthew 10:7-8**

These words are in red in the Bible and are spoken as a command of Jesus to his disciples. I believe the words are for us, too. Jesus attracted the multitudes through healing miracles. He then taught the people that the kingdom of heaven is at hand. Miracles are occurring in several churches in the USA where the people are believing for a break-through from God because the pastors are teaching and demonstrating these truths. There are twenty-four times in Mathew, twenty times in Mark and twenty-one times in Luke that mention healing individuals as well as multitudes. In fact, it says that He healed them all. It must be important.

PRAYER TARGET:
Pastors, priests and the body of Christ in Knoxville and East Tennessee.

PERSONAL PRAYER FOR KNOXVILLE:
Father, come alive in the hearts of our pastors, priests, and the body of Christ in Knoxville and East Tennessee. May each declare that You, Jesus, cane to demonstrate the goodness of God. I prayer for Your Kingdom to come here on earth as it is in heaven. I pray for the sick in the city to be healed.
Father, use each of us to demonstrate signs and wonders. Give us a desire to listen to the Holy Spirit and be bold enough to lay

hands on the sick and then have faith to believe they will recover through You. I pray this in Your Holy Name. Amen.

WEEK FOURTEEN: THURSDAY

AUTHOR: HANNAH JACKSON
FAMILY STRUCTURE: SINGLE
OCCUPATION: SPANISH TEACHER

THE LORD IS NEAR

"Rejoice in the Lord always. I will say it again: Rejoice! Let your gentleness be evident to all. The Lord is near. Do not be anxious about anything, but in everything, by prayer and petition, with thanksgiving, present your request to God. And the peace of God, which transcends all understanding, will guard your hearts and your minds in Christ Jesus." Philippians 4:4-7

Cancer; a word that brings immediate anxiousness and fear. A word that does not make anyone want to rejoice. This one word has been a constant in my life for over a year now. When I was first diagnosed this one word brought on more anxiety than I had felt in my entire twenty-four years of life.

As I began to seek the Lord and meditate on His word for some form of comfort Philippians 4 began to flood my mind and my soul. "Rejoice in the Lord always." Previously when I would read this passage I would focus on rejoicing and found myself coming up short without much peace; but when I began to focus on "the Lord" everything began to change. The joy, the peace, the comfort all came when I changed my focus from my situation to my God who is in control of the situation. When fear and anxiousness arise, I remind myself that "my Lord is near" and that is reason enough to rejoice.

PRAYER TARGET:
Those undergoing trials.

PERSONAL PRAYER FOR KNOXVILLE:

Father, I pray for those in our city who are undergoing trial and suffering. May they, during confusion and fear, know beyond a shadow of a doubt that You, Lord, are with them and that Your presence will bring peace that transcends all understanding. I pray Psalm 91:4 over their lives that Your wings would encompass them to be their strength and refuge. May You receive glory, oh God, through their seasons of trials. In Jesus' Name, Amen

WEEK FOURTEEN: FRIDAY

AUTHOR: PAUL METLER
FAMILY STRUCTURE: WIFE AND SON
OCCUPATION: LEADERSHIP CONSULTANT

STRATEGIC LEADERSHIP

> **"And I asked them concerning the Jews who escaped, who had survived the exile, and concerning Jerusalem. And they said to me, "The remnant there in the province who had survived the exile is in great trouble and shame. The wall of Jerusalem is broken down, and its gates are destroyed by fire." As soon as I heard these words I sat down and wept and mourned for days, and I continued fasting and praying before the God of heaven."
> Nehemiah 1:2-4**

The book of Nehemiah is a testimony of what was required to rebuild the walls of Jerusalem that had been destroyed during a Babylonian siege. Nehemiah's response is exemplary.

The catalyst for the rebuilding process began in a distant palace. An exile named Nehemiah was working as a cupbearer for the king of Persia when he received disturbing news about the condition of Jerusalem. Nehemiah responded with an immediate display of emotion and empathy. Yet, Nehemiah could move from utter distress into an inspiring display of prayer and leadership.

I am struck by Nehemiah's willingness to transition from significant emotional distress to fasting and prayer. He lifted his prayer to the *"great and awesome God."* Although Nehemiah's prayer includes requests, it is much more than a "wish list." Nehemiah acknowledges the sovereignty of God. For most of us, prayer seems an obvious response to distress. However, too often requests dominate our prayer and we lack a willingness to worship God and trust His provision for the future. Worship can become a catalyst for strategic action. Prayer can be the difference between becoming paralyzed by distressful news and empowered by God to move in a strategic direction.

PRAYER TARGET:
Focus for our current and future leaders in the city.

PERSONAL PRAYER FOR KNOXVILLE:
God in heaven, I thank You for hearing us. I thank You for Your power and Your presence in our lives. I pray for the current and future leaders in Knoxville. Together, we confess our need for Your help. Increase our vision. Empower us for faithful service in our communities. Refresh us with Your Spirit. Amen.

WEEK FIFTEEN: MONDAY

AUTHOR: KIMBERLY SEXTON
FAMILY STRUCTURE: HUSBAND, 2 DAUGHTERS, 1 SON, 1 SON-IN-LAW, AND 1 GRANDDAUGHTER
OCCUPATION: REGISTERED NURSE

CHARIOTS OF FIRE

**"And when the servant of the man of God arose early and went out, there was an army, surrounding the city with horses and chariots. And his servant said to him, 'Alas, my master! What shall we do?' So he answered, 'Do not fear, for those who are with us are more than those who are with them.' And Elisha prayed, and said, 'Lord, I pray, open his eyes that he may see.' Then the Lord opened the eyes of the young man, and he saw. And behold, the mountain was full of horses and chariots of fire all around Elisha."
2 Kings 6:15-17**

The scripture above is and always will be a special scripture for me. Yes, it is a majestic picture of the powerful unseen forces that fight for God's people, and for me God used this scripture to speak directly. For the first time in my spiritual walk I could hear him say, *"I've got this! I promise I am bigger than your battle and I always have been!"* I was new to daily scripture reading and at the time, I was trying to read through the bible in a year. One day I almost didn't pick up my bible at all. I had an incident at my child's school that left me mad, distracted, and hurt. I was crying out to the Lord that morning... crying out of a mother's desperation for her child. I had prayed all that was in my heart and then opened my bible to do my daily reading. I didn't expect God to speak to me, even though I had heard that He could speak to me through His word. I had just never experienced it myself. As I read this amazing story I could see the horses and chariots of fire around my child and her school. God gave me a picture of the unseen and it was comforting in a most powerful way! When I think about how many times since then He has used scripture to talk to me, I am ashamed that it took me by surprise that day. It was a faith building day.

I am convinced that a prayer of surrender and getting into the Word every day can change one's perspective and that change in perspective can give a different outcome for oneself and others. When we pray with a surrendered heart, our eyes are opened to the unseen, our heart is open to change, and Holy Spirit living inside of us can reveal what only He can reveal. We can receive the correction and courage we need to act in faith.

PRAYER TARGET:
Fellow followers of Christ Jesus seeking to strengthen their faith.

PERSONAL PRAYER FOR KNOXVILLE:
Thank you, Jesus, for revealing Yourself, Your power, and Your provision to me through Your word. I pray that those who have decided to follow You in our community will daily seek Your guidance through prayer and opening Your Word. May we never take for granted the freedom we have in You and the freedom we have to share Your saving, freeing power with others. Jesus, help us as a community of believers to rise unashamed to evangelize and disciple our community…. knowing that we are surrounded by chariots of fire! Lord, Your ways are higher than our ways. I pray that as we focus on You, that You protect us from the pride of self and frustration of the enemy. Help us to remember that answers to Our prayers do not always come in having the discomforts removed, but that through the comforts and discomforts You surround us with the unseen and are always present. Lord, I love You. Amen

WEEK FIFTEEN: TUESDAY

AUTHOR: DAVID LEACH
FAMILY STRUCTURE: WIFE AND CHILDREN
OCCUPATION: TEACHER

PRAYING THE LORD'S PRAYER

> **"This, then, is how you should pray: 'Our Father in heaven, hallowed be your name, your kingdom come, your will be done, on earth as it is in heaven. Give us today our daily bread, and forgive us our debts, as we also have forgiven our debtors. And lead us not into temptation, but deliver us from the evil one.'" Matthew 6:9-13**

In Matthew 6, the followers of Jesus ask him to teach them to pray. He gives them the model prayer that we call "The Lord's Prayer." I have found that this is a great prayer to use when praying for friends and family. We don't really know what people need for which we pray, we just know that they need to encounter the risen Christ. Fill in the blanks with the person that you are praying for.

Pause after each line, give the phrase time. Repeat often.
Our Father in heaven, hallowed be your name. In the life of
_____ I pray that your kingdom come. In the life of
_____ I pray that your will be done,
I pray that experience You on earth as it is in heaven. Give them today their daily bread.

And forgive them their debts and pray that they forgive their debtors. Lead _____ not into temptation, but deliver them from the evil one. For Yours is the kingdom, the power, and the glory, for ever and ever. Amen.

PRAYER TARGET:
Family members and loved ones seeking to learn personal praying.

PERSONAL PRAYER FOR KNOXVILLE:
Jesus, I pray for the people of this city to have a Kingdom encounter.Give them an experience with you, Jesus. Teach us to pray for ourselves and for others. In Your Precious Name. Amen.

WEEK FIFTEEN: WEDNESDAY

AUTHOR: LAURIE STONE
FAMILY STRUCTURE: HUSBAND, 4 ADULT CHILDREN AND 2 GRANDCHILDREN
OCCUPATION: NON-PROFIT ORGANIZATION

BE KIND AND HAVE COURAGE (CINDERELLA)

> **"For the Mighty One has done great things for me; and Holy is His Name!" Luke 1:49**
> **"I love the Lord because He hears my prayers and answers them. Because He bends down and listens, I will pray as long as I breathe." Psalm 116:1-2**
> **"Heal me/us, O Lord, and I/we will be healed. Save me/us, and I/we will be saved. For You are the One that I/we praise!" Jeremiah 17:14**
> **"And it was Jesus that made him well!" John 5:15**

I am not a writer, but I do believe in prayer, God's Truth, and the hope, joy, and peace that comes from being a child of The King. I enjoy the blessing of quotes with which God inspired others. Consider these:

Billy Sunday, the famous evangelist said, *"We have a God Who delights in impossibilities."* Louie Giglio says, *"Sin does not make you a bad person. Sin makes you a spiritually dead person."* Max Lucado quotes, *"A man who wants to lead the orchestra must turn his back on the crowd."* From William Booth we have, *"The greatness of a man's power is the measure of his surrender."* Johann Sebastian Bach gives us, *"Soli Deo Gloria-to the glory of God alone."* Peter in 1 Peter 2:16 says, *"Live as people who are free, not using your freedom as a cover-up for evil, but living as servants of God."* Timothy Keller finishes the listing of quotes with, *"The gospel is this: we are more sinful and flawed in ourselves than we ever dared believe. Yet at the same time, we are more loved and accepted in Jesus Christ than we ever dared hope."* I love our city, but God loves it more than I do. We must pray and share the Hope that we know.

PRAYER TARGET:
Believers to reflect Christ and the lost to receive Him.

PERSONAL PRAYER FOR KNOXVILLE:
Oh, Gracious Father, You are worthy of all our praise. You are our Redeemer, our Hope, and our Salvation is in Christ alone. We need You, Lord, to save our city, our county. We thank You for our government leaders, our law enforcement, our firefighters, our educators, all those making decisions for us, and pray that You would bless and guide them daily. Father, there are many people hurting, lonely, and sad. There are children that need to be rescued from the environment in which they live. I pray for those in authority to have insight and boldness to make change as Christ leads them. Protect and provide for those that are less fortunate and living in adverse situations. Raise up godly leaders and role models and compassion for those in need. I pray for peace in our homes and streets. I pray our public housing and all neighborhoods will have the Spirit of Christ to reside victoriously there. In the words of Thomas A. Kempis, Father, "Please write Your Blessed Name, O Lord, upon our hearts, there to remain, so engraved that no prosperity, no adversity, no temptation shall ever move us from Your Love." In Jesus' Holy Name we pray, praise, and trust, Amen.

WEEK FIFTEEN: THURSDAY

AUTHOR: BRENT BREWER
FAMILY STRUCTURE: WIFE AND 3 CHILDREN
OCCUPATION: UNIVERSITY PROFESSOR

ENGAGING OUR UNIVERSITIES AND COLLEGES

"Then the king of Babylon ordered his court officials, to bring into the king's service some Israelites from the royal family and the nobility, young men showing aptitude for every kind of learning, well informed, quick to understand, and qualified to serve in the king's palace. He was to teach them the language and literature of the Babylonians. They were to be trained for three years. Among those who were chosen were some from Judah: Daniel, Hananiah, Mishael and Azariah. To these four young men God gave knowledge and understanding of all kinds of literature and learning." Daniel 1:3-7

I was raised in a conservative, fundamentalist background that placed a high value on studying and learning the truths of the Bible, but was somewhat anti-intellectual with regards to engaging in secular academia due to the liberalization of higher education that happened in the twentieth century. This secularization has continued, especially in the physical and social sciences where the majority would consider themselves atheist or agnostic. Also in a recent Pew Religious Landscape Survey, thirty- six percent of eighteen to twenty-four-year-old people identified as religiously unaffiliated (the None's).

Despite the historic trend toward liberalism and the numbers above, we know that God is also at work in our universities and colleges. And it is encouraging to note that God is raising up faculty, staff and students to engage *"in the language and literature of the Babylonians."* And just as God blessed Daniel and his friends with knowledge and wisdom, He will bless His followers today as they seek Him and rigorously engage in their academic disciplines.

PRAYER TARGET:
Universities and colleges to seek truth.

PERSONAL PRAYER FOR KNOXVILLE:
Dear God, I thank You for the intellectual ability and wisdom with which You have blessed us. We especially lift those working and studying at our universities and colleges. Forgive us for the times we have failed to be Your salt and light in the world of academia. Thank You for Your servants, who have committed themselves to "learning the language and literature" of this world. We pray that just as You gave Daniel and his friends an extra measure of knowledge and wisdom, ou will pour out Your Spirit on Your followers here today. Show them favor as they interact with those who consider You non-existent or irrelevant. May they be as "wise as serpents, and as gentle as doves" in these interactions. Continue to bless the campus ministries and churches who invest time and energy sharing the Good News of Jesus on our campuses.
In the mighty name of Jesus, I pray! Amen

WEEK FIFTEEN: FRIDAY

AUTHOR: JENNIFER SMITH
FAMILY STRUCTURE: HUSBAND, 3 CHILDREN AND 4 GRANDCHILDREN
OCCUPATION: RETIRED RN, COMMUNITY AND CHURCH VOLUNTEER

IT'S TIME TO DEAL WITH PRIDE

"If my people who are called by my name, will humble themselves and pray and seek my face and turn from their wicked ways, then I will hear from heaven, and I will forgive their sins and will heal their land." 2 Chronicles 7:14

Pride…Why don't we dedicate more of our time and attention to fighting this destructive enemy? It's been the takedown of kings and kingdoms and the root of the rebellion of Satan and mankind. It destroys individuals, families, businesses, churches, and it blocks our communication with Almighty God. Pride continues through the ages to leave a trail of destruction.

Lately, the subject has been coming up often for me personally as I read the bible, and the conviction of the Holy Spirit has been becoming more evident. I believe God desires to work through each of us in our prayer times as we come before Him, but so many times, we are so filled with ourselves and our own ideas of how God should get things done, we end up talking to ourselves and missing any connection with Him at all. Pride even prevents us from seeing the lack of God's power in our lives. We simply pray to be able to mark it off our checklist. Then we feel better about the rules we have set for ourselves. We have gotten used to trite and powerless prayers. I hope you know, I'm speaking from experience here. The Holy Spirit has been convicting me and tenderly changing my heart and ultimately changing my prayers.

Dear friends, what would our city look like if pride was put aside in each of us and our focus became God's will and mission for this world, considering others better than ourselves, seeking God, rejecting sin, serving, expecting nothing in return, and staying united as the body of Christ? It's what Jesus taught and how He lived. Now make it so in our lives, Lord Jesus!

PRAYER TARGET:
God's people of Knoxville and surrounding areas seeking humility eliminating pride

PERSONAL PRAYER FOR KNOXVILLE:
Precious Father, forgive us of our pride and our attempts to take Your rightful place of authority. We have made a mess of things with our envy and selfish ambition.

Oh Father, heal us, create in us clean hearts, hearts that are tender and humble, breaking with the very things that break Yours. Holy Spirit, convict us when pride begins to rise in us and give us the strength and power to maintain a posture of humility as we serve You. Thank You for Your example, Sovereign Lord, as You left Your throne, came to earth as a servant, and suffered our penalty for sin. May we never forget what You sacrificed and may we proclaim it to the city of Knoxville and to this world until our last breath. Set our hearts on fire. Take us from the place of hearing Your Word, and move in our hearts to be doers of the Word. Breathe on us, Oh God. Bring life, bring healing, bring Salvation, and hear our prayers offered through humble hearts yielded to You. Amen.

WEEK SIXTEEN: MONDAY

AUTHOR: ANDREW WOOD
FAMILY STRUCTURE: WIFE AND 4 CHILDREN
OCCUPATION: EXECUTIVE DIRECTOR OF NON-PROFIT

MEET US AT THE WELL

> "Jesus said to her, 'Go, call your husband, and come here.'
> The woman answered him, 'I have no husband.' Jesus said
> to her, 'You are right in saying, I have no husband'; for you
> have had five husbands, and the one you now have is not
> your husband. What you have said is true. 'The woman
> said to him, 'Sir, I perceive that you are a prophet. Our
> fathers worshipped on this mountain, but you say that in
> Jerusalem is the place where people ought to worship.'"
> John 4:16-21

There is not enough space here to truly exegete (expound) on this text, but this snippet of what is commonly referred to as *The Woman at the Well* is profoundly important as we are given a glimpse into the heart of our Lord Jesus. He went to this well with intent to meet a broken woman and offer freedom. The brokenness found in this woman's life is deep-seated, but we quickly learn that her brokenness cannot hide itself from the Gospel.

This text has impacted my life in a big way as I wrestle with my own sin and as I serve at Hope Resource Center. The heart of the Father is one of truth and grace. Jesus exposed this woman's sin as He exposes our sin today, but this pulling back of the veil doesn't leave us broken and alone. Instead, Jesus exposes the void in our heart and the need for a Savior as He steps into and fills that need/void!

The result of the Father telling the broken that they are not alone has an eternal impact. I see this in my own life and I pray the people of this city would begin to see that today!

PRAYER TARGET:
Men and women facing unplanned circumstances.

PERSONAL PRAYER FOR KNOXVILLE:
Father, today I pray for the young mom facing an unplanned pregnancy, the young man facing a life-altering decision, and the young child without a voice. I pray that our brokenness would not be our identity or our reality. Lord,
I pray that you would meet us at our well and pull back the veil in order that we may be set free. Lord, intervene in the lives of young moms in our city to show them that they are loved, valued, and respected and that their current unplanned pregnancy does not point to their life and goals being dashed. Lord move us to stand for and with these moms as they choose life and their dreams.

Lord, help the young men involved in these unplanned circumstances to choose to stay when fleeing seems easy. Lord, forgive us for choosing self over the others in our lives. I pray for the baby in the womb. Let him or her be a gift to be stewarded and not a burden to be disposed of. I pray we would be their voice! We trust in Your plan, Lord, and we believe You will move. We love and praise You! In Jesus Name. Amen.

WEEK SIXTEEN: TUESDAY

AUTHOR: TIM HALEY
FAMILY STRUCTURE: WIFE AND 3 CHILDREN
OCCUPATION: PHARMACIST

DON'T BELIEVE YOUR PRAYERS ARE MEANINGLESS

**"So Peter was kept in prison, but earnest prayer for him was made to God by the church....he went to the house of Mary, the mother of John whose other name was Mark, where many were gathered together and were praying....but [Rhoda] ran in and reported that Peter was standing at the gate. They said to her, 'You are out of your mind.' But she kept insisting that it was so, and they kept saying, 'It is his angel!' But Peter continued knocking, and when they opened they saw him and were amazed."
Acts 12:5, 12b, 14b- 16**

Three or four years ago as God had been growing my faith in Him, He gave me the desire to share my faith. I prayed and prayed for God to allow me to share the Gospel and for someone to come to believe in Jesus as a result. For quite a while I saw no fruit, I felt very discouraged and felt, at times, like giving up in sharing my faith.

One morning through a series of circumstance which led me out of my normal route to work, I came across a young lady who needed a ride. I shared the Gospel with her and she believed in Jesus for the forgiveness of her sins.

Honestly, I was shocked! Much like the believers in Jerusalem who were praying for Peter to be freed from jail, I was praying but didn't really expect that God to allow my bold request to be fulfilled.

that, at times, is completely amazing and miraculous to us. And don't be shocked at the results of your prayers!

PRAYER TARGET:
Believers who have been praying and have not seen the results yet.

PERSONAL PRAYER FOR KNOXVILLE:
Oh Lord, You are our mighty, gracious and loving Father. You hear our cries for help and change in our lives, in our friends and family members' lives, and in this city. You know our struggles and our heart of compassion for the people in our lives and in this city. You are Almighty and you never stop working. Lord, let our prayers be bold and shocking to ask for Your hand to move in ways that are unimaginable. But Lord, let us not be shocked when we see You move in the unimaginable ways that we asked you to move. Let our faith in You always be strong and deep so that when You move mightily we are not surprised.

When the chains fall off and the doors are opened let us rejoice and be thankful but not be taken aback. Lord, we love You and we know You love us. We thank You for Your good, good gifts to us. We ask you now to move in ways that only you can imagine in our lives and in our city. In Jesus' name. Amen.

WEEK SIXTEEN: WEDNESDAY

AUTHOR: DOROTHY BRADLEY
FAMILY STRUCTURE: HUSBAND AND 1 SON, DAUGHTER-IN-LAW AND 2 GRANDSONS
OCCUPATION: RN CERTIFIED CASE MANAGER

WHAT IS STORED IN YOUR HEART?

> **"A good man brings good things out of the good stored up in his heart, and an evil man brings evil things out of the evil stored up in his heart...For the mouth speaks what the heart is full of." Luke 6:45**

Careless words. We all have heard them or even participated in using them in conversations that were "unwholesome" .... A little spark of gossip disguised as a prayer request ...A smidgen of bitterness and deceit disguised as concern...Prideful thoughts that come out as boastful words. The Bible has many passages regarding our conversations and the power of the tongue. These are just a few that warn us not to take our words lightly:

" *Set a guard, O LORD, over my mouth, Keep watch over the door of my lips."* Psalm 141:3

"If anyone thinks he is religious and does not bridle his tongue deceives his heart, this person's religion is Worthless." James 1:26

"Death and life are in the power of the tongue and those who love it will eat its fruit." Proverbs 18:21

When we can encourage a brother or sister, do we first give our opinion of what they should or should not do, or do we get on our knees before the Throne of Grace to petition for their burden and how we can share their burden? When people come to us and start to share gossip do we remind them that according to God's Word, how we love one another is how the world will know that we are followers of Jesus Christ. Gossiping not only hurts our witness but partaking in such activity grieves the Spirit. Gossiping has never, nor will ever be, a witness tool to reach the lost and isn't reaching the lost our mission while we are placed on this earth - To spread the gospel, not gossip?

PRAYER TARGET:
Church families dealing with destructive strongholds.

PERSONAL PRAYER FOR KNOXVILLE:
Father, You know our hearts, our motives, our mind, our thoughts. We ask that by the power of Your Holy Spirit You convict us of everything that is keeping us from doing what You have called us to do. You are the Vine and we need to abide in You alone. May we not tolerate evil but stand in Your strength. Keep the Armor of God securely surrounding us so we can stand strong and courageous against evil that wants to destroy our city. You have called us by name; You have written your law on our minds and on our hearts. You have plans for us to prosper not to harm us. Your plans give us hope and a future.
Father, we know that You alone are good and trustworthy. We thank You for what You are doing and going to do in our City. We pray a hedge of protection around the leaders of our city and for those who serve and protect us. May everything, we do bring glory to You. In Your Precious Name. Amen.

WEEK SIXTEEN: THURSDAY

AUTHOR: CARTER COUGHLIN
FAMILY STRUCTURE: FATHER, MOTHER, AND TWIN SISTER
OCCUPATION: STUDENT

LOOKING BACK

"The angels urged Lot, saying, 'Hurry! Take your wife and your two daughters who are here, or you will be swept away when the city is punished.'" Genesis 19:15

"Thus He overthrew those cities and the entire plain, destroying all those living in the cities—and also the vegetation in the land. But Lot's wife looked back, and she became a pillar of salt." Genesis 19:25-26

The city in which Lot lived was called Sodom, and the neighboring town was Gomorrah. Both cities were ripe with sin and disobedience, so God wanted to destroy them for the good of His Kingdom. The night before the destruction, He sent two angels into the city, and Lot invited them into his home to spend the night. The angels warned Lot to leave and take his family with him. God wanted to save them from the sin and destruction in Sodom and Gomorrah. As they were running away from the city, though, Lot's wife looked back towards the sin God was warning them of, and she turned into a pillar of salt.

Oftentimes, this is what my walk with Jesus feels like. He is calling me away from the city and warning me of the impending danger, but I keep looking back; I keep turning my eyes from God towards sin. God wants to call us deeper and closer to Himself, but He can only do that if we are looking towards Him and away from sin. So, let us turn our heads away from the burning world and towards our loving Father so that He may transform us.

PRAYER TARGET:
Those with heads turned.

PERSONAL PRAYER FOR KNOXVILLE:
Dear Lord, I pray that as you call us all away from the sinful world behind us, we would keep our eyes focused on You. I ask that you give us the desire to follow You and the plans that You have for us. Despite the temptations that exist in the world, I pray that You would help us keep our heads turned and our hearts focused on You. Lord, ground us in our faith and in Your power and strength. Give us the courage and bravery to keep walking in the other direction, away from the burning world. In Your Holy Name, we pray. Amen.

WEEK SIXTEEN: FRIDAY

AUTHOR: CHRIS YERGER
FAMILY STRUCTURE: WIFE AND 2 CHILDREN
OCCUPATION: INDUSTRY CEO

HEARING AND DOING

"But be doers of the word, and not hearers only, deceiving yourselves. For if anyone is a hearer of the word and not a doer, he is like a man who looks intently at his natural face in a mirror. For he looks at himself and goes away and at once forgets what he was like. But the one who looks into the perfect law, the law of liberty, and perseveres, being no hearer who forgets but a doer who acts, he will be blessed in his doing." James 1:22-25

In our technology-driven culture, it's easy for us to have quick access to scripture and sermons. Through social media and smart phones, a well-known preacher or bible verse is only a click away. We can fall into a trap of "snacking" on Christian messages without experiencing deep change. James (the brother of Jesus) provides us with one of the best word-pictures in the entire bible. Most of us wake-up in the morning and look into a mirror. Can you imagine if we looked into the mirror and did nothing about what we saw?! For most of us, it might be a little embarrassing as we walked into work or school! In these verses, James is indicating that we do a similar thing when we read scripture and don't act on it. We deceive ourselves into thinking that just by listening or reading we have changed. As followers of Jesus, we need a hunger and commitment to be transformed by the Holy Spirit and become more and more like Christ, especially in the way we love others. Let's ask God to help us be "doers" of His Word. We will be blessed (James 1:25), and we will become a blessing to others.

PRAYER TARGET:

Anyone in a leadership position-that they would hear and seek His substance.

PERSONAL PRAYER FOR KNOXVILLE:

Heavenly Father, I pray for every person that is in any type of leadership position. As we listen to or read Your Holy Scriptures, please help us to be doers of Your Word and not just hearers. Please fill us with Your Holy Spirit and give us the power to be transformed. Mold us more and more into Your image so that we can love and serve those around us. We need You Father, Lord Jesus and Holy Spirit. Please bless us as we become "doers who act" so that we can be a blessing to those around us. We ask this in the powerful name of Jesus, Amen.

WEEK SEVENTEEN: MONDAY

AUTHOR: BRYAN W. DAVIS
FAMILY STRUCTURE: WIFE, 3 CHILDREN, AND 1 SON-IN-LAW
OCCUPATION: COMPANY OWNER

AN ACT OF WORSHIP

> **"Whatever you do, work at it with all your heart, as working for the Lord, not for man." Colossians 3:23**

The Bible tells us we are made for worship and fellowship with God. Yet we often compartmentalize worship as something we do on Sunday morning with some folks who lead us in a few songs, and frankly are a lot better at "worship" than me. Surely God didn't create us to spend 167 hours a week separated from Him so that we could worship for only an hour on Sunday.

The fifty or so hours I spend each week at work should be an offering of worship. From my attitude, to how I engage others, to the actual work I produce, it should be done with humble excellence. We are not working for the approval of share-holders, bosses or even customers. As a follower of Christ, my standard must exceed those. Regardless of whose signature is on my paycheck. Or how little or much the amount may be. My work should be an expression of grateful worship, to an audience of One.

PRAYER TARGET:
The scared and the angry.

PERSONAL PRAYER FOR KNOXVILLE:
Dear God, our nation seems as polarized, frustrated and angry as we have been since at least the late 60's. Old wounds that perhaps have never fully healed have been re-opened or at least exposed. New wounds of gender, race and economic position

exposed. New wounds of gender, race and economic position are gaping open. Father, as a culture, we are led to believe that a political remedy exists. It is a cynical, false hope perpetrated by both political parties. We know that You, Jesus, said, "Come unto me all ye who are burdened and heavy laden. And I will give you rest." Dear God, give us eternal hope and joy unspeakable regardless of our personal circumstances. May our little town in the foothills of the Appalachian Mountains, become a city on a hill that is a place of eternal hope and joy. In Your Name, Jesus, I pray, Amen.

AUTHOR: BARBARA NICHOLS
FAMILY STRUCTURE: SINGLE
OCCUPATION: PROFESSIONAL PRIVATE MUSIC TEACHER

COURAGE FOR THE JOURNEY

> **"Only be strong and very courageous, being careful to do according to all the law that Moses my servant commanded you. Do not turn from it to the right hand or to the left, that you may have good success wherever you go. Have I not commanded you?**
> **Be strong and courageous." Joshua 1: 7-9a**

God's blessing of victory and success accompanied the command to not turn in either direction away from the laws given by Moses from the hand of God. In verse 8, Joshua is admonished to meditate on God's laws day and night and to walk carefully according to every word given by God.

What is our Lord directing you to do today that will require following His commands? Is He leading you to unfamiliar places where challenges await? Then "Only be strong and courageous." Is He moving you into a new career, a new ministry direction, or away from spiritually toxic people in your life? Then "Only be strong and courageous." Is He moving you to step out in absolute faith toward a door of opportunity that causes you to be fearful of possible failures? Then "Only be strong and courageous." Is He moving you to a newer and closer relationship with Himself which requires following Him without reservation? His promises will accompany you. "Only be strong and courageous." Is your Lord asking you to wait on your long-awaited answer to prayer? Then, "Only be strong and courageous."

God will honor your faithfulness to His Word and will never leave or forsake you. Can you step out this week in your neighborhood, your work place, throughout our city, to go as God's ambassadors to invite change in the lives of people around us? "Only be strong and courageous" as you let Jesus be seen through you today!

PRAYER TARGET:
Those who need to remain faithful to God's Word in meeting life's challenges.

PERSONAL PRAYER FOR KNOXVILLE:
Lord, help your people today to become ambassadors of the living God by remaining faithful to whatever task You set before us. Remind us of Your constant abiding presence that will give us the courage to undertake the challenges and obstacles which mount up to defeat us. Grant us grace for the journey and set our focus on the eternal things that matter. Amen.

AUTHOR: BAILEY EDWARDS
FAMILY STRUCTURE: I AM A DAUGHTER
OCCUPATION: STUDENT

JOY

> **"I am not saying this because I am in need, for I have learned to be content whatever the circumstances. I know what it is to be in need, and I know what it is to have plenty. I have learned the secret of being content in any and every situation, whether well fed or hungry, whether living in plenty or in want." Philippians 4:11-12**

My story is one of a desire for joy in all things. This is something I thought I had a grasp of early on in my life, and it wasn't until a series of serious breakages that I was truly brought into contact with our Lord. He broke down my castle. The things I once tried to find happiness in were ripped from me and I was experiencing lows I never saw coming.

Paul knew true hardship, hardships I will probably never fully understand. For him to declare what he does in verses 11 and 12 is a true testament to the peace he found in the Lord and this is something I so desperately wanted to have. It took the crumbling of the things I thought would fulfill me to look to Him for not just happiness, but for joy. A joy in the Lord that is not affected by circumstances. Happy and sad are a moment's feelings. Joy is knowing who is in control. Joy is knowing that we will never have the full picture of what things will look like, but the One who does loves us and wants more than we could ever design for ourselves.

PRAYER TARGET:
Anyone and everyone struggling to find joy in all things.

PERSONAL PRAYER FOR KNOXVILLE:

Father, my prayer is that all would see the fruit of their castles being torn down. This is a confusing process, and isn't always one that we are fully asking for or accepting of Father, help us to just keep pressing. God, You have more in store than is imaginable. The Bible tells us that Your greatness is immeasurable. You didn't promise us promised an "easy" life, but when the highs and lows hit us and the lows seem too great to conquer, we know that You, God, have it already finished. And with that, great peace comes. In Your Name, Amen.

WEEK SEVENTEEN: THURSDAY

AUTHOR: ERIN VANDERSTEEG
FAMILY STRUCTURE: HUSBAND AND 2 COLLEGE-AGE CHILDREN
OCCUPATION: WIFE AND MOM

SURRENDER

**"I will tear down your walls and demolish your defenses."
Micah 5:11**

Many years into my relationship with the Lord, I felt like there
was something missing. I would read in His Word about
abundant life and freedom and I knew I wasn't experiencing that
in my life. At the time, I was mentoring high school students in
our church and each week I would speak words of Truth over
their lives with conviction, but when I tried to claim those same
Truths for myself, something kept me from believing it. The
Lord brought people into my life who were really experiencing
abundant life with HIM, and I began to long for a more intimate
relationship with Jesus. I was doing all the right things: studying
the Word, praying, serving, and going to church…but something
was missing.

One night I sat in my room and I asked God to show me how to
get closer to Him, how to have freedom and intimacy with Him.
He led me to Micah 5:11. To have true intimacy with anyone, one
must be completely vulnerable. There were places in my heart
that I kept guarded and hidden from everyone, even God. There
were walls I had put up to protect myself for years! The Lord
was gently urging me to take down the walls in my heart or He
would take them down.

Trying to keep part of my heart hidden from the world and the
Lord was keeping me from becoming who God had created me
to be. One Bible commentary explains it this way, 'That I was
relying on something other than God for security and He will

cut off anything that compromises the holiness of His people.' That night I prayed the scariest and most thrilling prayer of my life! I asked the Lord into every corner of my heart and I released everything I'd been clinging to for security besides Jesus. Real intimacy and abundant life is possible when we surrender.

PRAYER TARGET:
Women of the city seeking a relationship with Christ.

PERSONAL PRAYER FOR KNOXVILLE:
Father, my prayer is that the women of Knoxville would have a spirit of power, love, and self- discipline. I pray they would be women who love their families well and not be afraid to be feminine and vulnerable. Jesus, I pray You will make these women bold in Your Name. May they will have a desire to serve others and to encourage one another to be the women you have called them to be. I pray for the single women to be pure in a crooked world, to shine out like beautiful lights in a dark place! I pray for the married women to love their husbands passionately and to speak gently to them. I pray for the working women to be bold and courageous. May they be set apart in the work place and let people know they belong to You. Father, I pray for the women who work in the home to do it as unto the Lord! I pray all these things in the Name of Jesus! Amen.

WEEK SEVENTEEN: FRIDAY

AUTHOR: MICHELLE PARDUE
FAMILY STRUCTURE: HUSBAND, 3 MARRIED DAUGHTERS, THREE GRANDSONS
OCCUPATION: ARTIST

HAVING YOUR CAKE AND EATING IT, TOO!

> **"Because everything that belongs to the world, the lust of the flesh, the lust of the eyes, and the pride in one's lifestyle, is not from the Father but is from the world."**
> **1 John 2:16**

Does Knoxville and surrounding areas belong to the world or do they belong to the Father? I guess the answer is "yes" to both. Consider the fact that Knoxville represents approximately 186,000 people. Each has the individual choice to devote his or her life to the world, its lust and pride, or to the Father and His goodness.

If we were to be completely honest, do we who call ourselves Christians try to ride the fence of having our cake and eating it too? In choosing both lifestyles we are really choosing one over the other and fooling no one. Especially God. The above verse is sandwiched in between despair and hope. In verse 15 it says, "If anyone loves the world, love for the Father is not in him." And in verse 17 it says, *"The world with its lust is passing away, but the one who does God's will remains forever."* Living in the world and not of the world is hard but the rewards are tremendous and worthy of our devotion.

I encourage us all to read 1 John and be totally honest in asking, *"Where am I in this? What do I need to confess?"* He is faithful and righteous to forgive us our sins and to cleanse us from all unrighteousness!

PRAYER TARGET:

Christians living in Knoxville and surrounding areas learning to be in this world but not of this world.

PERSONAL PRAYER FOR KNOXVILLE:

Father, may we as God's people be known as People of God and not as hypocrites who ride the fence and try to live in the world. Help us stop sending messages out in the neighborhood that it is okay to live in lust and pride and then go to church and act as if nothing is out of balance and acting as if You approve of our lifestyle. Father, would we know personally that You are the light and there is no darkness in You. I pray we would not deceive ourselves into thinking that we are good people without the goodness that Jesus has bestowed on us through His blood. I ask You, God, to draw our neighbors to Yourself, and if You choose us to join You in Your Mission that we would be willing and honored to share in Your love and story. It is because of Your Son, God, that we are even able to offer this prayer. Amen.

WEEK EIGHTEEN: MONDAY

AUTHOR: VONWAUNACA KAYRETTA STOKES
FAMILY STRUCTURE: DIVORCED MOTHER OF 3 CHILDREN
OCCUPATION: MINISTER; EXECUTIVE ASSISTANT

HOW TO REMAIN FAITHFUL IN ANOTHER MAN'S WORK

"And if ye have not been faithful in that which is another man's, who shall give you that which is your own?" Luke 16:12

Being faithful in another man's work can be a challenging task to the believer. Oftentimes we find ourselves struggling with carrying the burden that Christ has commissioned us to bear. It is difficult to help another man with his. We think like this because we have allowed the enemy to weigh us down in our spirits with things that only Christ can and has already taken care of. Jesus instructs us to take His yoke upon us, learn of Him, because His yoke is easy and His burden is light (Matthew 11:30).

Our assignments from Him are meant to be easy because we have transferred our lives for Christ's. We operate in the same power He does. As a body, we must start taking on this mindset. This is the only way we will be able to cheerfully serve and uplift another man in his work. This will allow us to fulfill the law of Christ, which is to bear one another's burdens (Galatians 6:2). We are commissioned to help our brothers and sisters carry the weight of Christ's ministry. We were birthed into this earthly realm for the sole purpose of finishing Christ's (another man's) assignment. It is in this act that is God able to increase us as we have are tried and proven worthy to receive the more that He promised.

PRAYER TARGET:
Unity in the body of Christ for the fulfillment of Christ's law, encouraging others.

PERSONAL PRAYER FOR KNOXVILLE:

Father, may Your Bride come together as one body. Help us uplift, uphold, encourage, and keep one another accountable, so that the Law of Jesus Christ can be fulfilled. I decree that the body will begin to put off a selfish mindset, and I declare that we operate in the same intellect, wisdom, and love as Jesus. I speak life into the body and I decree that the dead in Christ Jesus will arise as we remain faithful in the work, assignment, and mission that Christ has purposed in our lives. Thank You, Jesus, for girding us up with Your strength and making our way perfect unto You. Thank you for imparting healing and strength to any weak or broken place in our lives. I thank You, Holy Spirit, for imparting power to the faint and for increasing strength to those who are feeble and weary in heart. I thank You, Holy Spirit, for the fresh wind that You have blown our way that refreshes, revives and quickens us in our spirits for such a time as this. I seal this prayer in Jesus' Name. Amen.

WEEK EIGHTEEN: TUESDAY

AUTHOR: RICK KUHLMAN
FAMILY STRUCTURE: WIFE, 1 SON AND HIS WIFE AND 1 GRANDDAUGHTER
OCCUPATION: NON-PROFIT DIRECTOR

EXPECT THE UNEXPECTED

"Suddenly, there was an earthquake so violent that the foundations of the prison were shaken. All the doors immediately flew open, and everyone's chains were unfastened." Acts 16:26

When I was a young man, I felt I needed to have everything planned ahead of time to be successful. I needed a five-year plan, a ten-year plan, even a thirty-year plan. Recently I have realized that when I become so connected to "my plan," I leave no room for God to act. I, therefore, changed my way of thinking.

When this attitude changed, a whole new world opened to me. Each day became fresh and exciting as my eyes saw what God was accomplishing. He was doing this all along, but I would not notice or I explained it away as a coincidence or luck. As the scripture passage above so graphically illustrates, Paul and his fellow inmates were doing what prisoners do when they are incarcerated; however, suddenly God acted on their behalf. The message is clear. Continue to go about everyday life, but hold loosely to any plans. Look to see where the Holy Spirit is leading. That will give the Lord an opportunity to use us best to glorify Him.

When we have this mindset, we can look forward to every new day with excitement and anticipation as we expect the unexpected. To God Be the Glory!

PRAYER TARGET:
Those that seek an exciting life of following Jesus through the leading of the Holy Spirit and willing to step out in faith, knowing God is with them.

PERSONAL PRAYER FOR KNOXVILLE:
Lord, please fill us daily with your Holy Spirit. Create that excitement in each of us to follow You, trusting You one-hundred percent. Lord, give us the confidence to move forward as we seek the peace of our city, knowing that You are working all around us and are always calling us into Your plan. Surround us with others that will encourage us to take the risk of following You. We love You, Lord, and know that You have put us in Knoxville to glorify You through our service, making our community a better place to live and work. In Christ's Name we live and in Christ's Name we pray. Amen.

WEEK EIGHTEEN: WEDNESDAY

AUTHOR: STAN JOHNSON
FAMILY STRUCTURE: WIFE AND 2 CHILDREN
OCCUPATION: EXECUTIVE DIRECTOR OF ORGANIZATION

KEEP HOPE ALIVE

"May the God of hope fill you with all joy and peace as you trust in him, so that you may overflow with hope by the power of the Holy Spirit." Romans 15:13

"Dear children, let us not love with words or speech but with actions and in truth. This is how we know that we belong to the truth and how we set our hearts at rest in his presence: If our hearts condemn us, we know that God is greater than our hearts, and he knows everything. Dear friends, if our hearts do not condemn us, we have confidence before God and receive from him anything we ask, because we keep his commands and do what pleases him. And this is his command: to believe in the name of his Son, Jesus Christ, and to love one another as he commanded us. The one who keeps God's commands lives in him, and he in them. And this is how we know that he lives in us: We know it by the Spirit he gave us." 1 John 3:18-24

People succeed in life because of hope. It causes us to get things done even when it shouldn't be possible. Hope is far more powerful than we give credit. Every person, Christian or not, can have it. There are people who do not believe in God that succeed because they never lose hope. Simply put, people that believe in themselves and have hope are powerful. God is the creator of hope and offers Christians an advantage beyond human ability. It is supernatural power through the Holy Spirit. The problem is we rarely tap into it. If we lose hope then we have no advantage and no peace or joy. God is not going to give a lazy, apathetic

Christian an advantage over anyone else. When we are not obedient over the small stuff, God is not going to bless us with more.

The Holy Spirit is available to every believer. If we do not engage with Him then we put ourselves in the same place as everyone else, resting in human hope. Human hope can take us far, but it remains ordinary and is not the abundant life Jesus promised. We are supposed to be using God's power; when we don't, even our best efforts will not feel like enough because we are meant to be using something greater and it is not something we can muster up or reproduce. Prayer is important, but it is not the advantage. We must pray in faith. We must believe in Who we are praying to and what He says. We must trust and be obedient. And we must apply actions that reflect our faith. The same power that performed the miracles in the Bible exists today and is accessible to us. When we act in love, forgiveness and the fruit of the Spirit, we activate His power. If we will do right, taking the initial step, things will start to feel right.

PRAYER TARGET:
Citizens in the city of Knoxville and surrounding areas seeking hope and change.

PERSONAL PRAYER FOR KNOXVILLE:
God, we pray that Knoxville will learn the importance of keeping hope alive. We pray that our spiritual leaders will continue to orchestrate a sense of Godly faith that will drive others to have hope in You. Let us as a Christian community have patience with those who may cause us to lose our hope. Violence in our city has risen and many have lost all hope in our judicial system and our protectors. As we gain new leaders in political positions, help them to re-focus our city on efforts to bring unity and love back to Knoxville again. Protect through Your Amazing Spirit. In Your Name, Amen.

WEEK EIGHTEEN: THURSDAY

AUTHOR: LANCE HUFF
FAMILY STRUCTURE: WIFE AND 2 CHILDREN
OCCUPATION: DATA MANAGEMENT

NEVERTHELESS

> **"When He had stopped speaking, He said to Simon, 'Launch out into the deep and let down your nets for a catch.' But Simon answered and said to Him, 'Master, we have toiled all night and caught nothing; nevertheless, at your word I will let down the net.' And when they had done this, they caught a great number of fish, and their net was breaking." Luke 5:4-6**

Just like all of us, my family and I have faced many hardships in our lives. The death of a loved one, the lack of financial stability and the absence of life direction have been dark spots on the canvas of my life. It would have been easy to look at these situations and remain in those dark places. However, Luke encourages us in his letter to look past our situations and hold fast to God's word.

This passage gives us the encouragement to be a *"nevertheless"* believer. That kind of a believer is someone who doesn't remain a victim of their circumstances, but one who stands on God's promises, knowing that He is watching out for us. Many times, I get stuck at the first part of Simon's response. I like to make excuses and tell God everything He already knows. I don't always get to *"nevertheless"* as quickly as I would like. When I finally arrive, God's has always been faithful to meet me at my need and bless me abundantly. His faithfulness to me helps me say *"nevertheless"* a little more quickly each time.

PRAYER TARGET:
Struggling people who think they have no hope.

PERSONAL PRAYER FOR KNOXVILLE:

Father, I'm thankful that you are a God who loves all of His creation. You know what is best for Your children, even when we believe that You don't. When we feel like You don't love us, You're always there, watching and waiting. I'm thankful that You love this city and everyone in it, no matter what we're facing or what our situations look like. God, encourage us that You are faithful to Your word and that You are greater than any of our circumstances. Help us to keep our sights set on You and not on the world. Remind us that You are a God of love that can be trusted with our lives. I pray that this city would become a "nevertheless" city that is filled to overflowing with Your love. In Your Name, Amen.

WEEK EIGHTEEN: FRIDAY

AUTHOR: WENDY MCGAHA
FAMILY STRUCTURE: MOM AND BROTHER
OCCUPATION: FULL-TIME COLLEGE STUDENT

I AM ENOUGH

"Not that we dare to classify or compare ourselves with some of those who are commending themselves. But when they measure themselves by one another and compare themselves with one another, they are without understanding." 2 Corinthians 10:12

"Not that we dare to classify or compare ourselves with some of those who are commending themselves. But when they measure themselves by one another and compare themselves with one another, they are without understanding." 2 Corinthians 10:12 One of my biggest struggles that I endure daily is comparing myself to those around me. It's so easy to compare my looks, actions, words, and personality with those around me, especially with my sisters-in-Christ. The result from this struggle always ends with feeling like I am not good enough. One way or another, I always end up down on myself.

Once I came upon the above verse, Jesus began to reveal a sweet but important truth to me- I AM enough! I am enough for Him to lay His life down for me, and to continue to use me for His kingdom. I am uniquely designed and woven by the very hands of my Creator. He took the time to place every freckle and hair on my head. Even Isaiah 49:16 says, *"I have written Your name in the palm of my hand."* I am not forgotten or too flawed for His work. He is doing a work in me that is completely different than my sister beside me. To fully understand and love like Christ, I must realize that I am unique, loved, and called His daughter. We are all walking different paths and enduring different seasons, but we have the same end destination: Jesus.

PRAYER TARGET:
Unity in the Body of Christ independent of denominations, elimination of comparisons.

PERSONAL PRAYER FOR KNOXVILLE:
Father, You are our Creator, and You wove us together with Your very hands. You've given us seasons and stories to tell of Your steadfast love and new mercies every day. Help us to see and hold onto the Truth that we are created one-of-a-kind by You, for Your Kingdom's cause. Help us to lift our brothers and sisters and always show them daily how unique we are because of You. We praise You that we were wonderfully and fearfully made by You, to be used as vessels daily for Your kingdom. I pray that we see no need of comparing, and need only to sharpen and strengthen our brothers and sisters. I pray all these things in Jesus' Name, Amen.

WEEK NINETEEN: MONDAY

AUTHOR: BEN HEATH
FAMILY STRUCTURE: WIFE AND 2 SONS
OCCUPATION: ENGINEER

JESUS HAS AUTHORITY OVER ALL THINGS

> "And they began discussing with one another the fact that they had no bread. And Jesus, aware of this, said to them, 'Why are you discussing the fact that you have no bread? Do you not yet perceive or understand? Are your hearts hardened? Having eyes do you not see, and having ears do you not hear? And do you not remember? When I broke the five loaves for the five thousand, how many baskets full of broken pieces did you take up?' They said to him, 'Twelve.' 'And the seven for the four thousand, how many baskets full of broken pieces did you take up?' And they said to him 'Seven.' And he said to them, 'Do you not yet understand?'" Mark 8:16-21

In this passage, we see Jesus reminding the disciples of His power in some of the miracles He had just performed. Do we understand WHO Jesus is? Jesus is the Son of God! Jesus was in the beginning and all things were made through Him. Jesus became flesh and lived a sinless life to be the ultimate sacrifice for all our sins. This is who Jesus is, BELIEVE IT!

Do you understand the authority that Jesus has? Have you ever made anything? Have you ever made anything from nothing? Jesus has authority of all things and has the ability to make, create, orchestrate, prevent, and sustain far beyond what our minds can comprehend. Let us learn from the disciples' lack of understanding and live in this glorious truth: Jesus has authority over all things.

PRAYER TARGET:
Each person that struggles to comprehend Jesus' authority.

PERSONAL PRAYER FOR KNOXVILLE:
Father, I pray that each one of us can understand Jesus' authority. In this busy modern-day society with an endless supply of negativity and distractions from every direction, Lord, help us to remember that You reign. When we face obstacles that are not accomplishable, You reign. When there are needs, You reign. Lord, help us to understand and live in Your truth, grace, mercy, and authority. Amen

WEEK NINETEEN: TUESDAY

AUTHOR: LAWRENCE SEGREST
FAMILY STRUCTURE: WIFE AND 3 CHILDREN
OCCUPATION: CEO, LOCAL MANUFACTURER

LIVE AS A PRIEST

"Coming to Him as to a living stone – rejected indeed by men, but chosen by God and precious – you also as living stones, are being built up to a spiritual house, a holy priesthood, to offer up spiritual sacrifices acceptable to God through Jesus Christ." 1 Peter 2:4-5

"...and [Job] rose early in the morning and offered sacrifices for [his sons and daughters] according to their number, as well as one calf for the sins of their souls. For Job said, 'Lest my sons consider evil things in their mind against God.' Therefore, Job did this continually." Job 1:5

While there is a priesthood of the Melchizedekian order (that is, Christ), and an ordained priesthood with authority in Christ's church, there is also a holy, royal priesthood composed of all Christians. In our priestly role, each Christian must first reconcile himself to God through repentance, prayer, and fasting - the "spiritual sacrifices." We are then spiritually prepared to pray for the salvation of our family, our city and our world (I Timothy 2:1 - 4). Of particular focus, we need to pray for our families. St. Job, like Melchizedek, preceded the Levitical priesthood, yet he clearly understood his role as "priest of the family." Parents, grandparents, and particularly fathers need to follow the example of St. Job. Our responsibility for the salvation and faith of our children should be central to our priesthood. As for our "spiritual sacrifice" for the sins of our children, let us look to the Psalmist who says, "Let my prayer be set forth before You as incense, the lifting up of my hands as an evening sacrifice." (Psalm 141:2)

PRAYER TARGET:
All Christians (priests) who pray for this city, nation, and world, and particularly for fathers (priests of their families) and their children.

PERSONAL PRAYER FOR KNOXVILLE:
Father, I pray first that we desire holiness – that we not see our title of "a holy, royal priesthood" as a poetic nicety, but as the serious calling and responsibility of all Christians. Secondly, may we not grow weary in our priesthood or in the spiritual defense of our children. We fight not against flesh and blood, and, Lord, give us zeal to engage the spiritual battle for our children, this city, and the world. Finally, give us spiritual eyes to see that through our daily spiritual sacrifices we reclaim creation, offering this world, which we have disfigured through sin, back to God.

WEEK NINETEEN: WEDNESDAY

AUTHOR: ANNA MOORE
FAMILY STRUCTURE: HUSBAND 2 DAUGHTERS
OCCUPATION: NURSE PRACTITIONER, AUTHOR

A WALK IN THE WILDERNESS

"See, I am doing a new thing! Now it springs up; do you not perceive it? I am making a way in the wilderness and streams in the wasteland." Isaiah 43:19

Have you ever felt like you were personally walking through a wilderness in your life? Have you experienced a time when you felt the struggle, with no relief in sight? Have you wondered why you were experiencing what seemed to be a spiritual drought? When God's words seem to have dried up in your life? When you just could not seem to connect with God? I have. And not just once. I questioned God. I questioned myself. I felt so alone …

Wilderness experiences are part of life. Our human condition and our natural rebellion toward the Creator set the stage for such times. Yet, while we feel alone and dried up in that spiritual drought, God is at work in our lives. God goes before us to prepare the way. He goes with us through the wilderness, present even when we do not sense Him.

The children of Israel spent forty years in the wilderness. King David hid in the wilderness. John the Baptist preached in the wilderness. Jesus spent forty days being tempted by Satan in the wilderness.

I think we can safely assume that the wilderness is a sure thing for all of us at some point in our Christian walks. The question then becomes: How do we respond to wilderness times? We must remember that God has a purpose for the wilderness times. It may be to humble us and to test us like the children of Israel

(Deuteronomy 8:2). It may be to build our faith as He provides for us in that time. It may be to grow us spiritually and strengthen us as we come against the Evil One.

Whatever the purpose of our walk in the wilderness, we can rest assured that God is with us, He is for us and not against us, and He has a plan to use our wilderness times for our good and for His glory. See, He is doing a new thing....

PRAYER TARGET:
Wilderness Wanderers.

PERSONAL PRAYER FOR KNOXVILLE:
Father God, Creator of Heaven and Earth, I praise Your name, for You alone are worthy of our praise. I thank You, Lord, for the wilderness times, when we grow more dependent on You. Father, show us the path you would have us to walk in these times. Lead us, guide us, and give us wisdom for the journey. We want only what You want, Lord, for You want what is best for Your children. Lord, we long for the "New Thing" that You are doing in our city, in the surrounding areas, and in the mountains of East Tennessee. We see the wastelands, Lord, and anxiously desire the streams of Living Water that only You can provide. Refresh us with Your Spirit today, and give us boldness to share Your grace with those around us. Strengthen us. Draw us to Yourself, and teach us to humble ourselves before You in surrender and obedience. Pour out Your Spirit in a fresh and mighty way. May You be glorified in all we say and do. In the name of the living Lord, Jesus Christ. Amen

WEEK NINETEEN: THURSDAY

AUTHOR: ROY NICAUD
FAMILY STRUCTURE: WIFE AND 2 CHILDREN
OCCUPATION: REAL ESTATE

TRUST AND SERVE

> **""Trust in the Lord with all your heart and lean not on your own understanding. In all your ways submit to him, and he will make your paths straight." Proverbs 3:5-6**

No matter how old we are we will face circumstances in life that we are not expecting. No matter how it comes about it is not a good place to be, but the way we respond may move us to best place we could be.

In my life, I have had multiple scenarios where I have tried to push forward in a career only to come to a roadblock. I remember telling my Dad, now I know how people truly begin to lose hope, drive, or passion for life. It did not matter what direction that I went, whether I pursued my business career or full-time ministry goals, the roadblocks would come again and again. Then I read the passage in Acts 27:39-28:10 in which Paul showed me how to pursue life by the way he responded to the circumstances in which he found himself.

First, Paul trusted God. "Trust in the Lord with all your heart." Paul was heading to see Caesar and be sentenced to death. That alone is scary. However, during the journey he was in a shipwreck, stranded on an island, and bitten by a poisonous snake. Through it all, Paul continued to trust God with everything that he faced. Do you trust that God is at work even in moments that seem off the path of life?

Second, Paul responded in service. "Lean not on your own understanding, in all your ways submit to him." Many times, we want to be angry, blame others, and get revenge on for the circumstances we find ourselves in. We may even have every right to do so but Paul did not. He served! Even in the circumstances in which Paul found himself he helped the people with building a fire, then went and prayed over the Chief, and led many people to be healed by laying hands on them. Might I add it was the same hand that was bitten by a snake!! What would happen if we served people in every circumstance we were in good or bad? How might God use us to exalt His name?

PRAYER TARGET:
That Christians would reach out in trust and serve Him.

PERSONAL PRAYER FOR KNOXVILLE:
Father, help us as Christians in this city to trust You more in the circumstances in which we find ourselves, whether good or bad, and to serve those that are around us in the scenario we are placed. God, continue to reveal to those that feel they have been forgotten that You know right where they are and You have not forgotten them. Help us to understand that through our proper responses, You are revealing to those that do not know You that You have not forgotten them. Lord, help us to be the hands and feet of You to our city. Awaken our city to your Truth. Amen

WEEK NINETEEN: FRIDAY

AUTHOR: MARK BITHORN
FAMILY STRUCTURE: WIFE, 3 CHILDREN, AND 3 GRANDCHILDREN
OCCUPATION: HOUSE REHAB AND SUBSTITUTE TEACHER

FIGHTING BATTLES WHEN THE WAR HAS BEEN WON

"Be strong and courageous, for you shall give this people possession of the land which I swore to their fathers to give them." Joshua 1:6

God told Joshua to be "strong and courageous" and take possession of the Promised Land. To do so, he had to take the first step toward the land of Canaan. The Victory was already won, however, the children of Israel had to take possession of the land.

Lately, I have noticed the defensive prayers of friends. They are the prayers of a victim, not a victor. God gave us the victory by sending His Son to be crucified for our sins. The war has been won and we must be on the offensive, not dwelling on circumstances from the past that anchor us down. Instead, when we renew our mind daily with the Word of God, we are on the offensive. We are "strong and courageous." If we are not in and around the word purposely, then the Devil will weaken us with lies and condemnation, placing doubts in us to the point that we allow him to weigh us down with extra baggage that keeps us from holding our Lord's Sword.

PRAYER TARGET:
The body of Christ that are fighting battles that have already been won.

PERSONAL PRAYER FOR KNOXVILLE:

Jesus, we love You, praise Your name, and are thankful that You love us so, even unto interceding on our behalf to our Heavenly Father. As part of the Church that is Your bride, we want only to please you by walking out our Father's will. We were all lost but you found us. The world needs us to be the salt and light so that our examples can help them enter with You into an eternal life. Your word is a light unto our path and a lamp unto our feet.

Thank you for showing us the way. Our prayer for the city of Knoxville and surrounding areas is to be like the church at Philadelphia that Jesus talked about in Revelation, faithful and loving to the end. May denominations be united in the Truth: Jesus made the way to the Father. May we share Your love, even to our enemies, so that You may bring them into salvation! Amen

WEEK TWENTY: MONDAY

AUTHOR: JILL PRESNELL
FAMILY STRUCTURE: HUSBAND AND CHILDREN
OCCUPATION: REGISTERED NURSE, YOUTH CHAPLAIN

EXCERPT FROM CHUCKS IN CHAPEL

"Though I speak with the tongues of men and of angels, and have not charity, I am become as sounding brass, or a tinkling cymbal. And though I have the gift of prophecy, and understand all mysteries, and all knowledge; and though I have all faith, so that I could remove mountains, and have not charity, I am nothing. And though I bestow all my goods to feed the poor, and though I give my body to be burned, and have not charity, it profiteth me nothing. Charity suffereth long, and is kind; charity envieth not; charity vaunteth not itself, is not puffed up, Doth not behave itself unseemly, seeketh not her own, is not easily provoked, thinketh no evil; Rejoiceth not in iniquity, but rejoiceth in the truth; Beareth all things, believeth all things, hopeth all things, endureth all things." 1 Corinthians 13:1-7

"For I know the plans I have for you," declares the LORD, "plans to prosper you and not to harm you, plans to give you hope and a future. " Jeremiah 29:11

I sat on the floor next to the mattress, Queenie lying in a hospital gown, her back towards me. She was on the strictest "behavior modification" plan and allowed only her school books which lay untouched in the corner of the room. We were going on week three of this plan and my heart was breaking. "Jesus loves you so much," I whispered. "He has a plan for your life. You are better than this and I'm expecting great things for you. I love you too."

We are encouraged not to say I love you to the kids. But I do love them. More importantly, Jesus loves them and I represent Him. So, for me to make a difference, I must walk in His love. My time with these kids is way too short to not share His love for them in any way availed to me. I almost begged God to use me to reach this precious girl. She carried so much on her heart and I wanted her to be free from the heavy load.

One day she appeared in the youth group I'd started at work. "Nurse Jill! I made it!" She privately shared at conclusion that she'd been molested by her brother, and was now afraid she'd be taken from her home with no place to go. My powerlessness was excruciating. I feebly asked, "Do you want to pray?" Without hesitation she proclaimed, "Dear Jesus…I need you!" That was it! She had been listening!

PRAYER TARGET:
Teachers of Youth-- in His Love.

PERSONAL PRAYER FOR KNOXVILLE:
Dear Lord, You are such a good, good Father, and You love our youth. We come to You on behalf of those with an identity crisis, not having the blessing from their earthly fathers or turning away from their faith. Heal their brokenness and help them to receive the hope and future You intended for them. We speak purpose and direction to our youth. Show us who they are as we come across them and stop us in our tracks to be used as your hands and voice. It's when we think we must have the most eloquent words to reach a heart that we become as a clanging cymbal. It's when we become self-centered with who we are – instead of who we are in You – that we become nothing. We cannot truly love without knowing Your love. When we have that we cannot do anything but love. Amen.

WEEK TWENTY: TUESDAY

AUTHOR: TIM ADAMS
FAMILY STRUCTURE: WIFE, 2 GROWN CHILDREN, AND 2 GRANDSONS
OCCUPATION: NON-PROFIT EXECUTIVE DIRECTOR

WHY CAN'T WE ALL JUST GET ALONG?

> "Above all, maintain constant love for one another, for love covers a multitude of sins. Be hospitable to one another without complaining. Like good stewards of the manifold grace of God, serve one another with whatever gift each of you has received." 1 Peter 4:8-10

I see way too much hatred in our world today. My concern is that it is a problem that we, the world, have been dealing with for far too long. I am not sure we are getting a whole lot better at showing love and serving.

My mother grew up Jewish in pre-war Germany. She was a Holocaust survivor but the rest of her family did not survive. Therefore, I did not have grandparents growing up. I missed that element of family life. Grandparents can bring a new dimension of love to their grandchildren.

Because some youngsters today do not have love from parents or grandparents, my hope is that we can find ways to teach love and service to our young people. My further hope is that one day our world will "maintain constant love for one another." I want my grandsons to "be hospitable to other people without complaining." Just think of how wonderful the world would be if we all "served one another with whatever gifts we have been given!"

PRAYER TARGET:
All adults concerned for the future of children in this world.

PERSONAL PRAYER FOR KNOXVILLE:

Father God, we are Your children. We thank You for the love and Grace that You have shown us through Your ultimate sacrifice of Your Son. Father, please show us how to be better stewards of Your love and Grace. Help us to see that loving each other and serving each other will show our children a better way. Help us all to see that love, kindness, forgiveness and service will create a better future for Your children. Amen

WEEK TWENTY: WEDNESDAY

AUTHOR: DOUG SAGER
FAMILY STRUCTURE: WIFE, CHILDREN, AND GRANDCHILDREN
OCCUPATION: SENIOR PASTOR

SEE IT, SAY IT, AND SEIZE IT

> **"Now to him who is able to do immeasurably more than all we ask or imagine, according to his power that is at work within us, to him be glory in the church and in Christ Jesus throughout all generations, for ever and ever! Amen."**
> **Ephesians 3:20-21**

When the dynamic power of God is upon us, we must *See it, Say it, and Seize it!* When God gives us a vision, we have to see it or it will never happen. Next, we have to say it because with the mouth confession is made. Lastly, we have to seize it by moving in the direction of the vision with the expectation it is going to be fulfilled.

There was a time in our family where we owed a lot of money. We became convinced that God wanted us out of debt so we had a family meeting. During that meeting, we cut up all the credit cards and used cash only. I turned in my lease car and drove an old Plymouth for three years, which was the amount of time it took us to get out of debt. We experienced so many miracles during that time it never occurred to us how difficult it was. It was a great time! Since then, we have been able to do things for the Kingdom that we never felt we could do.

What we do in our thoughts and actions often limits what God would like to do in and through us. The tragedy comes when we wind up operating in the spiritual realm through the energy of the flesh. This can cause us to miss seeing the dynamic power of God in the moment. This is why I believe it is always important for us to stretch for something we cannot achieve. If all we accomplish is what we are able to physically do, then there is not a whole lot that is going to get done. There must always be that supernatural element that pervades every person, business, and congregation. There must be something there that none of us can explain in human terms. This has to be the dynamic of God in the midst!

PRAYER TARGET:
For God to clarify the vision over our lives.

PERSONAL PRAYER FOR KNOXVILLE:
Father, I pray that the eyes of our hearts will enlighten our lives. Let us see clearly with both our hearts and our eyes the purpose that You have for our lives. Give us Your vision for our ministries. Precious Lord, help us to be willing to walk in that narrow path that leads to You regardless of circumstances and consequences. Amen.

WEEK TWENTY: THURSDAY

AUTHOR: JONATHAN CHAFFEN
FAMILY STRUCTURE: SINGLE, NO CHILDREN
OCCUPATION: SERVER, DRUMMER, RADIO DEEJAY

BE A VOICE AND A LIGHT

> **"Finally, my brethren, be strong in the Lord, and in the power of his might. Put on the whole armor of God, that ye may be able to stand against the wiles of the devil. For we wrestle not against flesh and blood, but against principalities, against powers, against the rulers of the darkness of this world, against spiritual wickedness in high places." Ephesians 6:10-12**

My dear mother first introduced to me those scriptures as a young boy. They really became reiterated in my life through the mouth and teachings of my greatest collegiate mentor, Tyvi Small, as he helped guide my development into a faithful, God-fearing man.

More recently, upon returning to UT Spring 2017 to finish the last few years of my bachelor's degree, I've faced some major trials and tribulations: from moving back and feeling all alone, to almost becoming homeless, to almost losing my life in a car accident and destroying my car. The accident happened on July 14, 2017, just three streets over from my parents' home.

Through it all, I've kept in constant communication with Mr. Tyvi, and he's reminded me numerous times of staying optimistic, positive, and remaining "strong in the Lord" always. Having a man of God in front of me wearing the "Armor of God," and showing me how to walk right spiritually helped and still helps me stay out of darkness. His mentoring helps me be that shining light in someone else's life each day.

PRAYER TARGET:
Those who feel silenced and in darkness.

PERSONAL PRAYER FOR KNOXVILLE:
Heavenly Father, I pray that You let Your light continue to shine through us and reflect upon those in darkness. Heavenly Father, I pray that You place a voice in us so that we may be able to vocally plant seeds of life into those who feel as though they are without a voice. You said that no weapon formed against us shall prosper, and I believe it! Pierce our hearts. Show up and SHOW OUT in Your people's lives in every dark situation. We need a fresh rain of glory from You in our lives. We are nothing without You and cannot make it without Your constant input, God. Through all adversity, may every man and every woman be reminded of how great You are and that You have already worked out every situation before we even have a chance to face it. Grant me the constant opportunity to be a voice and a light in this great city of Knoxville, Tennessee for You always. I just thank You for all You have done, are doing, and will do. In this I pray. Amen.

WEEK TWENTY: FRIDAY

AUTHOR: TYVI SMALL
FAMILY STRUCTURE: WIFE
OCCUPATION: EDUCATOR

STRONGER TOGETHER

> "After this I looked, and behold, a great multitude that no one could number, from every nation, from all tribes and peoples and languages, standing before the throne and before the Lamb, clothed in white robes, with palm branches in their hands." Revelation 7:9

> "My brothers, show no partiality as you hold the faith in our Lord Jesus Christ, the Lord of glory. For if a man wearing a gold ring and fine clothing comes into your assembly, and a poor man in shabby clothing also comes in, and if you pay attention to the one who wears the fine clothing and say, "You sit here in a good place," while you say to the poor man, "You stand over there," or, "Sit down at my feet," have you not then made distinctions among yourselves and become judges with evil thoughts? Listen, my beloved brothers, has not God chosen those who are poor in the world to be rich in faith and heirs of the kingdom, which he has promised to those who love him?" James 2:1-5

People say the most segregated time in America is on Sunday at 11:00am. As believers in Christ we must re-examine ourselves. We can no longer see this as us versus them. We are in this together…. for the long haul. Brothers and sisters, we cannot sit by idly as racism, drugs, crime, unemployment, underemployment, homelessness, and hopelessness ravage our city. There are so many injustices that happen in Knoxville and in our country and we as Christians have been silent. As Christians (being Christ-like), we must realize those things that affect our brothers or sisters. The same affects us because when one of us hurts we all hurt. So, my challenge to you my brothers and sisters is to be bold and fight for those who cannot fight for themselves, be the voice for the voiceless.

Gods wants us to love all of his people regardless of who they or where they come from. Love is an action word that should force us to do something when we see injustices in our community. It should keep us at night when we think of the inequities that some of our neighbors face. God has called us to love our brothers and sister as we love ourselves Mark 12:30-31. It's time to put our love to the test.

PRAYER TARGET:
Unity in the body of Christ, not tied to denomination, race, color, culture.

PERSONAL PRAYER FOR KNOXVILLE:
Father, bring us together, regardless of race, ethnicity, socioeconomic status or denomination to solve the critical issues affecting our city. God, I pray that You will send a spirit of unity and empathy to our city. Remind us that we are our brothers' and sisters' keeper. God, convict our hearts so we know that You are not just God on Sunday or only in communities that that are familiar and comfortable to us. God, I pray for You to bring different denominations, churches, pastors and people who love You together in a mighty way to stand on Your Word. If we are going to move forward as a community, it's going to be the church to get us there. I know it's tough. I know it's uncomfortable, but that's how we move forward, together. Unity will make us stronger. Keep us together. In the Name of our Jesus. Amen.

WEEK TWENTY ONE: MONDAY

AUTHOR: ROBERT D. LAND
FAMILY STRUCTURE: PARENTS AND BROTHER
OCCUPATION: REGISTERED NURSE

WHAT DO WE DO WITH THE TIME GIVEN TO US?

> **"Make it your ambition to lead a quiet life, to mind your own business and to work with hands, just as we told you, so that your daily life may win the respect of outsiders and so that you will not be dependent on anyone."**
> **1 Thessalonians 4:11-12**

The American culture strives towards business and continual advancement. We see that in our obsession with entertainment e.g., music, news, sports and our huge personal phones. We can see that in our ongoing pursuit towards better grades, more degrees, that next promotion, and our inability to say no to signing ourselves up for that next social engagement, even though we are exhausted. This may be who we are as a culture, but it's not who we are as a Christian people. We often can't see this because we do not learn to adhere to God's instruction in Psalm 46:10, *"Be still, and know that I am God."*

Once, I went through several life changing events all in one brief time span. It stopped me and caused me to be still. I felt as if I had little will or purpose to live and all that mattered so dearly to me before, was burned away in the fire of my trials. I was left with a few Truths. What matters in our last moments on this earth can be concentrated to about three things: Our relationship with The Lord and how we have served and obeyed Him; Our conduct and relationships with our family; and How we loved and served our friends and those around us. The Apostle Paul tells us in 1 Timothy 6:6-7, *"But godliness with contentment is great gain. For we brought nothing into the world, and we can take nothing out of it."* Maybe we should stop striving to do so much with constantly seeking entertainment, but rather, learn to be content and live with some quiet times in our lives. Pray for contentment and more quiet time in your life.

PRAYER TARGET:
Youth and young adults seeking to grasp purpose in life.

PERSONAL PRAYER FOR KNOXVILLE:
Lord, may You help Your followers here in Knoxville know that You are our purpose, our identity, and our joy. Fill us with the deep contentment that only You can provide. Lord, help us know and use the times when it is quiet or boring to draw closer to You. Please, Lord, give peace and comfort to those who need it. Help us to honor You today with our thoughts, our words, and our actions. We want to live in obedience to You and so that we can bring glory to Your Name, Jesus. In your great and holy Name, Lord Jesus Christ, Amen.

WEEK TWENTY ONE: TUESDAY

AUTHOR: LORI S. ROBINSON
FAMILY STRUCTURE: SINGLE
OCCUPATION: EDUCATOR: LEARNING SPECIALIST

GROWING OUR SPIRITUAL GIFTS THROUGH LOVE

> "The end of all things is near. Therefore, be alert and of sober mind so that you may pray. Above all, love each other deeply, because love covers over a multitude of sins. Offer hospitality to one another without grumbling. Each of you should use whatever gift you have received to serve others, as faithful stewards of God's grace in its various forms. If anyone speaks, they should do so as one who speaks the very words of God. If anyone serves, they should do so with the strength God provides, so that in all things God may be praised through Jesus Christ. To him be the glory and the power for ever and ever. Amen." 1 Peter 4:7-11

1 Peter 4:8 tells us, "Above all, love each other deeply, because love covers over a multitude of sins. Each of you should use whatever gift you have received to serve others…" Constant prayer and love for everyone is what has helped me hold my peace as I transitioned to living in Knoxville. The experiences I've had here have changed my life spiritually, personally, and professionally. Most of the experiences were designed to distract me from developing my spiritual gifts and His purpose for my life.

Distractions are surrounding us every second of every day. A lot of the times, the events, circumstances, or situations we are fighting against are not the individual people themselves, but the spirit inside of them (see Ephesians 6:12-13). Never allow the distractions around you to keep you from realizing, growing, and developing the spiritual gift with which God has blessed you.

When those distractions rise, turn your focus to God. The unconditional love He has for us will remind us how to serve and love others unconditionally and use your spiritual gifts even in the face of adversity.

PRAYER TARGET:
Youth – all ages, seeking to understand their spiritual gifts.

PERSONAL PRAYER FOR KNOXVILLE:
Father, I pray for the young people here in Knoxville. I pray that each young person in the city will learn to love others even when love has not been displayed to them. As our youth experience situations, help us look for Your face during each. God, help us develop our spiritual gifts and share them with others, especially in tricky situations. As each young person's gifts are cultivated with love and service to others, may You lead each in this generation to change the world and build Your kingdom here on earth. Amen!

WEEK TWENTY ONE: WEDNESDAY

AUTHOR: KATHLEEN FALK
FAMILY STRUCTURE: HUSBAND, 6 CHILDREN, AND 23 GRANDCHILDREN
OCCUPATION: GRANDMOTHER

CHRIST'S COMPASSION FOR A GREAT CITY

> "As he [Jesus] approached Jerusalem and saw the city, he wept over it and said, 'If you, even you, had only known on this day what would bring you peace--but now it is hidden from your eyes." Luke 19:41,42

Imagine this scene. Jesus is approaching the great city of Jerusalem, and as He does, He begins to weep. The Greek word for weep can be translated "wail," so this is no mere moment of sentimentality. Christ is sobbing for the very people who rejected Him. *"He came unto His own, and His own received Him not,"* according to the words in John 1:11. He is not crying for Himself because He has been rejected. He is crying for them. They have stubbornly refused Him as Messiah because they were waiting for a Messiah who would bring them peace militarily. But Jesus had told them, *"Peace I leave with you; My peace I give unto you, not   as the world gives do I give you."* (John 14:27) They were rejecting their only hope of peace.

From what I've read, some old copies of the Bible omitted the statement of Christ's weeping, because it was believed that a perfect Messiah would not weep. But isn't it comforting for us to know that Jesus--Emmanuel, God with us--showed us that God does not delight in judgment, even when that judgment is deserved. His heart is full of grace and truth. Christ wept for Jerusalem, and He weeps today for those who reject their only Source of peace.

PRAYER TARGET:

The cities of Knoxville and surrounding areas to become cities of God.

PERSONAL PRAYER FOR KNOXVILLE:

Dear Lord, man is hardwired to look everywhere but to You, Christ, for peace. I pray that You, God, by Your Holy Spirit will draw the people of Knoxville and surrounding areas to Yourself, and that men and women everywhere in this great city will see the futility of all the counterfeit gods they have been worshiping, and turn to You, Christ. You are the only One who can give real, lasting peace--the peace of sins forgiven, the peace of the indwelling Holy Spirit, and the peace we will have in the presence of You, God, for eternity. All other sources of peace are fleeting and deceptive. And may we weep, too, for our families, neighbors and friends who do not know Christ as Savior. God, forbid that we should be callous to the lost and dying around us. In Your Name. Amen.

WEEK TWENTY ONE: THURSDAY

AUTHOR: LEILA MANCINI
FAMILY STRUCTURE: HUSBAND, 3 GROWN CHILDREN, AND
11 GRANDCHILDREN
OCCUPATION: HOMEMAKER

PRAYING WITH EXPECTATION

"The wise woman builds her house, but the foolish tears it down with her own hands." Proverbs 14:1

My favorite woman in the Scriptures is Mary of Bethany who anointed Jesus with her most precious possession, a vial of very expensive perfume, which probably represented her life and future. Jesus responded to those who complained about what they considered a waste by saying, "Truly I tell you, whenever the gospel is preached throughout the world, what she has done will also be told in memory of her." (Mark 14:9) Her extravagant sacrifice was the proper response to the One who would sacrifice Himself for the salvation of the world, and bring new life, eternal life.

Women sacrifice themselves, too, to bring life, through their bodies, through their words, and through their open arms. They bring life to their marriages by loving their husbands and they bring life to their families by loving and nurturing their children. They bring life to their homes by creating atmospheres of love and warmth, peace, and welcome. They bring life to their churches through their glad volunteer service. They bring life to their communities by caring for and sharing with their neighbors. Women that give of themselves to serve the living God… they are the women of influence.

PRAYER TARGET:
Women of the city who sacrifice themselves for others.

PERSONAL PRAYER FOR KNOXVILLE:

Father, God, how we thank You for the life-giving abilities You have created in women. We pray for the women of Knoxville, that You would open their eyes of understanding to work in concert with You to bring life to our families and communities. We pray that the light and love of Jesus Christ would shine through them to the hurting and dying in Knoxville. We pray that Knoxville families would be strengthened, that our churches would flourish in bringing new life into our communities, and that Knoxville would be known as a city that joyfully protects and nurtures life for its people. We pray that You would be bringing more and more women to the realization that they are called to raise life to a higher existence, as a response to the abundant and eternal life in Christ You have given us. In Jesus' Name and for His glory, Amen.

WEEK TWENTY ONE: FRIDAY

AUTHOR: STEPHANIE KOCH
FAMILY STRUCTURE: HUSBAND AND 4 CHILDREN
OCCUPATION: WIFE AND HOMESCHOOLING MOM

PRAYING WITH EXPECTATION

"I lift up my eyes to the hills. Where does my help come from? My help comes from the Lord, the Maker of heaven and earth." Psalm 121:1-2

The laundry, the dishes, vacuuming, and dusting. Doctor's appointments, piano practice, ballet, and football. And homeschooling 4 children. There is also the husband who works overtime so much that sometimes I forget what he looks like. Go to sleep, wake up, and do it all again. It gets overwhelming. I feel ready to snap. And I find myself frazzled, short-tempered, and angry. How do other moms do this?!?!?!? It is obvious that I can't do this.

One day I had enough. I found myself throwing my hands up in despair and yelling out, "I just need a little help here." I left the room to cool off. I was going to look up some Bible verses to help me get in control of my feelings. Psalms 121 was the very first one I found. I knew the instant I read it, it was for me. I was NOT alone. I had a helper. He soothed my troubled heart by showing me that what I thought of as a burden was really His calling. I finally found the joy in my calling when I realized I did have the help I wanted.

PRAYER TARGET:
Stay at home moms and homeschooling moms.

PERSONAL PRAYER FOR KNOXVILLE:

Lord, let every stay at home mom and homeschooling mom be filled with the soothing presence of You, Lord. If we have frustration, anger, resentment, hopelessness, or helplessness on our hearts, please remove it. Change our mindset from "this is a burden" to "this is my calling," Lord. Let us find the joy in our everyday life and in the simple tasks that make up our day. I ask that You give us authentic friendships that will help cultivate a joyful spirit instead of a complaining one. I thank You for the help we receive from You God, the mightiest of all Helpers. Amen.

WEEK TWENTY TWO: MONDAY

AUTHOR: JESSICA DAVIS
FAMILY STRUCTURE: HUSBAND AND 6 CHILDREN
OCCUPATION: WIFE, HOMESCHOOL MOM, WOMEN'S MINISTRY LEADER

OPERATING IN THE AUTHORITY OF CHRIST

> **"Now to Him who is able to do immeasurably more than all we ask or imagine, according to His power that is at work within us, to Him be glory in the church and in Christ Jesus throughout all generations, for ever and ever! Amen."**
> **Ephesians 3:20**

Sometimes I feel like we get so focused on our human and fleshly limitations that we miss the Truth of His Word, when the reality is that we are Spirit-filled believers with the same power that raised Christ from the dead living inside us! Not for our own glory, lest any man boast, but rather just as the scripture says, so that God may be glorified. Sometimes we are the only roadblock in unleashing the power of the Holy Spirit and operating in His authority.

If we just yield to His spirit and ask, I believe that God can do through us immeasurably more than all we ask or imagine! His word says that His name will be established. It's not a question. It will be. The question is, are we going to let it happen through us? Let's allow Him to shape us and change us to be more like Him. Let's yield to His power and let it work within us so that others may come to know the Jesus we love and with Whom we have a personal relationship!

PRAYER TARGET:
The Women of the city seeking true freedom.

PERSONAL PRAYER FOR KNOXVILLE:

Dear God, as women we are created to be our husband's helpmate. I pray that we would walk out that very calling and challenge with all the authority that Christ has given us through supporting not only our husbands, but the church as well! We want to rise with all boldness to speak the truth in love. Father, help us lead and encourage other women to walk in humility, to truly love their husbands and home first, and then reach out to the hurting.

I pray against the spirit of division among women. Father, the only one with Whom we should compare ourselves is Christ, and the good news is we all fall short! I pray that as our eyes are opened to our desperate need of a savior, that the eyes of our understanding may be opened to all that Christ has for us! Let women no longer compare themselves with others just to beat themselves up or to compete, but rather compare to learn. Help us learn with humility how to be more Christ like. I pray for the spirit of unity to operate in the women of this city, throughout all generations. May the unity affect young and old and may the light of Your glory shine brightly through us as we join to operate in the ministry of reconciliation to You, Christ. In Your Name. Amen.

WEEK TWENTY TWO: TUESDAY

AUTHOR: GRANT STANDEFER
**FAMILY STRUCTURE: WIFE, 3 GROWN, MARRIED CHILDREN, AND
7 GRANDCHILDREN**
OCCUPATION: NON-PROFIT EXECUTIVE DIRECTOR

INCARNATIONAL MINISTRY

**"The Word became flesh and blood and moved into the
neighborhood." John 1:14**

The business world was a very different experience for me
since I had worked in paid ministry with a church all my adult
life. In the midst of normal everyday circumstances, problems,
conflict, or high- pressure situations my co-workers looked for
my reaction since they knew I was a follower of Jesus and that
I had been a pastor. God was doing a work in me, teaching me
in powerful and personal ways that we are to be the loving,
serving presence of Christ wherever God has us at any given
time…our neighborhoods, in the stands of the sporting events
of our children and grandchildren, our places of employment,
our schools, or our hobbies and clubs. In the words of Douglas
John Hall, *"…Christ is always going toward this world…and
discipleship, when it is authentically so, is always a matter of
being taken up into this world-directedness despite one's own
preference for security and peace."*

PRAYER TARGET:
The Christians of Knoxville and surrounding areas that may not
be aware of His eternal presence.

PERSONAL PRAYER FOR KNOXVILLE:
I pray, God, that the Holy Spirit would so move in Your people
all across this city that we would, every one of us, come to
understand and grasp that we are all the presence and aroma of

Christ wherever we go and whatever we do. I pray that the Christ in us would move us toward the pain, brokenness and darkness of our city and give us sacrificial, servant-hearts so that we will be light, love, and a healing presence. Amen.

WEEK TWENTY TWO: WEDNESDAY

AUTHOR: AMANDA SHAVER
FAMILY STRUCTURE: HUSBAND AND 2 CHILDREN
OCCUPATION: HOMEMAKER

FIRMLY PLANTED

"That person is like a tree planted by streams of water, which yields its fruit in season and whose leaf does not wither-- whatever they do prospers." Psalm 1:3

"Consider it pure joy, my brothers and sisters, whenever you face trials of many kinds, because you know that the testing of your faith produces perseverance. Let perseverance finish its work so that you may be mature and complete, not lacking anything." James 1: 2-4

Have you ever stopped to consider the roots of a tree? Since I was a kid I have always loved when tree roots protruded from the ground a bit. For me it is like a little peek into just how strong the tree is. I like to imagine how deep and wide its unseen root system goes beneath the surface. I recently learned that trees need wind to blow against them to deepen their root system and make them stronger. No wind pressure means the tree will be weak and topple over easily in the face of a storm.

I've always been one to shy away from confrontation, challenges and unfamiliar territory. To be honest, I could never understand how someone might consider it joy to be in the midst of a trial. That is until, I faced a season where everything seemed out of my control. During that time, I was diagnosed with skin cancer, lost loved ones, and moved to a new city. Just like a tree during an East Tennessee wind storm, I felt the pressure being applied from every direction. Yet, instead of toppling over I experienced God in a new way.

Through letting go of my fears and trusting Him I saw fruit in my walk with Him that hadn't been there before. I am thankful that God can use even the storms in our lives to strengthen and deepen our root system in Him. Now that is something to consider pure joy.

PRAYER TARGET:
Those that are facing storms.

PERSONAL PRAYER FOR KNOXVILLE:
God, thank You that amid trials and tests that you never leave us and you never forsake us. Thank You that You are a friend who sticks closer than a brother. You are our comfort when we are desperate for relief from the worries of this life. I pray specifically for those facing big trials and storms in their lives. Please meet them during the chaos. May their roots and character be strengthened and deepened because of this season. In your Precious Name I pray, Amen.

WEEK TWENTY TWO: THURSDAY

AUTHOR: PORSCHIA CLARK
FAMILY STRUCTURE: ENGAGED
OCCUPATION: STUDENT AND FAMILY SUPPORT COORDINATOR

YOU ARE DOING A GREAT WORK

> **"So, I sent messengers to them, saying, "I am doing a great work, so that I cannot come down. Why should the work cease while I leave it and go down to you?" Nehemiah 6:3**

I heard Joyce Meyers quote this verse a few years ago and it has never left my heart. What I heard God say through Nehemiah is that what you are doing in the Kingdom and your community is good work. Don't quit. Just remember that God always honors your sacrifice.

When I tend to get distracted or tired, and find myself ready to give up I just remind myself, "I'm doing a great work." I also find myself quoting this scripture when people question or doesn't agree with my calling. Remember that your calling and assignment is from God and it is between you and God. Don't allow the tricks of the enemy to discourage you or put fear in your heart.

In times of doubt and fear, remember Nehemiah's faithfulness and his words, *"I am doing a great work and cannot come down."* Never come down from the work God has called you to do until you're finished with the assignment.

PRAYER TARGET:
Educators and community leaders who need encouragement.

PERSONAL PRAYER FOR KNOXVILLE:

Father, I pray to You, asking that You lead the educators and community leaders in continuing to serve our city with the heart of Jesus Christ. I pray that we always remember why we started and go back to our "Why" in times of struggle, doubt, and fear. Father, guide us as we continue to move forward! Amen.

WEEK TWENTY TWO: FRIDAY

AUTHOR: GEORGE MCRAE
FAMILY STRUCTURE: MARRIED WITH 2 GROWN DAUGHTERS
OCCUPATION: RETIRED CHEMICAL ENGINEER

HOW TO PLEASE GOD

"With what shall I come before the Lord, and bow myself before God on high? Shall I come before him with burnt offerings, with calves a year old? Will the Lord be pleased with thousands of rams, with ten thousands of rivers of oil? Shall I give my firstborn for my transgression, the fruit of my body for the sin of my soul?" He has told you, O man, what is good; and what does the Lord require of you but to do justice, and to love kindness, and to walk humbly with your God?" Micah 6:6-8

Years ago, I took a course in Old Testament at the University of Florida. My professor said that the above passage is as complete a summation of the messages of the Old Testament Prophets as there is. It assumes that one wants to please God. Many today do not seem to have that concern. For those who are interested in pleasing God, one often finds them "doing things" to accomplish that. Micah lists burnt offerings, rams, rivers of oil, calves, and child sacrifice, as some of the things people were "doing" in his day that they thought would please God. "Doing" is not what God wants!

This passage also points out man's greatest need, to have the "sin of my soul" taken away. Micah knows we have a problem in that our sin keeps one from coming *"before the Lord, and bow myself before God on high."* Until that problem is fixed, one cannot please God. We know, from the New Testament, that the ultimate fix for "the sin of my soul" is Jesus and His atoning death. Micah was not fortunate to see Jesus, but he does lay out what a life that has its sin problem fixed would look like. That person would do, and seek, justice; would be kind, and love being kind; and would put God, and His wishes before all other claims (walk humbly with God) on his or her life.

PRAYER TARGET:
Citizens of Knoxville, Knox County & surrounding areas seeking to please God.

PERSONAL PRAYER FOR KNOXVILLE:
Heavenly Father, we all want to see Knoxville become a place where justice is found, where kindness is routine, and where people are not selfish. Help us Father, desire to have what the Prophet Micah gave us a view into on what people who are in relationship with You are like. We ask forgiveness, Father, for our "doing" things to please You. Help us desire the "humble walk" with You. We can't have a meaningful walk with someone without having a relationship with that person. Father, we know we have a sin problem that must be fixed because the Bible indicates that sin has broken our relationship with You. Therefore, Father, please grant us an awakening of sin awareness and an awakening of desire to be in relationship with You. Please grant that we will become so burdened with the sin that we carry and the need for a relationship with God, that we will stop trying to "do" and throw ourselves on Your Grace as provided by the atoning death of Jesus. We acknowledge that we cannot have the city we desire to live in and leave to our children and grandchildren, unless we can exhibit the life traits You revealed to Micah so long ago.
Father, help us step aside and let You rule Knoxville as we humbly walk with You. Amen

AUTHOR: TY ROBERTS
FAMILY STRUCTURE: HUSBAND
OCCUPATIONS: CREDENTIALS COORDINATOR

THE TRUTH ABOUT WORSHIP

> "Woman,' Jesus replied, 'believe me, a time is coming when you will worship the Father neither on this mountain nor in Jerusalem. You Samaritans worship what you do not know; we worship what we do know, for salvation is from the Jews. Yet a time is coming and has now come when the true worshipers will worship the Father in the Spirit and in truth, for they are the kind of worshipers the Father seeks. God is spirit, and his worshipers must worship in the Spirit and in truth." John 4:21-24

Worship. The perceived mystery of this thing called "worship" seems complex to most. However, worship is simply an intimate encounter with our Father. But, to be intimate, there must be a space for vulnerability. The kind of vulnerability that allows one to bare all. In that moment, you are acutely aware that the One with which you are being intimate can see everything about you. There's nowhere to hide. Every scar and blemish is exposed. Everything that you try to cover becomes obvious.

The good news is that the person with which You are being intimate can see your imperfections and still chooses to join you in intimacy. That's how our Father is. When you worship, you invite Him into those places that you don't want anyone else to see. You become exposed. And yet, you realize that His love for you causes Him to not only see those imperfections, but allows Him to bring healing and beauty to those places. However, worship is not a one-time event. It's daily and lifelong. We experience true and authentic worship when we open up and expose every aspect of our lives up to our Father and allow Him into those hidden places…..when we give Him our truth.

PRAYER TARGET:
Citizens of Knoxville and surrounding areas to worship the one true God!

PERSONAL PRAYER FOR KNOXVILLE:
Father, as we humble ourselves before you, help our city to return back to the true heart of worship. Allow us to become vulnerable before you once again. Father, allow our worship to bring healing to this city. Remind us that we are all Your children and that You desire to spend intimate quality time with us. Bring us back to You. Bring our children back to You. Raise up a generation that will worship You in spirit and in Truth. Make us sensitive to Your voice like never before. We reverence and honor You. In Jesus's name, Amen.

WEEK TWENTY THREE: TUESDAY

AUTHOR: MICHELE RENEE DANIEL
FAMILY STRUCTURE: 3 CHILDREN
OCCUPATION: MINISTER, MOTHER, AND PROFESSIONAL

SUIT UP FOR BATTLE

> "" Wherefore take unto you the whole armor of God, that ye may be able to withstand in the evil day, and having done all, to stand. Stand therefore, having your loins girt about with truth, and having on the breastplate of righteousness; And your feet shod with the preparation of the gospel of peace; Above all, taking the shield of faith, wherewith ye shall be able to quench all the fiery darts of the wicked. And take the helmet of salvation, and the sword of the Spirit, which is the word of God:"
> Ephesians 6:13-17

God provides 360-degree protection against all attacks of the enemy, whether personal or corporate. From head to toe, I am reminded that in any battle, fight, or war, I am completely covered. We can stand with peace shoes on – standing on His principles and His ways.

The only offensive weapon is the Word of God (not my words or yours). Knowing that I don't have to make my own provision and cover myself has comforted me and emboldened me in the most difficult times. How God keeps me in a helmet of salvation of both my mind (emotional), my brain (intellect as the epicenter of my body), and covers my vital organs with the breastplate of righteousness, gives me joy even during trying times. Salvation is the gift of God, as is His righteousness. Both protect vital organs. The Belt of Truth keeps my pants from falling and exposing the parts of me that make me most vulnerable. The Shield of Faith protects me and puts out the fires sent to consume me. Faith in the one and true Living God allows one consume me. Faith in the one and true Living God allows one to trust that He is still working, still saving, still protecting, still healing. Still…

PRAYER TARGET:
The mothers of the city- donning the Armor of God!

PERSONAL PRAYER FOR KNOXVILLE:
Dear God, my prayer is that every mother in this city feel the presence, the power and the protection of You. May every mother recognize that the protection and arsenal against the things that come against our youth and our community are found in You, God, and You alone. Trade our weariness for refreshment, and hopelessness for hope as we allow You to outfit us with Your complete protection.

Your armor, God, is tailor-made for the believer and cannot be duplicated. Expose and remove the things that masquerade as solutions. Bring to our memory all the battles that You have already brought us and ours through. May Your grace and mercy cover each of us. Guide us as we walk in the promises of Your provision and rest in the peace and knowledge that whatever You have called us to, You have already made provisions for success. May our city feel the refreshing breeze of the Holy Spirit blowing through and removing the debris of racism, classism, sexism, and all other divisive weapons of the enemy. May we stand up in Your full armor, knowing that we overcome because Christ overcame. In the matchless name of Jesus, I pray, Amen.

WEEK TWENTY THREE: WEDNESDAY

AUTHOR: DONNA AVANT
FAMILY STRUCTURE: HUSBAND, 3 ADULT CHILDREN AND THEIR SPOUSES, 4 GRANDCHILDREN
OCCUPATION: PASTOR'S WIFE, SPEAKER, AND WRITER

THE FATHER'S HEART

> "I urge, then, first of all, that requests, prayers, intercession, and thanksgiving be made for everyone…. This is good and pleases God our Savior who wants all men to be saved and to come to a knowledge of the truth." I Timothy 2:1-4

My father was not a good man. He left my mom when I was sixteen. By age fifty he had been married four times, was on the brink of divorcing his fourth wife, was about to be laid off, and was close to bankruptcy. My dad's heart was all about himself. My heart was broken for him.

I believed that apart from my dad coming to know Christ, he would spend eternity in hell. I began to pray boldly for his salvation. I asked others to pray for his salvation. The church we were pastoring at the time had a card in the prayer room with his name on it. So many people prayed for my dad that the card was just a blob of blue and black ink initials.

In February of 1995 the phone rang. It was my dad telling me he was in Atlanta. John, my husband, was there preaching at a local church. My dad was desperate. Desperate people do things they normally would never do. Out of desperation my dad went to hear John preach.

After 30 years of praying, dad walked down the aisle of the church and fell into my husband's arms crying, *"Every good thing the Lord has given me I have thrown away. I need Jesus in my heart."*

When my husband called that night his shouted "Donna, you have a new daddy!" My father began to grow as a believer. He became a great father and grandfather. Dad did not start well, but he did finish well.

Dad's heart became like the Father's heart!

PRAYER TARGET:
All men and women of the city, praying for the Father's heart.

PERSONAL PRAYER FOR KNOXVILLE:
Father, I pray that every man, woman, student and child in our city will have the Your heart if they do not know You. I pray that we will truly know that apart from salvation, there are thousands that will spend eternity in hell.

Jesus, I pray that we will fall on our faces and cry out to You for those who are lost. I pray that if there are those who do not have lost family, friends, neighbors or co-workers, that that they will repent and ask God to open their hearts to those who do need You. Help us intercede on behalf of all lost.

May You, God Almighty, move across our city and bring the lost to Yourself. Amen.

WEEK TWENTY THREE: THURSDAY

AUTHOR: STACEY GRINDSTAFF
FAMILY STRUCTURE: WIFE AND 3 CHILDREN
OCCUPATION: SMALL BUSINESS OWNER AND SALES REPRESENTATIVE

SERVANTHOOD WITH SACRIFICE

"And whoever desires to be first among you, let him be your slave – just as the Son of Man did not come to be served, but to serve, and to give His life a ransom for many." Matthew 20: 27-28

As a business leader, father, husband, and active church member, there seems to be an endless demand for my time. I am reminded what the Bible says in Luke 12, that "…to whom much is given, much will be required…"

Being a Christian does not make these demands any different from those of my contemporary peers, Christian or non-Christian. However, the way I approach them is…through Grace. Just as Christ served sacrificially during His time on Earth, we have the same obligation to serve others sacrificially. "Putting off" our desires to meet the needs of others is a basic requirement to being a sacrificial servant. When someone asks if I can help them, saying, "No," has long been a character weakness. I always try to find the time to serve them as Christ served by example. All too often, our efforts out speak our words.

Serve with grace and humility!

PRAYER TARGET:
Individuals who claim the title of "Leader" who seek to lead as Christ lead.

PERSONAL PRAYER FOR KNOXVILLE:

Dear God, let every leader be burdened to serve others sacrificially. True change in any culture can only be achieved when dependence on You for every aspect of life is recognized and that acceptance of Jesus as Savior and Lord of our lives is acknowledged.

Heavenly Father, I ask that Your Will be fulfilled in the life of every leader. May their service to others be provided in an attitude of grace and a spirit of humility. May every servant acknowledge that their ability to lead comes from You, and as your Word states, "Blessed is the man who trusts in the Lord, and whose hope is in the Lord." I pray that everyone with the attitude of servanthood allows their actions to be of service to Christ. May Your light shine in their lives so brightly that others see the radiance of God.

In the name of Jesus, I claim these promises. Amen

WEEK TWENTY THREE: FRIDAY

AUTHOR: CARL BRIDGES
FAMILY STRUCTURE: WIFE, 2 MARRIED CHILDREN, 4 GRANDCHILDREN
OCCUPATION: PROFESSOR OF BIBLE AND THEOLOGY

A PRAYER FOR THE DOUBTERS

"If anyone's will is to do God's will, he will know whether the teaching is from God or whether I am speaking on my own authority." John 7:17

Jesus spoke these words to a mixed crowd in Jerusalem at the Feast of Tabernacles. Some believed in Him; others doubted; still others would not be convinced. He tells us today the same thing He told the crowd on that day: that our will comes before our intellect with God. Often when we *"don't understand"* or *"can't believe,"* we have a problem with our will and not with our mind. But when we decide to align what we want with what God wants, the difficulties go away. The Bible calls this realignment repentance.

PRAYER TARGET:
People who have a hard time believing.

PERSONAL PRAYER FOR KNOXVILLE:
Our Father in heaven, please speak to the minds and hearts of our friends and relatives, our neighbors and coworkers who struggle with their belief in You and Your Son. Free them from pride. Free them from enslavement to harmful ways of living. Bring each of them to the point where they want to do Your will more than anything else, and when they reach that point, reveal to them the truth of Jesus Your Son. Amen.

WEEK TWENTY FOUR: MONDAY

AUTHOR: BRITTON SHARP
FAMILY STRUCTURE: WIFE AND 3 CHILDREN
OCCUPATION: MINISTER AND ARTIST

WHEN THE WATERS RUN SWIFT

**"The Lord is my shepherd; I shall not want. He makes me lie down in green pastures. He leads me beside still waters."
Psalm 23:1**

When we picture a shepherd, it is usually in a field with rolling green hills. However, in the context that the familiar Psalm 23 was written, this was not the case. The land is arid and hostile. When the writer says, the Lord is my shepherd, it is not just some cozy metaphor, it is a declaration. God is my provider amidst this hostile land. When you realize the context of Psalm 23 it shifts from the common comfy green hill interpretation, into the realization that God is my provider amidst a difficult and broken world. Green pastures are not plentiful, and in fact they move. The shepherd does not lead the flock to the same spot every day, but instead has the foresight to see where the green pastures will be.

This often messes with my desire for routine and formulas. This formulaic approach is often because I am trying to minimize the amount of faith required in following my Shepherd. The shepherds' provision continues with leading the sheep to still water. Sheep will not drink from fast moving water. Even if they are in dire thirst, they are intimidated. In these moments, the shepherd finds a still pool, and when there is not one available, will dig out a channel to create one for the thirsty sheep.

How often has this been seen in my life. I desire to be close to God, yet fear stops me. Yet my Savior comes to me, my Shepherd leads me. Life changes, our environments change, our city changes, yet God is our Shepherd, and He will lead us.

PRAYER TARGET:
The flock of Christ, when life is in disarray.

PERSONAL PRAYER FOR KNOXVILLE:
Lord, may You be our Shepherd. May You lead us to your green pastures, even as they may move and not be in familiar places. May You lead us to still waters so that our hearts may be filled and quenched by Your presence. May You guide us and teach us how to live. Where there is darkness may You bring light. Where there is pain may You bring healing and where there is despair may You bring hope. May You bless us and keep us, may You cause Your face to shine upon us and grant us peace. May You give us faith to follow You. Amen.

WEEK TWENTY FOUR: TUESDAY

AUTHOR: JOSH HOWARD
FAMILY STRUCTURE: WIFE AND 1 CHILD
OCCUPATION: MUSICIAN

SEASONS

"These are the appointed times of the LORD."
Leviticus 23:4

From the beginning of 2017 I knew that my family's life was going to go through some changes. I have been praying and trying to figure out what God has in store for us but I kept being met with something that my sixteen-year-old self would have been mortified to hear: *Continue to do your daily tasks.* When I was younger the idea of doing the same things day after day was a sign that your life was dead. I looked horrified at the people with 9-5 jobs and thought that what they were doing was just mindlessly going about a routine with no dreams or visions for the future.

I know now that I was very wrong. Fast forward so many years and I know now that the Lord uses times where there is a lot of repetition to mold you into a clearer image of Christ. God uses the circumstances in your life currently to prepare you for the circumstances and opportunities that he has for you in the future. And just like the parable of the talents in Matthew 25:14, God looks very fondly on those who take opportunities to invest in the things He has put before them. So, if it's your own prayer life, being Christ to the people you see every day, a skill or trade you're working on, or practicing being in the presence of God, take that time seriously because God ordains every season in your life.

PRAYER TARGET:
Those struggling with the mundane of their day-to- day lives.

PERSONAL PRAYER FOR KNOXVILLE:

God, I pray that as You move this city from one season to the next that You would show us what our daily assignment is so we may do the work of Christ. Do this so we can worship You with our obedience and so that we may be prepared for the amazing things to come. Amen.

WEEK TWENTY FOUR: WEDNESDAY

AUTHOR: VICKIE DUNCAN
FAMILY STRUCTURE: HUSBAND AND 2 MARRIED CHILDREN
OCCUPATION: BUSINESS OWNER

SHARE ONE ANOTHER'S BURDENS

> **"Carry each other's burdens, and in this way you will fulfill the law of Christ." Galatians 6:2**

> **"Be devoted to one another in brotherly love. Honor one another above yourselves." Romans 12:10**

Leading a new Bible study one evening, I had an eclectic group of women. Some I knew, some I didn't. As we began studying God's Word together in James 1, the women began to share and open up about considering it pure joy when we face trouble. As we finished the time we had together that night, one lady asked if she could say something. She told this group of women that she had walked in that night thinking, *"Oh great, a group of Barbie doll women who have it ALL together."* She quickly learned that the women sitting around that circle were anything but "perfect." Some of their problems looked similar to hers and some were very different, but they all had "stuff." This group of women gathered around our new friend and prayed over her and encouraged her in her situation.

God asks us in His Word to bear one another's burdens, lifting them up in prayer, encouragement and love!! Not only does it help the other person, it allows us to know that we are not alone as the Enemy would like us to think. It doesn't matter our financial status, skin color, sex, or age, we all need each other, and we need Christ as our Savior.

PRAYER TARGET:

That everyone in our city would learn to bear one another's burdens, caring for each other.

PERSONAL PRAYER FOR KNOXVILLE:

Father God, my prayer for our great city is that we would put ourselves in others' lives to tell them about You, encourage them, love them, pray for them - being the hands and feet of Jesus. May we also allow those in our lives to share in our burdens. I pray You would bind the Enemy's lie that we are all alone and that no one cares. Help us to love You with all our heart, soul, mind, and strength, loving our neighbor as ourselves as we are told in Luke 10:27, and in so doing, looking like a picture of You! Amen.

WEEK TWENTY FOUR: THURSDAY

AUTHOR: SPENCER HALL
FAMILY STRUCTURE: WIFE AND 3 CHILDREN
OCCUPATION: FINANCIAL PLANNER

CASTING OUR ANXIETIES ON JESUS

**"Cast all your anxiety on him because he cares for you."
1 Peter 5:7**

At 3 PM on Easter afternoon three years ago, gunshots erupted through our Parkridge block as competing gangs littered the street in front of our home with bullet shells. We yanked our children from the front room of our home and darted to the kitchen for safety.

Despite God's providential protection, we were deeply shaken and felt significant anxiety for weeks. Sadly, other neighbors have not escaped unharmed from similar incidents and have much more significant reason for anxiety.

Violent events that touch us usually generate anxiety in us. They have the capacity to debilitate us. If not for Jesus' life, the world's unsteadiness and the violence and pain that each of us have experienced could push us to constant anxiety.

Almost two thousand years ago, Christ dealt definitively with the violence of our world. He endured a truly gruesome crucifixion to conquer death. As a result, we have a place to take all our anxiety. The Apostle Peter instructs us to cast all our anxieties on Jesus because He cares for us. He cared enough to die for us, and He sent the Holy Spirit to inhabit our lives so that we can live in abiding peace.

PRAYER TARGET:
Releasing anxiety.

PERSONAL PRAYER FOR KNOXVILLE:
Lord Jesus, we ask You to bring peace to our city. Through Your life, death, and resurrection, remind us during the course of this day that You bring shalom. Keep us from trusting in our strength, insight, or acumen to bring peace. Remind us that You care for us, that You call us to cast our anxieties upon You. Help us to abide in You.

Holy Spirit, please also remind us of those faithful saints who have walked before us, casting their anxieties on you during violence and even persecution. Thank You for so many examples of how to cast our anxieties on You in the midst of trying times. Thank You for ancient examples like Stephen, Polycarp, Perpetua, and more recent examples like William Wilberforce, Dr. Martin Luther King, Jr. and many of our Christian brothers and sisters currently living in the Middle East under the specter of ISIS. Help us to emulate their faith and the way that they cast their anxieties upon You. Give us Your perspective, Your strength, and Your peace that passes understanding. Amen.

WEEK TWENTY FOUR: FRIDAY

AUTHOR: JOHN MCMICHAEL
FAMILY STRUCTURE: WIFE, 2 SONS, AND 5 GRANDCHILDREN
OCCUPATION: RETIRED PROJECT MANAGER

FROM IDOL WORSHIP TO WORSHIPING THE ONE TRUE GOD

"You are my witnesses. Is there any God besides me? No, there is no other Rock; I know not one. All those who make idols are nothing, and the things they treasure are worthless. Those who speak up for them are blind; they are ignorant to their own shame. Who shapes a god and casts an idol, which can profit him nothing? He and his kind will be put to shame; craftsmen are nothing but men. Let them all come together and take their stand; they will be brought down to terror and infamy." Isaiah 44:8-9

No doubt we no longer are too enlightened to worship the idols of the Old Testament; e.g., Ashtoreth, Baal, Chemosh, Dagon, Golden Calf, etc. But what about our modern-day idols such as career, business, entertainment, pursuit of pleasure, money, automobiles, sex, athletics, politics, power, wealth, influence, prestige, fame, and family? What consumes our private thoughts and public motivations?

A.W. Tozer wrote, *"The essence of idolatry is the entertainment of thoughts about God that are unworthy of Him."* The germination of all idolatry is rooted in our diluted understanding of God. We undervalue His worthiness, dismiss His holiness, disregard His love, dilute His truth, or forget His jealousy. We begin to erect idols as our affections drift away from the exclusive worship he requires.

Tozer also said, *"An idol of the mind is as offensive to God as an idol of the hand"*. The danger of idolatry is not found simply in the things we can hold and label as idols. Idols are conceived deep in the human soul, evolving in the mind and poisoning the will long before they are evidenced in behavior of objects.

Blaise Pascal identified our serious propensity when he said, *"There is nothing so abominable in the eyes of God and of men as idolatry, whereby men render to the creature that honor which is due only to the Creator".*

Whatever you love more than God is an idol.

PRAYER TARGET:
All brothers and sisters in Christ to identify idols in their lives.

PERSONAL PRAYER FOR KNOXVILLE:
Dear God, we implore You to send the Holy Spirit to search our hearts and identify those idols that we have set up in our lives that replaced You as the object of our devotion and love. Forgive us of our spiritual adultery. Renew our lives, reset our priorities and purpose, to give You the full measure of our devotion. For You alone are worthy, Oh God! Amen.

WEEK TWENTY FIVE: MONDAY

NAME: DOROTHY MOSS
FAMILY STRUCTURE: SINGLE
OCCUPATION: CUSTOMER SERVICE REP AND BUSINESS OWNER

HEIR CONDITIONING

> **"Study to shew thyself approved unto God, a workman that needeth not to be ashamed, rightly dividing the word of truth." 2 Timothy 2:15**

Recently, I found myself in a predicament. A moment every woman faces, from time to time, trying to find something to wear. So, I went to the closet and found a "suitable" blouse. I put it on and walked to the mirror. While standing in front of the mirror, I noticed an unsightly bulge through the blouse. Shocked and dismayed (*as if I did know it was already there*), I was determined to rid myself of this intruder as quickly as possible.

So, the next day I began to workout. However, my zealous determination would be short lived and after a few days, I relegated myself to an alternative plan- SPANX.

Just as the lack of exercise produced the unsightly bulge, the lack of discipline in studying God's word will leave all of us out of shape. Consequently, when trouble arises, our faith will fail the strength test. The scripture above tells us to study to show ourselves approved unto God. That is a tall order for all of us to follow. As heir's we must condition ourselves with the Word of God daily. Just as our physical body requires conditioning; our spiritual body requires the same.

PRAYER TARGET:
Women seeking discipline in their lives.

PERSONAL PRAYER FOR KNOXVILLE:

Father, I ask You to give us the desire to study Your Word and to set aside some quite time to commune with You daily. We need Your wisdom to navigate this world. Open our eyes and help us understand that we cannot allow daily distractions. Take away the social media and the cares of this world that are feeding our spirits and replace them with a yield of nutritional harvest of wisdom, power and authority. Help us to set aside every weight that so easily beset us. For without You, we are nothing. Amen.

WEEK TWENTY FIVE: TUESDAY

AUTHOR: CHRIS MARION
FAMILY STRUCTURE: WIFE AND 5 CHILDREN
OCCUPATION: RADIO/TV PRODUCER

LIVING FOR GOD IS LIFE; IS FUN; IS FREEDOM

"Let the beloved of the Lord rest secure in him, for he shields him all day long, and the one the Lord loves rests between his shoulders." Deuteronomy 33:12 "Do you think anyone is going to be able to drive a wedge between us and Christ's love for us?" "Absolutely nothing can get between us and God's love because of the way that Jesus our Master has embraced us." Romans 8:31, 39

"I want to give you good things." Matthew 7:9-11 "The truth says God "richly provides us with everything for our enjoyment." 1 Timothy 6:17b

I used to be like a lot of people who think that to live for God means giving up Life, giving up Fun and giving up Freedom, but I've come to realize that nothing could be further from the truth. Because once you decide to live for Him; Once you say Yes, then you can relax and rest in His love, His grace, His forgiveness and His mercy.

Rick Warren says, *"As a Christian, you can enjoy life because your conscious is clear. You can enjoy life because you are secure within God's love."* In other words, He's got you! You can chill out. You don't have to worry about anything...AND there is absolutely nothing that could ever come between You and Him or cause Him to let you go. That's a promise; not from me, but from the Lord Himself.

He loves to see you Happy and "Joy-Full." That brings Him so much joy.

He wants you to enjoy your life. Give it (your life) to Him and then go out and live it…trusting Him the whole way.

PRAYER TARGET:
Folks who struggle with FULL commitment.

PERSONAL PRAYER FOR KNOXVILLE:
Father, I prayer for folks who think like I once did. I pray for folks who really love You, but struggle with full commitment to You because they feel that You would have them forfeit fun and enjoyment. Father, they may think their lives would somehow become dull or stagnant or that they would have difficulty living up to Your standard of worthiness.

God, I pray that through the Holy Spirit…You would speak to their hearts and reveal to them that they don't have to "live up" to anything. All they must do is trust You and let You give them a life that is far more enjoyable than they could ever imagine…a life full of joy, of love, of hope, of fun and eventually a life of eternity. Amen.

WEEK TWENTY FIVE: WEDNESDAY

AUTHOR: KAITLYN KERRIGAN
FAMILY STRUCTURE: 2 BROTHERS
OCCUPATION: STUDENT

MAN'S APPROVAL VS. GOD'S APPROVAL

"For am I now seeking the approval of man, or of God? Or am I trying to please man? If I were still trying to please man, I would not be a servant of Christ." Galatians 1:10

Recently I have been finding myself caught in that wheel of comparison and am constantly seeking man's approval. Whether it be in my leadership skills, my hair, my face, my grades, whatever. Satan has done an excellent job at bogging me down.

I came across this verse the other day and it spoke so much truth into me. The task of pleasing man is quite daunting. Man will never be one-hundred percent satisfied because man is constantly changing.
But God is unchanging; He created us. We are created in His image (Genesis 1).

I realized that when I am in a leadership position, I am meant to be serving God not comparing myself. If I am seeking man's approval I am not a servant of Christ. I am no longer seeking man's approval because it is not man's approval I care about. I am serving an audience of one.

PRAYER TARGET:
People struggling with insecurity

PERSONAL PRAYER FOR KNOXVILLE:
Dear God, I pray that any and every person struggling with insecurity or comparison will have those comparisons knocked

down in Jesus' name. I pray that Christ will be above, below, before, behind, and all around them. May they see that they are created in the image of Christ and know that He has formed them from their head to their toes. I pray that they would see the beautiful creation they are in Christ. And most of all, Father, I pray that they would continue to serve You in a humble spirit. Amen.

WEEK TWENTY FIVE: THURSDAY

AUTHOR: ATLEE HAMMAKER
FAMILY STRUCTURE: WIFE, 5 DAUGHTERS, AND 3 SONS-IN-LAW
OCCUPATION: SELF-EMPLOYED

INDEPENDENCE VS INTERDEPENDENCE

"Is not this the fast that I have chosen? to loose the bands of wickedness, to undo the heavy burdens, and to let the oppressed go free, and that ye break every yoke? Is it not to deal thy bread to the hungry, and that thou bring the poor that are cast out to thy house? when thou seest the naked, that thou cover him; and that thou hide not thyself from thine own flesh? Then shall thy light break forth as the morning, and thine health shall spring forth speedily: and thy righteousness shall go before thee; the glory of the LORD shall be thy reward. Then shalt thou call, and the LORD shall answer; thou shalt cry, and he shall say, Here I am. If thou take away from the midst of thee the yoke, the putting forth of the finger, and speaking vanity; and if thou draw out thy soul to the hungry, and satisfy the afflicted soul; then shall thy light rise in obscurity, and thy darkness be as the noon day: and the LORD shall guide thee continually, and satisfy thy soul in drought, and make fat thy bones: and thou shalt be like a watered garden, and like a spring of water, whose waters fail not. and they that shall be of thee shall build the old waste places: thou shalt raise up the foundations of many generations; and thou shalt be called, The repairer of the breach, The restorer of paths to dwell in." Isaiah 58: 6-12

We ask, "Where does God fit into the story of my life?" When the real question is, "Where does my little life fall into the great Story of God's mission?" My life was operating on the premise of the first question. I believed if I lived morally and lived with heroic effort for the Lord, chances are things would work out in my favor. It did not take long to figure out this was a faulty belief system.

Our relationship with the Lord is a mystery. We live by faith and trust, and put our confidence in the character of God when things seem to not make sense. The Lord has blessed me with people who have poured their lives into me, speaking Truth at times when it was hard to hear it. I began to realize that the second question gave me the right perspective. Then the Lord revealed the verses above in Isaiah. The True Fast became my North Star. It has forced me to change from chasing life so I could become independent, to a life as a believer of interdependence. This new paradigm shift has not been easy, but as I continue to grow in my faith, I am learning to embrace it as God's way of accomplishing His work.

PRAYER TARGET:
Church of Knoxville and surrounding areas grasping to have a biblical worldview.

PERSONAL PRAYER FOR KNOXVILLE:
Father, I pray for a biblical worldview. As believers accept You, God, as the Creator of all things, may they see You as the sovereign Ruler of the universe. Show us our life's purpose and let us love and obey You. Help us love and serve other people. May we live according to the guidelines You provided and set forth in Your Word. Give us the power and guidance of the Holy Spirit that indwells us as we continually surrender to You. I pray for our city to know You! Help us see bonds of wickedness loosened, the bands of the yoke undone, the oppressed set free, and every yoke broken. Divide our bread with the hungry, bring the homeless poor into a house, and cover the naked. Let our lights break out like the dawn, our recovery spring forth, and Your righteousness go before us. May the glory of the Lord be our rear guard so that when we call, You, Lord, You will answer. Call us to be the repairer of the breach and the restorer of the streets in which we dwell! Amen.

WEEK TWENTY FIVE: FRIDAY

AUTHOR: STEVE HALL
FAMILY STRUCTURE: WIFE, 2 ADULT CHILDREN, 5 GRANDCHILDREN
OCCUPATION: FINANCIAL PLANNER

PRIDE, MOTIVES, AND BROKENNESS

"All a person's ways seem pure to them, but motives are weighed by the Lord. Commit to the Lord whatever you do, and he will establish your plans." Proverbs 16: 2-3

Am I continually broken before God and humble before others? Or, am I self-serving and bitter when others offend me? Are my motives honestly pure, even when I do something "good"? (Or, are my motives deeply intertwined with making myself "look good")? When I reflect on these and even deeper questions during devotional times I find myself in awe of God's grace… *"He who saved a wretch like me."*

Am I drawing closer to the Lord every day? On my journey through life, do I know Him better and walk with Him closer than I did yesterday, last week, or last month? I have come to the realization that the transformation of my motives requires a daily refresh and commitment to His plans for me. In this process, I have become very thankful for the assurance that His sovereign hand is in control of the world in which we live, including the lives that we touch each day.

PRAYER TARGET:
Community seeking the ways of the Lord.

PERSONAL PRAYER FOR KNOXVILLE:
Father, I praise You for all Your creation and thank You for placing us in the beautiful surroundings of East Tennessee. Please forgive us when we sin by the harsh words that we've spoken,

disgraceful things that we have done, and opportunities for good that we've left undone. Forgive us for our pride and for the deceitful motivations of our hearts.

I thank You for Your forgiveness, grace, and mercy in our lives. I pray that You would grant us a spirit of reconciliation within our community, of brokenness before You, and a genuine humbleness in our relationships with each other. Father, break down any hardening in our hearts that would cause suffering to those in need. Please draw us closer together as a unified community and closer to Yourself. Give wisdom to our elected officials and community leaders, that they would seek Your ways and thoughts. I pray that all that we do, say, and think, Father, would bring honor and glory to You.

In the name of Jesus and for His sake, Amen.

AUTHOR: MARCIA MECHLIN
FAMILY STRUCTURE: WIDOWED AND 2 GROWN DAUGHTERS
OCCUPATION: PERSONAL ASSISTANT

THE BEST NEWS!

> **"I have been crucified with Christ; it is no longer I who live, but Christ lives in me; and the life which I now live in the flesh I live by the faith of the Son of God, who loved me and gave himself for me." Galatians 2:20**

Imagine! This is the verse that explains how we are created in His image. It assists in deciding to die to our imagined godhead and our imagined right to self! That Christ lives in us now as our Born-Again self in Him is the best news! I only have to die to the lie that I have a right to be offended and a right to have myself be a god. It brings a change to my right of attitudes of shame, fear, resentment, lust, and self-righteousness. Oh my! Christ is our freedom! I am so grateful to learn this.

To lay down my life as I lived it in self-interest and find the answer to all the yearnings in me for love is the best news. Christ lives in me now! I now know that as Christians, we are His Beloved and all the chasing after self-realization have been answered by Him, His faith, and His presence. So, I have chosen to seek Him first in all things, to be inspired, and be loved by Him.

He is our breath, He is our life! We are created anew in His image. We are one with the Father through Him as He is one with the Father. Just this little thing about dying has to be done. I came to realize that my way had only brought misery. I was so grateful to understand this simple yet profound truth. He came to bring us back to our original creation, to our belovedness. Now, I am no longer an "I" but a "We." Christ and me! He in me! He is leading, loving, and creating. I hope to meet each Christian so we can look into each other's eyes, see Him, and laugh and say "Hello, Beloved."

PRAYER TARGET:
Everyone in Knoxville and surrounding areas seeking revelation from Him through His body of believers.

PERSONAL PRAYER FOR KNOXVILLE:
Dear Lord, thank You for loving us. Thank You for every single beloved soul in Knoxville. I claim each one for the Body of Christ. As Christians, we are all Your beloved. I pray for revelation from You. For hearts broken by love, may Your presence be known. I pray for sincere love to be spread by each awakened soul and for Christ to be presented in their lives. Make Your Grace known. I love you, Lord. Amen.

WEEK TWENTY SIX: TUESDAY

AUTHOR: MEGAN HOLLAND
OCCUPATION: COLLEGE STUDENT

THE NATIONS ARE HERE

> "How beautiful on the mountains are the feet of those who bring good news, who proclaim peace, who bring good tidings, who proclaim salvation, who say to Zion, "Your God reigns! "Listen! Your watchmen lift up their voices; together they shout for joy. When the LORD returns to Zion, they will see it with their own eyes. Burst into songs of joy together, you ruins of Jerusalem, for the LORD has comforted his people, he has redeemed Jerusalem. The LORD will lay bare his holy arm in the sight of all the nations, and all the ends of the earth will see the salvation of our God." Isaiah 52:7-10

We see God's heart for the nations over and over again in scripture. He WILL be glorified among the nations. It's a promise we see. I think some people end up overlooking these passages of scripture and writing them off as only applying to overseas missionaries. My heart is utterly shattered when I hear people in churches saying that reaching the nations just is not their role. The Great Commission, in Matthew 20:16-20, is a command to all believers. It is the mission of all believers. Having a love to see the nations come to know Christ should be a mark of being a Christian, because it is our calling.

I love to see people move and go to the nations, but do you know what so many are missing? The nations are here! We have people, here in the city of Knoxville and surrounding areas, who are from the ends of the earth. We have people in Knoxville and surrounding areas who come from dangerous countries. We have people coming from countries without access to the gospel. Specifically, our college campuses are

FULL of international students. These are soon-to-be educated professionals who can take the gospel back to their countries and make a bigger impact than we can ever imagine. The nations are here, so let's run with those beautiful feet and live the mission we have been called to by reaching them.

PRAYER TARGET:
International students and international people groups.

PERSONAL PRAYER FOR KNOXVILLE:
Father, we see Your plan of redemption for the nations all through your Word. Help us to love You more, and as we grow closer to You, help us to know Your heart for the lost. Stir in us a love for the nations and a desire for Your glory to fill the earth. We ask for You to go before us and work in people's hearts. Our prayer is that the nations would be reached here in Knoxville. We ask for You to do more than we could ever imagine and may revival break out in this place. We pray that "all the ends of the earth will see the salvation of our God." It's all for Your glory, God. Amen.

WEEK TWENTY SIX: WEDNESDAY

AUTHOR: DONNA MITCHELL
FAMILY STRUCTURE: HUSBAND AND 4 CHILDREN
OCCUPATION: BUSINESS OWNER AND SOCIAL WORKER

CALLED TO BE A COVENANT FOR THE PEOPLE

> **"I, the Lord, have called you in righteousness; I will take hold of your hand. I will keep you and will make you to be a covenant for the people and a light for the Gentiles, to open eyes that are blind, to free captives from prison and to release from the dungeon those who sit in darkness."**
> **Isaiah 42:6-7**

Hearing mother calling us for dinner after a day outside and ignoring her call was never an option. Why? First, we'd be in trouble, and secondly, we knew that something good was waiting on the other side. Now as an adult, when God calls, I experience the same feelings. If I ignore His calling I have "troubles," and miss out on His goodness. His call to us is in righteousness, He personally takes us by the hand to empower and help others.

While writing this devotion, God is prompting me, "Get real. Are you willing to help people get free by sharing what I've done and continue to do for you?" Oh man, my first inclination when asked to write this devotion, was, "Are you serious? Okay God, You know I don't have time." I quickly thought, "Did I just say that?' An answer followed immediately of, "Oh well, Donna, just check-it off your list." This attitude quickly subsided because God is calling. I am honored to answer!!

God is calling many of us to be a Covenant to the people. That may mean to allow others to be free and show them what Christ has done in our lives. We live and interact with hurting people every day. God has called each one of us to open the eyes of the blind that they may see Him, free those who are imprisoned by various trials of life, and release captives from darkness. Many of those people are the ones who say they believe in our Lord and Savior Jesus Christ, but continue to limp through life pretending to be believers. We must answer the call of righteousness by admitting we all were once blind and we were captives who sat in darkness. Thanks be unto God, Who sets us free, we are now free captives to Him!!!

PRAYER TARGET:
Those with mental health challenges, especially in the church.

PERSONAL PRAYER FOR KNOXVILLE:
Father, You promised to take us by the hand, keep us, and make us a covenant and light for the people. There are so many people, bound by mental health challenges: depression, substance abuse, suicidal thoughts, attempts, and family conflicts - even among believers. You promised You would make us worthy of Your calling, and that by Your power, You would bring to fruition every desire for goodness and every deed prompted by faith. (II Thessalonians 1:11) We choose to believe You and not the distractions around us. Thank You, Father, for Your faithfulness and unwavering covenant of redemption of salvation and freedom. Amen.

WEEK TWENTY SIX: THURSDAY

AUTHOR: RAY MEADE
FAMILY STRUCTURE: WIFE AND 4 CHILDREN
OCCUPATION: EDUCATOR

LOVE THY NEIGHBOR

"The second is this: 'Love your neighbor as yourself.' There is no commandment greater than these." Mark 12:31

While sitting in church today I started thinking, "What if I really love our neighbors as myself?"

My neighbors are a very diverse group, both racially and religiously. Jesus commands me to love all of them, not just the ones that look like me or just the ones with which I agree. He tells me to love all of them. When we stop looking at each other as "different" and start looking at each other as God's chosen people we will then experience a true change in our community.

PRAYER TARGET:
That all in the city would learn to love each other as Christ loves us all.

PERSONAL PRAYER FOR KNOXVILLE:
Father, my prayer is that we can all take off the prejudices that blind us and keep us bound, and truly start to love one another. Father Your word says, "If My people, which are called by My Name, shall humble themselves, pray and seek My face and turn from their wicked ways, then I will hear from heaven, and will heal their land." Today, Father, we stand before you humbled asking You to heal our city. Let it start with me. I pray this in the precious Name of Jesus. Amen.

AUTHOR: J. JEROME PRINSTON
FAMILY STRUCTURE: WIFE AND 3 ADULT DAUGHTERS
OCCUPATION: PROFESSOR

FROM TROUBLE TO HOPE

> "There I will give her back her vineyards, and will make the Valley of Achor a door of hope.
> There she will respond as in the days of her youth, as in the day she came up out of Egypt." Hosea 2:15

One of the most enduring metaphors about life is that it is a journey. As we journey through life, it is virtually guaranteed that we will go through valleys of trouble where we will suffer and be tested and challenged.

Many times, the figurative valleys we experience in life are associated with real places where we get to experience God's discipline and grace in various ways. One such valley in the life of the people of Israel is the Valley of Achor. In Joshua 7, this place, which literally means "Valley of trouble," is associated with a real geographical location where grievous sins were committed, and God's punishment was inflicted.

But later, in the prophecies of Hosea, after God has done his work of transformation in the life of the people of Israel, the same Valley of Achor is heralded not as a place of shame and dread but as an avenue for forgiveness and hope. Only a gracious, loving God can heal our land and transform our sins and shame into hope and glory.

This a divine promise: Surrender to God's will through faith and obedience, and our sin-styled valleys of trouble will become "A Door of Hope."

PRAYER TARGET:

The leaders of our city to be a light to those who are troubled.

PERSONAL PRAYER FOR KNOXVILLE:

Father, my prayer is that every leader of this city may be empowered by the Holy Spirit to lead in a way that is pleasing to God. Lord, first we thank You for all those who serve as leaders in various capacities in our city. We thank You for their dedication and commitment in service. We pray for all those who serve in government positions. Give them wisdom and discernment to rightly administer the law and carry out the responsibilities of their office. We pray for all religious and educational leaders that they may lead in a way that inspires their students and disciples to greater heights of maturity and conformity to Your image. Give to all our leaders the courage to surrender to Your will, to lead by example, to be motivated by Your precepts, to promote peace, unity, and reconciliation in our city. Teach us Your ways that we may be found faithful in service to You and Your people. As we surrender to Your will, may our every valley of trouble be transformed into a land of hope, justice and opportunity for all. We pray because of Christ, the Lord, and in His Name. Amen.

WEEK TWENTY SEVEN: MONDAY

AUTHOR: KEVIN COWART
FAMILY STRUCTURE: WIFE AND 4 CHILDREN
OCCUPATION: PRODUCT MANAGER

SEEING THE UNSEEN

> **"So we do not lose heart. Though our outer self is wasting away, our inner self is being renewed day by day. For this light momentary affliction is preparing for us an eternal weight of glory beyond all comparison, as we look not to the things that are seen but to the things that are unseen. For the things that are seen are transient, but the things that are unseen are eternal." Corinthians 4:16-18**

When you lose a limb, a part of you is tossed in the trash and sent to decompose somewhere. It's hard to explain what it's like to live on while part of you dies, but it brought to life passages like this, "Our outer self is wasting away."

There is nothing in this world that can restore what was lost. I will always have the brokenness of waking up each day missing a part of me that has already died. Yet, my loss is only temporary.

Each morning brings new mercies with my "Inner-self being renewed day-by-day." Christians are given one hope. We aren't promised that we will have our health. We don't get trees that grow cash. Our relationships aren't suddenly made easy. What we get is greater than these and all other hopes this world creates in us, but it's not easy to see. In fact, it's unseen.

Peter, in 1 Peter 3-4, describes it for us as being, "Born again to a living hope through the resurrection of Jesus Christ from the dead, to an inheritance that is imperishable, undefiled, and unfading, kept in heaven for you." My home and my hope are both in heaven.

PRAYER TARGET:
Those seeking hope in a troubled world.

PERSONAL PRAYER FOR KNOXVILLE:
Father, take hold of our city and all the believers that call her home. We long for so much, feel such brokenness, and hurt for a reality that we can't yet have. Teach us that this is a gift from You, but please never, never leave us in it.

May Your Spirit instead give us eyes that lift to heaven. Let us behold Your unseen glory. Let us find rest in the richness of Your heavenly hope. Give us a voice to sing for joy. We have eternal days coming where tears, pain, and loss can reach us no longer. May Your glory be our treasure and Christ our life's King. Amen.

WEEK TWENTY SEVEN: TUESDAY

AUTHOR: LAUREN COWART
FAMILY STRUCTURE: HUSBAND AND 4 CHILDREN
OCCUPATION: HOMEMAKER

ENTRUSTING MY SOUL IN THE MIDST OF TROUBLES

"Therefore, let those who suffer according to God's will entrust their souls to a faithful Creator while doing good."
1 Peter 4:19

Peter writes these words to the elect who have been scattered throughout Asia Minor into cultures much like the one in which we find ourselves. Injustice, debauchery and foolishness surround the believers. They may not yet be facing death for their belief in Christ, but their souls are plenty battered by sin and circumstance.

Over the last several years, my family has faced quite a bit of suffering. A couple of my children have had bizarre medical issues, and my husband lost his right leg six years ago. In the midst of this, I have had bouts of sometimes debilitating anxiety and my faith in God has been put to the test. What if the worst happens? Will Christ still be enough? What does it mean for a loving God to put his people through such pain?

When I am scared or facing something unknown, when I find that God's will holds suffering for me, I remind myself of Peter's words to God's people. I remember that He is faithful. He will not abandon my soul. Though His will may wound my body or those of my loved ones, His glory is so much more revealed as I share in His sufferings. As Christ entrusted Himself to His Father, so can I. He who calls me is so faithful that I can be obedient with total confidence. He will not put me to shame.

PRAYER TARGET:
Those who are suffering.

PERSONAL PRAYER FOR KNOXVILLE:
Good Father, You are faithful. You hold us in Your hand, and nobody can pluck us out of it. Whatever our circumstances, whatever we stand to lose, You will never abandon our souls. You promise that in our suffering, there is purpose, there is glory, and there are eternal rewards. Spirit, supply us with strength to be faithful like You are faithful, that we may not live in fear but rather be freed to do good all the days of our lives. Amen.

WEEK TWENTY SEVEN: WEDNESDAY

AUTHOR: GINDY HOUSTON
FAMILY STRUCTURE: PARENTS
OCCUPATION: GREETING CARD DESIGNER

CHRIST IS ENOUGH

> **"Therefore, in order to keep me from becoming conceited, I was given a thorn in my flesh, a messenger of Satan, to torment me. Three times I pleaded with the Lord to take it away from me. But he said to me, "My grace is sufficient for you, for my power is made perfect in weakness." Therefore I will boast all the more gladly about my weaknesses, so that Christ's power may rest on me." 2 Corinthians 12:7-9**

It may seem strange that God would direct His strength through our weaknesses, but He does. He promises that His grace is sufficient. How true! The saving blood of Jesus is enough for anyone. Christ is enough for any situation because through Him you will receive everything else you need.

A huge weakness (or thorn) for me is loneliness. Like Paul, I've prayed for relief, but still feel alone sometimes. However, in 2011, God helped me start a greeting card ministry from within my home. The ministry is for the homebound, elderly, and others who are lonely. Today, the ministry is still going and it is expanding. What was intended to bring me down is exactly what God is using to assist me in reaching and comforting others. God should, and does, receive all the glory for this!

The thing that is bringing you down or holding you back, whether it is illness, alcohol, drug abuse, anger, or your own loneliness, I relate to you and I personally know the thorn hurts. Jesus knows it most of all. He sees any helplessness we have and understands. He wore a painful whole crown of thorns for us on the Cross, suffered, died, and rose. Therefore, He understands our thorns, but in mercy He gives us grace daily. That is sufficient for each.

PRAYER TARGET:
Lonely Souls.

PERSONAL PRAYER FOR KNOXVILLE:
Hi, God. I come to You in Jesus' Name. I praise You for being an all- sufficient Redeemer and enough for me and anyone who comes to You through Your Son, Jesus Christ. I thank You for hearing this prayer, for knowing what we need before we ask. I lift all the lonely souls of Knoxville and ask You to let them know that You are with them and You will never leave. Thank You, Jesus, that You experienced the deepest loneliness of all on the cross so that we don't have to be alone at any time! Revive us with Your Holy Spirit across Knoxville and across our nation. Thank You Father. In Jesus' Name, I pray this. Amen.

WEEK TWENTY SEVEN: THURSDAY

AUTHOR: EMILY MATNEY
FAMILY STRUCTURE: MOTHER, FATHER, AND 2 SISTERS
OCCUPATION: STUDENT

FINDING THE TRUTH IN A WORLD OF FALSEHOOD

> "You, dear children, are from God and have overcome them, because the one who is in you is greater than the one who is in the world. They are from the world and therefore speak from the viewpoint of the world, and the world listens to them. We are from God, and whoever knows God listens to us; but whoever is not from God does not listen to us. This is how we recognize the Spirit of truth and the spirit of falsehood." 1 John 4:4-6

I am a college student majoring in biology. The very essence of the truths I hold in my heart are directly contradictory to the core of what I am taught daily. I have always found that science and the Bible never contradict one another, but rather it is people and their interpretations of scientific evidence which contradict the Word.

These verses so clearly demonstrate that we cannot expect nonbelievers to interpret things the way we as believers would, and we cannot become discouraged when they disagree with us or do not listen. In the scientific community, I have received many reactions for my faith, from curiosity and respect to mockery and patronization. It is so comforting to me to recognize this simple reminder from the Father. The One Who is in us is greater than the one who is in the world.

Be encouraged my brothers and sisters. When you feel ridiculed for your faith, know that it is not what you preach but rather who is listening which determines the response. You never know. One person in a crowd of Saul's may become a Paul; so speak Word-rooted Truth, and let the Father handle the outcome.

PRAYER TARGET:
The college students of the city seeking truth.

PERSONAL PRAYER FOR KNOXVILLE:
Dear Father, I pray that You would wrap Your arms tightly around my brothers and sisters being taught things that they know are not Truth. I pray that You would give them wisdom, guidance, and discernment. Help them to find Truth in Your word, and to ignore falsehood. I pray that You would allow Truth to prevail in what they think, hear, and speak, that they might shine as beacons for You in a dark and stormy world. Thank You so much for Your blessings, Lord. We are undeserving and eternally grateful for Your grace. Amen

WEEK TWENTY SEVEN: FRIDAY

AUTHOR: WALTER L. GHOSTEN
FAMILY STRUCTURE: WIFE, 2 DAUGHTERS, AND 3 GRANDCHILDREN
OCCUPATION: CHAPLAIN

LOVE CONQUERS HATE

> "Love is patient and kind; love does not envy or boast; it is not arrogant or rude. It does not insist on its own way; it is not irritable or resentful, it does not rejoice at wrongdoing, but rejoices with the truth. Loves bears all things, believes all things hopes all things, endures all things. So now faith, hope, and love abide, these three; but the greatest of these is love." 1 Corinthians 13:4-7, 13

The Apostle Paul gives us a clear definition of love. He tells us what love is as well as what love is not. He makes it plain to all humanity that we have a responsibility as brothers and sisters in Christ Jesus to love each other unconditionally. So, whenever we show our compassion in various ways and deeds, we are expressing the love that we have toward one another. However, when a person is rude to others, they are not expressing love but rather their actions suggest a lack of understanding about the need to be respectful. The Apostle places love above all other gifts that we might possess. He said that love is greater than hope or faith. The clarion call to each person is to place love first above all else and when we do this, we will pattern our lives after Him.

PRAYER TARGET:
To leaders of our city to walk in Love in all actions.

PERSONAL PRAYER FOR KNOXVILLE:

Oh merciful and gracious God, I call upon You to continue blessing the people of this great city with Your unconditional love. And then Father, make us to understand the need to love each other unconditionally for the betterment of our great city. Bless our leaders with a double portion of wisdom so that they will have full knowledge about the needs of the citizens in Knoxville.

I pray, oh God, for those who have lost hope and faith, who find themselves living on the streets, in the woods, and in the most deserted places of this city. I pray oh God that their hope is restored through the goodness of Your grace. Then bless the religious leaders so that they might continue their work, ministering to all people. Father, we pray this prayer in the Name of Your Son, Jesus Christ. Amen.

WEEK TWENTY EIGHT: MONDAY

AUTHOR: JACOB GALLAHER
FAMILY STRUCTURE: SINGLE
OCCUPATION: MEDICAL PATIENT CARE ASSISTANT

THE RIGHTEOUSNESS OF CHRIST

> **"The way of the wicked is an abomination to the LORD, but he loves him who pursues righteousness." Proverbs 15:9**
> **"... for apart from me you can do nothing." John 15:5**
> **"And without faith it is impossible to please him..." Hebrews 11:6**

What is a righteous life? What does it mean to seek righteousness? These are words within the church that get thrown around, but do we understand what they truly mean? To be righteous, or pursue righteousness, is to live according to God's way. We live in a world where pursuing righteousness is difficult, especially for those who are entering and leaving college. Society and culture scream at us to live in a way that denies God, and the devil often tells us that God would never choose us to live for Him. Living a righteous life is seemingly impossible—and on our own, it IS impossible. Luckily, we have Jesus who tells us it isn't through our power to live a righteous life, but through His power.

This is our freedom in Jesus! We no longer rely on our own strength for righteous living, but we are filled with Christ's power through the Holy Spirit. By pursuing righteousness, how amazing it is that we can bring pleasure to our Father in Heaven! It can be hard for us to believe this Truth, at least for me, but in those times that we fall short, praise God that we have a Savior who helps us back to our feet, wipes the dirt away, and tells us to take one more step!

PRAYER TARGET:
Young adults seeking righteousness.

PERSONAL PRAYER FOR KNOXVILLE:
I pray all the young adults in the Body of Christ would pursue righteousness in this broken world, just
as Christ did! Lord, may You wash away the grime on our hearts with the powerful blood of Jesus! May You take the temptations, sins, and scars that plague our hearts and replace them with love and joy. May we seek lives that are not only good in Your eyes, but ones that also bring You pleasure. May we truly live as sons and daughters of our Father in Heaven, and seek to serve our King Jesus! May we be truly be the light of Christ in a dark world—bringing love, peace, happiness, and truth through all of our words, thoughts, and actions. I pray this in the Name of our Savior and King, Jesus Christ! Amen.

AUTHOR: KEVIN WINES
FAMILY STRUCTURE: WIFE AND 2 GROWN CHILDREN
OCCUPATION: CHURCH VIDEOGRAPHER

DO IT MORE AND MORE!

> **"Now about your love for one another we do not need to write to you, for you yourselves have been taught by God to love each other. And in fact, you do love all of God's family throughout Macedonia. Yet we urge you, brothers and sisters, to do so more and more."**
> **1 Thessalonians 4:9-10**

In the Scripture above, Paul is writing to the Thessalonians and encouraging them on how to live to please God. In the verses before these two he basically tells them to be holy, to quit doing what they are doing wrong. He gets specific on the type of sins they should avoid because he knows them. In verses nine and ten Paul then reverses this by telling them what they are doing right. They know how to love each other. He doesn't get real specific on how they love each other because it seems to be a given and they get it. He doesn't stop with just the praise either. He exhorts them to do it more and more.

Knoxville and surrounding areas, you know how to love each other. My prayer for you is that you do it more and more, not in a way that meddles in other's lives; but in a way that the world will truly be able to look at us and know us by our love.

PRAYER TARGET:
Christians that will reach out and love each other unconditionally.

PERSONAL PRAYER FOR KNOXVILLE:

Father, thank You for Your love and for teaching us how to love. I pray that the Church here in Knoxville will be known not because of its political stance, power, or wealth but by its love. Help us to love each other and our neighbors as You have taught us. In Jesus' Name. Amen.

AUTHOR: MICHAEL CLARK
FAMILY STRUCTURE: WIFE, 2 CHILDREN, AND FOSTER PARENT
OCCUPATION: URBAN YOUTH MINISTRY AND PASTOR STAFF

A SPIRITUAL REFUGEE

> **"He who dwells in the shelter of the Most High will abide in the shadow of the Almighty. I will say to the Lord, "My refuge and my fortress, my God, in whom I trust." For he will deliver you from the snare of the fowler and from the deadly pestilence. He will cover you with his pinions, and under his wings you will find refuge; his faithfulness is a shield and buckler. You will not fear the terror of the night, nor the arrow that flies by day, nor the pestilence that stalks in darkness, nor the destruction that wastes at noonday. A thousand may fall at your side, ten thousand at your right hand, but it will not come near you. You will only look with your eyes and see the recompense of the wicked. Because you have made the Lord your dwelling place - the Most High, who is my refuge, no evil shall be allowed to befall you, no plague come near your tent." Psalm 91:1-10**

While I have never experienced fleeing my home and country for life and safety, I realize that the Lord has called us all to be refugees. We have been summoned to take refuge in the Lord Most High. There are snares and even death awaits at times, but the promise of being overshadowed by the Lord Almighty brings comfort and peace. Words like "dwells" and "abides" convey a life lived in constant connection with our Lord. John, Chapter fifteen, reminds us that apart from Christ we can do nothing. He is the vine; we are the branches. BUT when abiding, we see our Deliverer at work. It is in these moments we see His faithfulness active on our behalf. So, take heart no matter what may be surrounding you. Take heart, and take refuge. He is bidding us to dwell in His covering, to abide in His shadow.

PRAYER TARGET:
Refugees in Knoxville.

PERSONAL PRAYER FOR KNOXVILLE:
Gracious Father, we magnify Your Great Name in our city. May Your shelter and shadow become our longed-for home. And for those who have found themselves here in Knoxville as refugees, we pray Knoxville will be a safe-haven and a harbor where Your Presence reigns. Mobilize Your Church to surround and encourage. For all the spiritual refugees, lost and without their way, lead them back to Yourself. Break the bonds of sin and addiction, as we declare this is the year of the Lord's favor in our city. Let revival sweep the most unlikely streets, as it is Your good pleasure to confound the wise and reveal Yourself to Your creation. Thank You for Your abundant mercy and grace, upon which we depend. In Jesus' Name, Amen!

WEEK TWENTY EIGHT: THURSDAY

AUTHOR: RUBY MILLICAN
FAMILY STRUCTURE: OLDEST OF 4 SISTERS
OCCUPATION: STUDENT

GOD'S PROVISION

> "For this reason I say to you, do not be worried about your life, as to what you will eat or what you will drink; nor for your body, as to what you will put on. Is not life more than food, and the body more than clothing? Look at the birds of the air, that they do not sow, nor reap nor gather into barns, and yet your heavenly Father feeds them. Are you not worth much more than they? And who of you by being worried can add a single hour to his life? And why are you worried about clothing? Observe how the lilies of the field grow; they do not toil nor do they spin {...}"
> Matthew 6:25-34

I have heard this verse many times growing up in a Christian culture. However, these verses in my current season of transition and change have been such an encouragement for me. The season of change and unknowns can be very unsettling for someone like me who likes to have a plan. So, I am prone to worry and stress about the future and what God has in store for me. But these verses remind me that if God cares about the birds, how much more does He care about me?

The first part of this is trusting that God has a plan. As a child of God, I need to constantly remind myself of His provision. He has fully provided for me by Jesus dying on the cross. That should be enough for me. It is also a perfect example of God providing for His people. If God loves us enough to send Jesus to die so we can be His, how much more does He love us to provide us with a future?

The second part of this is trusting that God's plan is better than mine. I have a lot of goals, hopes, and dreams. Some of these I know God desires for me to have, but maybe not some of them. But because God is all knowing, I rest assured in Him, knowing that He has the best in store for me.

PRAYER TARGET:
People in transition.

PERSONAL PRAYER FOR KNOXVILLE:
Father, help the people in this city who are going through changes. Help them trust in God. Romans 8:28 says, "And we know that God causes all things to work together for good to those who love God, to those who are called according to His purpose." You, God, have a bird's eye view of our situation, and we are trusting You to work it all for our good and give us comfort. I pray that each person in transition will find a community to help them with change and decisions. I pray that they will understand that they are a part of Your mission of sharing the gospel no matter where they are. In Your Name. Amen.

AUTHOR: NATHAN BINGHAM
FAMILY STRUCTURE: FATHER, MOTHER, AND OLDER BROTHER
OCCUPATION: COLLEGE STUDENT

BROKEN CISTERNS

> **"My people have committed two sins: They have forsaken Me, the spring of living water, and have dug their own cisterns, broken cisterns that cannot hold water."**
> **Jeremiah 2:13**

I had reached a place in my life last year where it was evident to me that I was not satisfied by the spring of living water. A year ago, I would honestly would have rather been in Neyland Stadium worshipping the Vols than in a church worshipping God. I would have rather been spending time talking to the girl I liked than spending time acquainting myself with the Father, and I would rather have spent time serving myself than serving God. I had built all these cisterns in my life with which I was trying to fill myself, but there simply was not enough water in them to satisfy me. I was settling for droplets while God was offering an ocean.

This verse pointed out to me that my sin was exactly the same as Israel's. The question I ran into was simply, *"How do I go about repenting of this sin and being satisfied by the spring of living water?"* The only answer I could find was simply the gospel. Now I know to fill your mind with the gospel so all you think about is the saving love of Christ. Practice drinking from the fountain of life and the leftover water at the bottom of your cisterns will begin to taste like sewage. Be satisfied in the Lord, because He is the only one worth it.

PRAYER TARGET:

The people of Knoxville and surrounding areas seeking living water that is permanent not temporary.

PERSONAL PRAYER FOR KNOXVILLE:

Father, my prayer is that the people in the city of Knoxville would be satisfied with God. Nothing more; Nothing less; and Nothing else. May the believers in You, Lord, live their lives with such joy and passion for You that no one could ever say, "They don't love God." May we share this spring of living water with those who are outsiders to us in the same way that Christ shared this message with the Samaritan woman at the well. Jesus, You are all we want. Point out to us any cisterns that are stealing Your glory. It is through Christ alone that I pray. Amen.

WEEK TWENTY NINE: MONDAY

AUTHOR: ZACK DURHAM
FAMILY STRUCTURE: SINGLE
OCCUPATION: COLLEGE STUDENT

FINDING PEACE IN THE BACKGROUND

"In your relationships with one another, have the same mindset as Christ Jesus: Who, being in very nature God, did not consider equality with God something to be used to his own advantage; rather, he made himself nothing by taking the very nature of a servant, being made in human likeness. And being found in appearance as a man, he humbled himself by becoming obedient to death— even death on a cross!" Philippians 2:5-8

When most people think of the church today they think of pastors and worship leaders leading hundreds of people through teaching and worship. Or we even think of Sunday school teachers or elders and deacons. But what happens if we do not fall into one of those lists? What if we can't teach and we can't carry a tune to save your life? Can we still contribute to the Church?

In 1 Corinthians 12 speaks of the Church in terms of a human body. Sure, the hands, feet, internal organs, and eyes are important, but the body must have other parts to be fully functional. What about elbows? Or taste buds? Or finger nails? Every piece is critical to the body. A church can't function without janitors, greeters, parking lot attendants, kid's workers, and prayer teams. Jesus was God in nature, yet came to earth to serve mere humans. He is the model of humility, and He is the embodiment of what we are called to be.

This is easy to say and hard to practice. Serving behind the scenes can seem like a thankless job. Nobody acknowledges your hard work and diligence. Nobody gives you praise for your work. But Galatians 6 calls us to not become weary in serving, knowing that our reward is waiting for us. The sacrifices and diligence do not go unnoticed, and they will be rewarded if we persevere.

PRAYER TARGET:
Church members that are serving behind the scenes.

PERSONAL PRAYER FOR KNOXVILLE:
God, I pray for the thousands of people in churches in Knoxville that aren't serving in visible positions, but that are doing good for Your Kingdom. I pray that You don't let them become discouraged and tired, but that You give them the power and strength they need to serve faithfully. Help them to rely on You and not the praise of others as they serve well. I also pray for those who attend Church regularly, but aren't actively serving because they feel inadequate and not talented enough to serve. Give them confidence through You to serve faithfully. Help them fill whatever role You have equipped them to fill. May all the glory go to You, God. Amen.

WEEK TWENTY NINE: TUESDAY

AUTHOR: MEGHAN RUSSELL
FAMILY STRUCTURE: DAUGHTER
OCCUPATION: COLLEGE STUDENT

LIVING IN THE WILL OF GOD

"So whether you eat or drink or whatever you do, do it all for the glory of God." 1 Corinthians 10:31 "Rejoice always, pray continually, give thanks in all circumstances; for this is God's will for you in Christ Jesus."
1 Thessalonians 5:16-18

Like most young college-aged Christians, I have always struggled with determining what God's will is for my life. Am I supposed to pursue this major? Am I supposed to attend this church or that one? Is my current job specifically where God wants me to be? There are so many questions we can ask ourselves that pertain to the will of God, and these questions can really spark some stress and anxiety in our day to day lives if we are actively seeking to please God. The big picture that I think most Christians fail to realize is that the will of God for our lives is already revealed to us in God's Word. Many times, we sit and we pray and we wait for God to show us a concrete task that He wants us to do, when really He has already told us!

In I Corinthians 10:31 He instructs us to do "whatever" we do to the glory of God. The language of this verse brings so much freedom to our lives! Whether it's being a full-time missionary, or a receptionist at a dentist's office, if we are doing what we do intentionally to the glory of God, we are doing the will of God!

In 1 Thessalonians 5:16-18 He gives us specific instructions to do in our day to day lives that are literally considered "God's will for you." In every circumstance, God wants us to be rejoiceful, prayerful, and thankful. This isn't always easy, but God is not limited, and He can help us observe all these things if we entrust Him to do so.

Let this be an encouragement to you if you have struggled with wondering if you are living in God's will. Know that God gives us different passions to pursue different things, but we can do ALL THINGS to the glory of God according to His will for us!

PRAYER TARGET:
People who are struggling with living in God's will.

PERSONAL PRAYER FOR KNOXVILLE:
Father, we thank You for Your goodness and Your mercy. You are always good and You are always worthy to be praised! Thank You for moving in Knoxville and showing the city Your great love. We pray that You continue to move in our city, and You move people to come to know You, Lord. Cause a great revival to move among the streets in every individual who does not know You as their personal Lord and Savior. We believe that You are the Ultimate Helper for the helpless and Comforter for the hurting. You are good in all that You do, Father. We love You. Amen.

NAME: CRYSTAL FREEMAN
FAMILY STRUCTURE: WIFE AND 2 STEP-CHILDREN
OCCUPATION: ADMINISTRATIVE ASSISTANT

HELP MY UNBELIEF

> "And Jesus asked his father, 'How long has this been happening to him?' And he said, 'From childhood. And it has often cast him into fire and into water, to destroy him. But if you can do anything, have compassion on us and help us.' And Jesus said to him, 'If you can'! All things are possible for one who believes.' Immediately the father of the child cried out and said, 'I believe; help my unbelief!'"
> **Mark 9:21-23**

The other day as I was praying the Spirit revealed a pattern I had never noticed. He sweetly whispered, "Do you see how you aren't afraid to ask the Father for action in the lives of others but don't ask Him to take action in your own life?" I found myself continually asking, "Help me to be kind" or "Help me to be patient" while asking the Father to "Change him" or "move her." I was fearless in my prayers for others. All the while I prayed down the heavens in the lives of those around me yet I lacked the faith in the goodness of the Father's Character to call down heaven in my own life. When I asked, "Help me" what I really was saying was, "Now, Father, don't do too much. Help me and I'll do it until I'm uncomfortable so I'm the one in control, but You can help me." Nice, right?

I've read this story in Mark 9 a dozen times. I felt compassion on the man for his lack of faith and recognized the same in myself but I had never noted the man kept asking for help; the same thing I kept asking for in my prayers. Jesus, being rich in mercy, gets to the heart of the issue by speaking Truth to the fear in the heart of the man. Jesus declared then and declares now, *"All things are possible for one who believes."* Oh, how sweet the Lord is to us when we cry out, "I believe; help my unbelief." In its purest form, unbelief is fear. And perfect love casts out fear according to 1 John 4:18. So, our Perfect Loving God casts out the unbelief and fear.

Friends, maybe you are super spiritual and you don't struggle with unbelief like me. Or maybe you are like me and have let a spirit of unbelief take up residency in your thoughts without even knowing it. Or maybe you know you struggle with unbelief because it's just hard to trust God after what you have been through. Where ever you are in your journey, can I encourage you with this? —Jesus loves for us to cry out to Him, "I believe; help my unbelief." He is trustworthy, kind, gentle and faithful. He is sure and steadfast and willing to walk with us. Trust His character. Believe His promises. Trust Him and allow Him to cast out the fear and replace it with His unfailing love.

PRAYER TARGET:
Increased faith.

PERSONAL PRAYER FOR KNOXVILLE:
Father, thank You for this city. Thank You for Your Spirit that is already working, constantly drawing others to Yourself. We ask You to increase our faith. Allow us to focus on things unseen because what is seen is temporary but what is unseen is eternal. Father, change our hearts to see others the way You do. Make us intentional in our relationships and in our prayer life. We ask all this in Jesus' Name. Amen.

AUTHOR: CHRIS STEPHENS
FAMILY STRUCTURE: WIFE AND 3 CHILDREN
OCCUPATION: SENIOR PASTOR

THE WAY BACK

> **"Brethren, I do not regard myself as having laid hold of it yet; but one thing I do: forgetting what lies behind and reaching forward to what lies ahead, I press on toward the goal for the prize of the upward call of God in Christ Jesus."**
> **Philippians 3:13-14**

Not only is today a brand-new day, but a brand-new year! Last year really did end last night and today is the beginning of an exciting new future. He calls each of us to a future as unlimited as the God we serve. None of us are all the way back, but like Paul, we must keep reaching forward to the future ahead. I have a biblical belief that your past can hold you back, or point you back to all God created you to become. Look at how far God has brought you. And how much further will He take you? But the choice is yours. Which way will you see it?

Far too many believers allow the pain of the past to block the path to their future. They allow the voices and experiences of yesterday to map out their life for them. Even though God offers a way back and a way forward, they choose a life looking backwards. They choose a life of doubting in the desert and wandering in the wilderness.

Other believers choose to trust the promises of the Word and allow their past to point them towards God's preferred future. My past was horrific, but when I met Jesus He rescued me, forgave me, called me, and blessed me. The former things were forgotten. Now my life serves as a sign pointing the way back for thousands to be set free. It is the will of God to use your story just like He does mine. Launch into His blessing and favor in this new year.

The choice is yours.

PRAYER TARGET:
Believers in Knoxville and surrounding areas who carry strongholds from their past.

PERSONAL PRAYER FOR KNOXVILLE:
Father, by faith, I declare this will be Knoxville's best year yet. I cannot wait to see all the Lord will do. I am praying believers choose to forget what's behind and look forward to this new year with expectation. I pray believers trust that You, Lord, will do something new this year, pour out rivers of provision in the desert, and pave roadways of vision through the wilderness. I pray believers will follow Him this year and go wherever He leads. The way back begins today!

WEEK TWENTY NINE: FRIDAY

AUTHOR: ZAC STEPHENS
FAMILY STRUCTURE: WIFE AND 2 CHILDREN
OCCUPATION: CAMPUS PASTOR AND GLOBAL STUDENTS PASTOR

SPIRIT-FILLED VISION

"For the one who sows to his own flesh will from the flesh reap corruption, but the one who sows to the Spirit will from the Spirit reap eternal life. Let us not lose heart in doing good, for in due time we will reap if we do not grow weary." Galatians 6:8-9

Understanding and listening to the Holy Spirit is near and dear to my heart. My focus for last year was, "Spirit-led," and it was life altering! It is hard to choose just one verse to pull from that encompasses the Holy Spirit, but the above verse from Galatians kept coming back to me. We sow in the flesh all week long, and then pray for crop failure. We all have tried trusting in our own ways, but our ways lack the vision to lead us where we want to go. And our ways never reap life in the long run, instead leading to dead-ends of destruction and death. Maybe you find this to be true in the choices you make each day, which lead to frustration, problems, and pain. Maybe you found this to be true in trying to restore a relationship, lead a Christ-like lifestyle, or escape addiction on your own – leading to confusion, distrust, and doubt. Whatever it was, we have all reaped the results of following our own ways. The frustrating part is we know we should plant seeds in the Spirit and trust in His ways. And yet, we still tend to choose the flesh. Why? Because planting in the flesh seems to grow faster! Our ways seem to be a shortcut to where we want to go. But, it is just not true.

Walking with Spirit-filled vision is the fastest and best way to get where you want to go. Although shortcuts and seeds planted in the flesh end in instant gratification, they inevitably lead us to dead-ends on down the road. Our culture and flesh encourage this short-sighted approach to life, which is exactly why the enemy wants us to travel without seeing.

Sowing in the Spirit is harder, because most of the time it grows slower. This is why verse nine says, "Let us not lose heart in doing good." Another translation says, "Let us not grow weary of doing good." One of the reasons sowing in the Spirit seems slower is because God makes it grow, not us. His timing, however frustrating it may be, is perfect and bigger than we can imagine. We want to travel down roads marked by the supernatural. And this means we will need to sow in the Spirit and let our lives be fertile soil for the supernatural to grow, expand, and open new roads for ourselves and others. Wisdom from the Holy Spirit requires humility to trust God knows best, patience to believe God is as work, and endurance to hold on until God's "proper time" to move. With Spirit-filled vision, the way will always be easy to find and follow. We will talk more about this tomorrow.

PRAYER TARGET:
Believers in Knoxville and surrounding areas who struggle with waiting on Gods timing.

PERSONAL PRAYER FOR KNOXVILLE:
Father, I pray for everyone to live a life focused on God's Kingdom in a world focused on personal kingdoms. I pray men and women of Knoxville and surrounding areas receive wisdom from the Holy Spirit. I pray when people feel the still small voice of God, they will follow wherever He leads. Holy Spirit, speak to us. Give us the humility, strength, and boldness to walk it out. Amen.

AUTHOR: ALMAZ GEMECHU
FAMILY STRUCTURE: SINGLE MOTHER OF 3 ADULT CHILDREN, AND 1 GRANDCHILD
OCCUPATION: DIRECTOR, REFUGEE/INTERNATIONAL MINISTRIES

THE LIVING GOD

> **"For I know the plans I have for you, declares the LORD, plans for welfare and not for evil, to give you a future and a hope. Then you will call upon me and come and pray to me, and I will hear you. You will seek me and find me, when you seek me with all your heart." Jeremiah 29:11**

Our God is in constant pursuit of us because of His great love and mercies toward us! As He saw the ancient Israelites drifting away from Him and worshiping idols, so He sees the subtle idols of our hearts today. He loves us too much to look the other way; therefore, He chastises us as a good father chastises his children whom He loves. At the same time, He's the God who seeks to turn us around and bring forth so much beauty out of our ashes when we cry out to Him with our whole heart. But are we willing to seek His help to move to a life of faith and repentance from our pride and unbelief?

Isaiah 30:15 says, *"In returning and rest you shall be saved; in quietness and in trust shall be your strength."* My fellow believer, what are the idols of your heart that separate you from the living God and staying in your life miserable today? Let us examine ourselves before the Throne of grace and confess our own sins, the sins of our families, and our city to the One who promises to hear us and cleanse us from all unrighteousness. Let's also stand in the gap and intercede on behalf of those who don't know their left from their right and have lost hope. Let's seek the Lord together to bring the healing & restoring touch of Christ to those who are untouchables in the world's eyes.

PRAYER TARGET:
Fellow Believers seeking the Healing of our Living God.

PERSONAL PRAYER FOR KNOXVILLE:
Father, I pray for repentance from
our complacency and for a new passion and zeal to advance the
gospel of Jesus Christ into the greater Knoxville area. May we
as Christians be a sweet aroma of Christ through our love and
actions. May Knoxville and surrounding areas, Lord, be a truly
welcoming city to the nations. You, Lord, are bringing others
to our doorstep. Let this be a city of refuge for them. Let our
actions translate into a concrete empowering outreach to the
strangers in our midst, both physically and spiritually. Amen.

WEEK THIRTY: TUESDAY

AUTHOR: TORI QUINTON
OCCUPATION: KNOX YOUTH INTERN

FOR EVERYTHING THERE IS A SEASON

"There is a time for everything, and a season for every activity under the heavens: a time to be born and a time to die, a time to plant and a time to uproot, a time to kill and a time to heal, a time to tear down and a time to build, a time to weep and a time to laugh, a time to mourn and a time to dance, a time to scatter stones and a time to gather them, a time to embrace and a time to refrain from embracing, a time to search and a time to give up, a time to keep and a time to throw away, a time to tear and a time to mend, a time to be silent and a time to speak, a time to love and a time to hate, a time for war and a time for peace." Ecclesiastes 3:1-8

Oh, our sweet Father has been teaching me so much lately but He has been showing me His timing, patience to wait for Him, and contentment in the right now more than anything. This summer the Lord has been working to show me that there is a time for it all, a time for joy, a time for pain, a time for laughter, but that all this comes in His time. The Lord shows how all the activities of life are described in these verses along with their polar opposites. IN each, He reveals His plan for our life has each of these events lining up in just the perfect time.

I used to be a person who had to have complete control over it ALL. I wanted to know when I was going to get hurt and by what or whom, what that day was going to consist of, and the fun/ exciting times before they even happened. I needed COMPLETE control. Then a friend told me to read the whole book of Ecclesiastes and I found Chapter three where the Lord assures us that His plans are higher than ours. He assured me that He knows when all these activities come and that He won't leave or forsake us during those times. I now know that it is best to fully trust in the promises behind these verses. He promises to ALWAYS be present with us, to ALWAYS have our back, and to ALWAYS know what is best for us and when.

Recently, I read a blog that had the statement, "God knows just what you need." I think these verses sweetly back up this statement with the thought that God knows the time, the place, the person, etc. and just how, when, and in what form to give it to your heart. Trust our sweet Father that He knows what your heart needs and when it needs it. Rest in the promises behind His word, that He is here and alive and will NEVER leave or forsake us. He loves so well and that never changes.

PRAYER TARGET:
Those struggling with trusting the Lord.

PERSONAL PRAYER FOR KNOXVILLE:
Father, help those struggling with trusting Your timing in everything. Help them see that the Lord is sovereign above all! Father, You have a time for everything and I pray for an ability to see and trust in the knowledge that You know our needs, as well as our desires. Lord, provide peace and understanding for things we don't understand. Help us ask You, seek Your will and guidance over our lives, and accept Your provision. Amen.

WEEK THIRTY: WEDNESDAY

AUTHOR: JOHNNY SHORT, JR.
FAMILY STRUCTURE: SINGLE
OCCUPATION: CAMPUS MISSIONARY

CROSS CULTURAL BARRIERS FOR THE GOSPEL

> "A woman of Samaria came to draw water. 'Give me a drink,' Jesus said to her, because his disciples had gone into town to buy food. 'How is it that you, a Jew, ask for a drink from me, a Samaritan woman?' she asked him. 'For Jews do not associate with Samaritans.' Jesus answered, 'If you knew the gift of God, and who is saying to you, 'Give me a drink,' you would ask him, and he would give you living water.'"
> John 4:7-10

Are you ever fearful of sharing your faith? What are the biggest barriers that prevent you from doing so? Is it fear of misspeaking, lack of knowledge on how to share your faith, or perhaps there are cultural elements that are preventative factors. If these are true for you, take heart. Let's look together at how Jesus handled this culturally sensitive situation for the glory of the Father and the good of this woman.

During this conversation, we see Jesus break through two cultural stigmas. First, it was completely taboo for Jews to associate with Samaritans. The Samaritans had intermarried with the Jews, and because they were not fully Jewish, the Jews looked down on them and viewed them as unclean. Second, similarly to many Middle Eastern cultures today, there was a cultural stigma for men to talk to woman in public alone.

So why did Jesus initiate conversation with this Samaritan woman? Jesus knew His purpose. He had come to reconcile people to the Father, and He knew that was exceedingly more important than any cultural barriers of His time. Was it uncomfortable? I am sure that it was! However, we are not called to comfort but to share the Father's love with a dying world.

PRAYER TARGET:
Believers to boldly share their faith.

PERSONAL PRAYER FOR KNOXVILLE:
Father, You have loved us with such a deep unconditional love! Remind us of this daily and give us opportunities to share that love. As opportunities arise, help us to look to Jesus as our example of crossing cultural barriers to share truth with those around us. Also, Holy Spirit, guide us and give us wisdom and boldness as we share our faith. For Your glory and the good of our neighbors. Amen.

WEEK THIRTY: THURSDAY

AUTHOR: WILL BEVERLY
FAMILY STRUCTURE: FATHER, MOTHER, AND 2 SIBLINGS
OCCUPATION: COLLEGE STUDENT

REPLACING OBLIGATION WITH COMMITMENT

> "Do not fret because of those who are evil or be envious of those who do wrong; for like the grass they will soon wither, like green plants they will soon die away. Commit your way to the LORD; trust in him and he will do this: He will make your righteous reward shine like the dawn, your vindication like the noonday sun. The LORD makes firm the steps of the one who delights in him; though he may stumble, he will not fall, for the LORD upholds him with his hand." Psalm 37:1-2, 5-6, 23-24

These verses were revealed to me while reading scripture on a mission trip last spring. Amazed by the strength the church planters we worked with seemed to have, I wondered why, how, and from where they got their strength, and why I could not duplicate it.

I soon realized the answer to my questions after praying and reading this scripture. My problem was a lack of trust. I had not been looking to God for strength, I had been looking to myself. The nervousness, lack of motivation, and hesitation I had faced when speaking to non-believers on this mission trip was indicative of my lack of trust in God.

I was afraid of what people would think about my beliefs. I was scared to speak to people about my beliefs or how I could pray for them. Knowing I shouldn't be, I realized the only motivation I had at the time was an obligation to God and the people with which I was working.

I encourage you all to look at these verses. They affirmed for me the fact that trust in God, and God alone, was the thing I needed. God spoke to me through scripture to replace the negative obligation I felt to God and those people around me with a positive commitment to trust in God alone.

PRAYER TARGET:
Those who feel a negative obligation to God and people.

PERSONAL PRAYER FOR KNOXVILLE:
Father, my prayer is that believers who are hesitant to share their faith freely would be filled with strength from You, Lord. Help these people delight in the Lord and make their footsteps firm. I pray that people would feel led to share their faith and testimony rather than feeling an obligation to talk to other believers. Break down walls of hesitation, lack of confidence, or fears that hinder us from sharing the gospel. Tear each blockage down and replace it with trust in You and Your love. In Christ Jesus' Name. Amen.

WEEK THIRTY: FRIDAY

AUTHOR: HUNTER BECKHAM
OCCUPATION: STUDENT

LOVE LIKE CHRIST

"No, in all these things we are more than conquerors through him who loved us. For I am convinced that neither death nor life, neither angels nor demons, neither the present nor the future, nor any powers, neither height nor depth, nor anything else in all creation, will be able to separate us from the love of God that is in Christ Jesus our Lord." Romans 8:37-39

"There will be trouble and distress for every human being who does evil: first for the Jew, then for the Gentile; but glory, honor and peace for everyone who does good: first for the Jew, then for the Gentile. For God does not show favoritism." Romans 2:9-11

"Accept one another, then, just as Christ accepted you, in order to bring praise to God. For I tell you that Christ has become a servant of the Jews on behalf of God's truth, so that the promises made to the patriarchs might be confirmed." Romans 15:7-8

"In your relationships with one another, have the same mindset as Christ Jesus: Who, being in very nature God, did not consider equality with God something to be used to his own advantage; rather, he made himself nothing by taking the very nature of a servant, being made in human likeness.And being found in appearance as a man, he humbled himself by becoming obedient to death—even death on a cross!" Philippians 2:3-8

Love is something that we too often fail to accurately represent. So often we try to put human boundaries on the love we exhibit and receive. Instead, we should open ourselves to the vulnerability of Christ's perfect example of love. In the first scripture above we can see and be reminded that Christ's love never fails or ceases to exist. His love for us cannot be stopped. If we could come to peace and understanding that Christ's love surrounds us constantly we could then be the love of Christ to others. True love can only come from the overflow of our heart which is filled by Christ's love.

In Romans 2:9-11 we understand that Christ's love does not show favoritism. His love casts a shadow on all, not missing one individual. Additionally, His love has been shown to all, accepting everyone as His creation. We see this in all the scriptures above. Lastly, we see Christ demonstrating love through humility. As the perfect example of love, Christ humbled Himself to being a servant, becoming the least of these and making Himself last, to the point of death on a cross. Even while we might never be put on a cross, we should love others to the point of putting ourselves last, and follow Christ's model as He humbled Himself to be a servant. Christ is all around us, we just must look. His face is on everyone. His grace is in every sunrise and sunset. His love is in our every breathe. So, love. Love others. Love life. Love, because you are loving Christ in every moment.

PRAYER TARGET:
Individuals we meet daily, approached in love.

PERSONAL PRAYER FOR KNOXVILLE:
Lord, God of love, may we, as the body of Christ, learn to accurately represent Christ's love as His love overflows from our own heart. May we understand that His love is exhibited to all without condition, judgement, or favoritism. As we go through our daily lives may others see Your love through us. God, we know that You are love so we ask for You to fulfill us in Your love and let the overflow of our heart be solely from You. In the name Christ, we pray. Amen.

WEEK THIRTY ONE: MONDAY

AUTHOR: MARTI RICHARDSON
FAMILY STRUCTURE: 2 MARRIED CHILDREN AND 3 GRANDCHILDREN
OCCUPATION: AUTHOR, STRATEGIC PLANNER, CONSULTANT

SAVE OUR YOUTH AND CHILDREN

"Righteousness exalts a city, but sin is a reproach to any people." Proverbs 14:34

We are losing our children! The following general facts about our young people concern me:

• The fastest growing segment of criminal population is children.

• The average child will watch 100,000 plus activities of violence on TV by the time he or she leaves school.

• Teen suicides have more than tripled.

• The top problems in high schools are bullying, alcohol, drug abuse, pregnancy, suicide, rape, and robbery.

It has been said, as goes the home, so goes the nation. If that is true, it is time for Knoxville to become a "City of the Concerned," and bring our homes back to God. I am suggesting two positive actions that we all can take to get biblically promised, widespread results for each problem.

1. Pray fervent and focused prayers. Prayer is the engine that will drive our city down a positive path of reform.

2. Develop a "Discipline of Delay." Stop the frenetic activities that take us away from the responsibility of nurturing our children and spend time with them daily to let them know how precious they are to God and us. Through these steps we can develop a depth of character in the youngsters and a strong culture of respect, integrity, and self-control within our community and begin to save our youth.

PRAYER TARGET:
Parents of children and youth longing to train children biblically.

PERSONAL PRAYER FOR KNOXVILLE:
Father, I pray for Your hand of protection to be over the children and youth of Knoxville and surrounding areas. Protect them physically from all accidents, diseases, infirmities, acts of violence by others, and sudden dangers. Help them learn to dwell in Your shadow and under Your umbrella of protection. Lord, when they go through times, please be their Defender. Arm them with strength for the battle and keep them safe. In our city, Lord, help them know that they can lie down and sleep in peace, for You alone, Lord, make them dwell in safety. Amen.

WEEK THIRTY ONE: TUESDAY

AUTHOR: LUIS CAMILLO ALMEIDA
FAMILY STRUCTURE: WIFE AND 2 CHILDREN
OCCUPATION: PROFESSOR AND KEYNOTE SPEAKER

DON'T OVEREXTEND YOURSELVES

> **"For the love of money is the root of all evil: which while some coveted after, they have erred from the faith, and pierced themselves through with many sorrows."**
> **1 Timothy 6:10**

I was changed by the Holy Spirit on this topic many years ago. The answer to professional success is not extravagance. It is simplicity instead. This piece of wisdom was shared with me by a poet. He was clear about what matters most to the Lord. These verses have helped me immensely to not live for man and guide my life by faith, not material possessions.

The former isn't to say that I was never tempted to accumulate great wealth. Having been born in a wealthy family of golfers didn't make my life any easier. I lived a life of materialism. At a very early age, I remember thinking about Christ in Mathew 19:16-24 when He said to the rich man, *"If you want to be perfect, go, sell your possessions and give to the poor, and you will have treasure in heaven. Then come, follow me."* A personal friend once told me to trust and live a simple life. His words were, "Just do it." It will change your life. It most definitely changed mine.

PRAYER TARGET:
Fathers of overextended families.

PERSONAL PRAYER FOR KNOXVILLE:

Father, guide every father of a family to make God first in their lives. Help them to not focus on possessions first. May every family leader experience the power of the Holy Spirit with passion, celebrating the gift of just being with God. Lord, please be with every father of a family and forgive their obsession with money. Inspire them to seek You, not the idolization of wealth.

Father, we are nobody without You. Work on our hearts and shake our earthly foundations in order to make us more like You. Do miracles, push aside evil desires, and with love forgive our spirits. Be our everything and anything. Let Your love save and bring Your sheep back home. We ask this in the name of the Most High Jesus Christ. Amen.

AUTHOR: JAKE LAMBERSON
FAMILY STRUCTURE: ELDEST OF 8 CHILDREN
OCCUPATION: STUDENT

SPEAK BOLDLY

> **"Now when they saw the boldness of Peter and John, and perceived that they were uneducated, common men, they were astonished. And they recognized that they had been with Jesus. But seeing the man who was healed standing beside them, they had nothing to say in opposition."**
> **Acts 4:13-14**

Peter and John spoke with confidence because they knew the truth in the words they spoke. They had received instruction from Jesus Himself, and did not doubt the truth of it. The Pharisees themselves recognized that they had been with Jesus because of this. Jesus' presence in Peter and John's lives is shown in two ways:
1.   Bold words
2.   A visible testimony

That's it. There were no eloquent words or advanced theology degrees involved. In fact, they were uneducated. Peter and John didn't have the theology background the Pharisees had, but they didn't need to engage them in a debate. The testimony of the healed man and the simple words of Peter and John were enough to convince the Pharisees that Jesus was involved. It wasn't until I truly admitted the Lord's work in my life that He transformed my life and I spoke the truth of the Gospel. testimony is. For this devotion, I encourage you to share the works God has done in your life with someone, then speak the same truth that Peter and John did (the Gospel). Practicing your own testimony prepares you to share it with more people, and affirms its importance in your own life.

PRAYER TARGET:
The believers of the city that will speak boldly.

PERSONAL PRAYER FOR KNOXVILLE:
Father, I pray that the believers of Knoxville will recognize the
This is more than a call to speak the Gospel boldly. It is a
reminder of how important a personal power of their own
testimonies. May they realize that their testimonies are the
application of the Gospel in their own lives. May they speak
boldly the simple message of the Gospel and boldly proclaim
the works of God they have witnessed in their lives. Help them
to see how broken the people of Knoxville are without Jesus and
then recognize the role He has had in their lives. May preaching
the Gospel to themselves open their eyes to the need of all other
people for the Gospel. Let them know, Father, that the Gospel is
the reason we can even pray this prayer to our Lord. I pray this in
the name of Jesus. Amen.

WEEK THIRTY ONE: THURSDAY

AUTHOR: JEFF DAVIS
FAMILY STRUCTURE: WIFE AND 2 DAUGHTERS
OCCUPATION: ASSOCIATE WORSHIP PASTOR

JESUS PUT THE "YOU" IN "UNITY"

"My prayer is not for them alone. I pray also for those who will believe in me through their message, that all of them may be one, Father, just as you are in me and I am in you. May they also be in us so that the world may believe that you have sent me." John 17:20-21

I will never forget my amazement when I first came across this passage! Jesus was in the upper room during what we call the "last supper" with His disciples. Knowing that He would soon be crucified, He began praying for them. But beginning in verse 20, Jesus began praying for you and me!! *"Those who will believe…".* Jesus was thinking ahead to us…and prayed for us!

In this, one of His last spoken prayers on earth, He could have prayed on our behalf for strength or courage, but what did He choose? Jesus chose unity. He prayed for the believers who were yet to be (you and I), that we would be "as one" for the purpose of giving the world reason to believe in Christ. This was His prayer because He knows that unity is not something that always happens organically, but it takes effort. It takes commitment. It takes the willingness to change and the determination to take action. But we can do this! Is there anyone we would rather have pray for us in this than Jesus?

PRAYER TARGET:
Personal introspection.

PERSONAL PRAYER FOR KNOXVILLE:

Father, thank You for the prayers of Your Son that were offered to You on our behalf. I pray that we will all search our hearts and begin to make unity and love, in the name of Jesus, the priority in whatever little corner of the city we may live. Help us, in both speech and action, to change our hearts, our homes, our workplaces and any area where we have any influence or presence. We are bold enough to ask You to bring about revival and unity in this city, realizing it begins with me. This, we ask and submit to, in Jesus' name. Amen.

WEEK THIRTY ONE: FRIDAY

AUTHOR: RODNEY NORVELL
FAMILY STRUCTURE: WIFE AND 3 CHILDREN
OCCUPATION: COLLEGIATE MINISTRY DIRECTOR

EQUIPPING FOR UNITY

> **"So Christ himself gave the apostles, the prophets, the evangelists, the pastors and teachers, to equip his people for works of service, so that the body of Christ may be built up until we all reach unity in the faith and in the knowledge of the Son of God and become mature, attaining to the whole measure of the fullness of Christ."**
> **Ephesians 3:11-13**

Each and every day as I work with students I see that many of them have a lot of book learning, but some have not been taught the common things to run a household. They may be great at taking an exam but fail at being able to cook a meal, doing their own laundry, or cleaning their own bathroom. As it turns out these things have been done for them so long they expect someone else to take care of that.

As a religious leader, I find that I do the same thing very easily. I have been taught a lot about the Bible, but I sometimes fail at equipping God's people to carry out works of service. Works of service can be tiresome, repetitive, thankless, and even dirty sometimes. Nonetheless according to scripture there is a great benefit: unity in the faith.

Just as students that begin to do household tasks have a greater understanding of how much work others have been doing for them, when God's people are equipped they have a greater understanding of how much they need each other. And when you realize how much you need someone else, there is a bond that begins to knit your hearts together in unity.

PRAYER TARGET:

All leaders who are governed by Jesus, seeking His Unity.

PERSONAL PRAYER FOR KNOXVILLE:

Dear Father, we repent of the times that we have failed to equip Your people to do works of service. We admit that we are often separated by our desire to make a good grade or pass the exam in Your sight instead of seeking unity. May we appreciate how much we do for one another, recognize how much we have done for each other, and may You bless how much we will do for one another in the future. May we be thankful for one another. May we seek the promise of unity as we equip those that follow us to do the task of serving one another. And may You, Father, receive the praise and glory as our knowledge of You fills us! Amen!

WEEK THIRTY TWO: MONDAY

AUTHOR: EUNICE ITOI NORRIS
FAMILY STRUCTURE: HUSBAND AND 3 TEENAGERS
OCCUPATION: CHILD CARE EMPLOYEE

GOD TURNS FEAR TO FAITH

> **"For God did not give us a spirit of fear, but His Spirit of Power, Love, and Self-discipline." 2 Timothy 1:7**
> **"Be still and know that I am God." Psalm 46:10**
> **"Without faith it is impossible to please God. Jesus is the author and finisher of our faith." Hebrews 11:6, 12:2**

My mother was on bedrest when she was pregnant with me. She told me that during that time she saw a dark figure that kept standing in the door of her room. It scared her to death. After freaking out a bit, she started to recite "The Lord is my Shepherd…" The dark figure disappeared. Numerous times, my mother told me that Satan exists. This scared me then and it scares me now.

The enemy always brings fear, deceit, and destruction with him as is seen in the Bible. The enemy's work here on earth is scary to experience. God understands that we as humans are full of fear, nervousness, and anxiety. God in the Bible as the Good Shepherd to His sheep assures us, "Do not fear." In times of fear, let us discipline our minds to focus on Jesus, the Prince of Peace. Let us train our minds to focus on the amazing character of God. He is all powerful, all good, all wise, all loving, and all just. He is ever present, our comforter, protector, provider, perfect friend and perfect Father - just to name a few of His amazing attributes.

PRAYER TARGET:
Anyone in the city who is afraid.

PERSONAL PRAYER FOR KNOXVILLE:

Dear Father in Heaven, thank You that You are the Author and Finisher of our faith. You tell us three-hundred, sixty-five times in Your word not to be afraid. You are in the business of bringing us through our worst nightmares in life to show us that we have and had nothing to fear. Help us have an awe-filled and holy fear and respect of You. Please guide us through our valleys of fear as You author the faith You desire us to have within us. In the Name of Jesus, I pray. Amen.

AUTHOR: ALISA LIM
OCCUPATION: STUDENT

CREATED IN THE IMAGE OF GOD

> **"Then God said, 'Let Us make man in Our image, according to Our likeness; and let them rule over the fish of the sea and over the birds of the sky and over the cattle and over all the earth, and over every creeping thing that creeps on the earth.' God created man in His own image, in the image of God He created him; male and female He created them."**
> **Genesis 1:26-28**

With all the events that have been happening within these past years, these verses have been speaking to me. As a student who goes to a secular college and works a part-time job in retail, I do not always think about how I treat others. But, this summer I was reminded of the creation account as I studied Genesis. Just as it is said in the verses above, God made all of us in His image.

The Hebrew word for *man* verse 27 is *adam*, which refers to mankind. This means that both men and women are made in God's image. As believers who know this, one thing that we need to ask ourselves is if we are treating non-believers as people created in the image of God. Also, am I as a man or woman treating people of the other gender as human beings who were each created in the image of God?

PRAYER TARGET:
Believers of the city created in His image, for confidence.

PERSONAL PRAYER FOR KNOXVILLE:
Father, I pray that God will constantly remind us that each of us are created in His image, believers and non-believers,

heterosexual and homosexual, and people of all ethnicities. I pray that we would treat each other as images of God and that love and mercy would be overflowing in our actions to each other. May God give us what we need to show others, especially those who are in broken worlds, that they are created in the image of their Creator and have self-worth. Amen.

WEEK THIRTY TWO: WEDNESDAY

AUTHOR: PAT BRYANT
FAMILY STRUCTURE: WIFE AND 3 CHILDREN
OCCUPATION: CONSUMER GOODS ANALYTICS CONSULTANT

STOP, LISTEN - AND LEAD!

> **"A fool takes no pleasure in understanding, but only in expressing his opinion. When wickedness comes, contempt comes also, and with dishonor comes disgrace. The words of a man's mouth are deep waters; the fountain of wisdom is a bubbling brook." Proverbs 18:2-4**

When you spend your life leading, directing, motivating, and encouraging, it's difficult to not speak. Speaking is the gateway to leadership, since communication is the currency of leaders. But not speaking reflects the spiritual gift of discernment – which is sorely missing in our current culture.

What is a fool? It's a person who knows better than to do something, and does it anyway. So – we often know that it's better to be silent and to listen for understanding, but we can't bear the silence of our own opinions, and we jump right in. I can't count the number of times I've been convicted by the Spirit for speaking out of turn, and being the fool.

The secret is to realize the strength that God has given to each of us through our words, and to be both powerful in our spiritual wisdom ("deep waters"), but gentle in our approach ("bubbling brook"). When we do this, we're creating space that God can use to help us see what we can't see on our own. We gain influence through a caring and gentle spirit – rather than the clanging bell to which we default under our own counsel. God can soften my spirit, and open my ears!

PRAYER TARGET:

Leaders of Knoxville and surrounding areas – in businesses, communities, and homes.

PERSONAL PRAYER FOR KNOXVILLE:

Father, may our leaders realize that theirs is a role – not a position – ordained by God to guide, encourage, equip, and enable the people under their authority. From this role, I pray that leaders will realize that words can both enable and disable, and that we would allow You to help us discern the difference. Father, you are the master communicator, and through your Holy Spirit you have gifted us to speak with kindness, gentleness, love, joy, peace, and patience, and to control ourselves and our tongues. Keep us from the foolish pursuits of our own hearts and minds, and transform us into being more like You. Lord, this city needs strong leaders who love You and love Your people. Help the people in our city to see Your leaders as men and women who are anything but fools; help them to see a fellowship of leadership that focuses on seeing what you see, and doing what You say. Help us to listen first, then speak through clearer understanding. Help us to be strong, relying only on You, but gentle in our speech as a "bubbling brook." Change us – for Your sake and for the precious Name of our Lord, Jesus Christ. Amen.

WEEK THIRTY TWO: THURSDAY

AUTHOR: ABIGAIL WALDROUP
FAMILY STRUCTURE: MOM, DAD, BROTHER AND SISTER
OCCUPATION: HIGH SCHOOL STUDENT, PIANO, AND VOICE TEACHER

SPIRITUAL WARFARE

"Be strong in the Lord and in the strength of his might. Put on the whole armor of God, that you may be able to stand against the schemes of the devil. For we do not wrestle against flesh and blood, but against the rulers, against the authorities, against the cosmic powers over the present darkness, against spiritual forces of evil in the heavenly places. Therefore, take up the whole armor of God, that you may be able to withstand the evil day, and having done all, to stand firm." Ephesians 6:10-13

Everyone in this life has something with which they wrestle, something that the devil throws in our faces whenever he wants to bring us down. We try so hard to fix this broken world and when we realize we can't do it in our own power, we run to God and give it all to Him. For a while we are happy and feel full. But then, the devil begins to attack. He tests our faith and opens our eyes to the world crumbling around us. We believe his lies and begin to think that God isn't there anymore when He really is.

The devil is out to seek, kill, and destroy this beautiful world God created. He tries to accomplish this goal by lying to God's people and putting out their fire. But God has given us all the tools and weapon to combat the devil's lies. When the devil tries to destroy your faith or bring you down, you can pick up that shield and that sword and beat the devil at his own game.

The bible says that we are at war people. But not against the government, ISIS, or any other organization out to destroy our physical world. We are at war against the spiritual forces of this world. We are at war against Satan himself. But don't be afraid. For God has given you his armor that has the ability to squash the devil. All you must do is put it on and God will help you do the rest.

PRAYER TARGET:
The people of Knoxville and surrounding area that are in spiritual warfare!

PERSONAL PRAYER FOR KNOXVILLE:
Father, I come on my knees today to pray that the men and woman of this city will realize we are at war against Satan and his minions. I pray that they will take this armor that You have given them to combat the devil and his lies. I pray that You will strengthen them with the power of the Holy Spirit that lives inside of them, so that You may dwell in their hearts through faith – that they, being rooted and grounded in love, may have strength to comprehend Your strength and length and height and depth. May they know Your love that surpasses all knowledge, that they may be filled with all the fullness of You. You, Father, are able to do far more than all that we could ever ask or think, so work within us so that Your glory can shine throughout all generations forever and ever. Amen.

WEEK THIRTY TWO: FRIDAY

AUTHOR: GREGORY LINTON
FAMILY STRUCTURE: WIFE AND 2 CHILDREN
OCCUPATION: ACADEMIC ADMINISTRATOR

THE FATHER WHO ADOPTED US

> **"And because you are children, God has sent the Spirit of his Son into our hearts, crying 'Abba! Father!'"**
> **Galatians 4:6**

Jesus was the unique Son of God. His unique relationship with God is reflected in the fact that He addressed God as Abba. Abba was an Aramaic word that children used to address their fathers in an intimate way. It is similar to our "Daddy" or "Papa."

Jesus invited His disciples to share His close relationship with God. When we surrender our lives to Christ, God adopts us as His children, and He becomes our Father also. As parents who adopted a child, my wife and I know the special bond that exists between adoptive parents and their children. Because we are adopted as children of God, we know that He dwells in our heart. As our heavenly Father, He wants to be close to us. He wants to spend time with us. He wants to talk with us. He wants to give us the good things we ask for.

Augustine said: *"He loves us everyone as though there were but one of us to love."* If we have accepted Christ as Lord, then God is our Father and we are His children. Let us draw close to the One who is as close as our heart.

PRAYER TARGET:
Those who need to feel God's love.

PERSONAL PRAYER FOR KNOXVILLE:

Abba, Father, we thank You for not being a distant, remote, uncaring God but a God who loves us and draws near to us. We thank You for reaching out to us and adopting us as your children. And we thank You for sending the Spirit of Your Son into our hearts so that we can confidently call You "Abba, Father." We pray that Your love would flow through our hearts to others so that they might also be drawn to You. We pray that those who are alone or hurting or lost would find the comfort and peace that comes only from Your love. Help us to be the channels of Your grace so that all might become one in You., In your Son's Name we pray. Amen.

WEEK THIRTY THREE: MONDAY

AUTHOR: BART DYKES
FAMILY STRUCTURE: WIFE, 2 ADULT CHILDREN, AND 1 PRE-TEEN.
OCCUPATION: RETIRED POLICE OFFICER

YES, I SAID I AM A HOME SCHOOL STAY AT HOME DAD

"Train up a child in the way he should go: and when he is old, he will not depart from it." Proverbs 22:6

You may be like me. You may not like all the things your kids are being taught in school, or you may complain about how kids these days talk, dress, or just spend too much time in front of a TV. You may say to yourself, "No wonder kids don't understand the importance of showing respect to our military, the American flag, know the words to the Pledge of Allegiance or about the great sacrifices that have been made by others so that we can all enjoy the freedoms we do." To mention "Jesus" has become an offensive politically and incorrect word in many places. I have pondered on these things at one time or another. However, I never really thought about stepping up and doing something about it until I was nudged one morning by the Holy Spirit.

It was not an audible voice, but I heard Him clearly. God said, "Bart, I want you to home school your daughter." I said, "Not me Lord. I am not a teacher. I am unqualified." But no matter how much I argued about why I was unfit the Lord said, "I have chosen you." So, I stepped out of my comfort zone and decided to become the primary home school teach for my twelve-year-old daughter. I can honestly say that it is one of the most rewarding things I have ever done. My daughter and I are closer than we have ever been and she is progressing in her studies with high marks, while I teach her basic core classes along with God's Word and how they relate to one another. We also start the day off by reciting the Pledge of Allegiance together in front of the American Flag! When God speaks of the American Flag! When God speaks to you and tells you to do something for Him you may feel like I did at first. But rest assured. He will be with you and guide you all the way. I have high hopes for my daughter and I know that she will be a well-rounded young lady who will contribute to society one day. Most importantly she has Jesus in her heart and she will pass that truth on to others as she goes through life. So, when someone asks me what I do now that I'm retired, I am used to repeating myself saying, "Yes, I said I am a Home School stay at home Dad." And I am proud to say it!

PRAYER TARGET:
Homeschool parents of children.

PERSONAL PRAYER FOR KNOXVILLE:
God, I pray for the families of Knoxville, Tennessee. I ask You to lift them up and give fathers confidence and encouragement as they lead their families. I pray that mothers will be recognized and appreciated for all the outstanding care they pour into their families. I pray that children will listen to the words of wisdom, instruction, advice, and guidance they receive from their parents. But the main thing I ask of You, Almighty God, is to come into each father, mother, and child's heart so that they can experience the peace and love that only You can provide. I am a simple man so if my words can inspire just one person to step up for their family then I am humbled and honored. I pray these things in the Name of our King, Jesus Christ. Amen.

WEEK THIRTY THREE: TUESDAY

AUTHOR: CARRIE DUGAN
FAMILY STRUCTURE: HUSBAND
OCCUPATION: MINISTRIES

TREES DON'T MOVE

"And he shall be like a tree planted by the rivers of water, that bringeth forth his fruit in his season; his leaf also shall not wither; and whatsoever he doeth shall prosper." Psalm 1:3 "To appoint unto them that mourn in Zion to give unto them beauty for ashes, the oil of joy for mourning, the garment of praise for the spirit of heaviness, that they might be called trees of righteousness, the planting of the Lord that he might be glorified." Isaiah 61:3

We are like the trees planted by the river that bring fruit in due season. The Lord said, "Trees don't move." We are the tree and the river is the supply God provides by the river. It's our nourishment! Our bloodline, if you will. It's a continuous flow of the supply from our Heavenly Father. He provides the supply continually; therefore, we are to meditate on this and in season, our leaves will not wither and we will bring forth fruit.

See yourself as that tree. You are the tree that is planted by Him. The water is the Word of God. By the washing of the water of the Word you are renewed if you feed on the Water of the Word daily. Don't move yourself from the water of "The Word of God." The analogy of the tree makes sense because we too are planted, rooted and grounded, even in storms. Trees may get blown by the winds; so will we. When they face storms, they can be made stronger. The water brought in by the storms nourish the tree to grow deeper roots, thus increasing its stability. Similarly, the Word of God spoken to you through the Bible will strengthen you. The deeper your roots go into the water through the Word, the stronger you become. When the next storm arises, therefore, you are much better prepared. Previous experiences pave the way through storms. With each passing storm of life, we become stronger.

We are trees of righteousness. Strong like oak trees. We can learn a lot from the trees. They don't move from their life source. Neither should we. Let's remember that our life source is the Lord God Almighty.

PRAYER TARGET:
Those who feel weak and need to be strengthened.

PERSONAL PRAYER FOR KNOXVILLE:
Father, I thank You that You have given us all things we need for life and godliness including Your Word, which brings us Your life by watering us in every season. Thank You for showing us that we are made to be the righteousness of God in Christ Jesus. It is a gift that we didn't earn and can't lose because it came from Jesus on the cross. I thank You that through the storms of life that I have You to help me bounce back. Just as Noah bounced back after the flood; Abraham after offering Isaac; and Paul after shipwreck and imprisonment, with Your help I will bounce back through the storms in my life. Help me stand on Your Word and the promises of Your Word. I thank You, Father God, that I am a "tree" You designed to withstand the storms that may come my way. With Your help I can bend but I will be able to stand right back up. Father, help us all to stand straight and tall and not be moved by adverse circumstances. In Your Name, Jesus, I pray. Amen.

WEEK THIRTY THREE: WEDNESDAY

AUTHOR: PAUL STANDIFER
FAMILY STRUCTURE: WIFE, SON AND DAUGHTER-IN-LAW, AND 2 GRANDSONS
OCCUPATION: RETIRED ENGINEERING AND MAINTENANCE

FINDING JOY, HOPE, AND PEACE IN WEARY CIRCUMSTANCES

"May the God of hope fill you with all joy and peace as you trust in him, so that you may overflow with hope by the power of the Holy Spirit." Matthew 15:13

Years ago, I spent a period of time assisting people who were suffering in many ways. The work was hard, but very rewarding because of the grateful response of those being helped. However, as the time extended in the remote location we were in, I began to focus more on the things I didn't like. The food was bad, the living conditions were awful, sanitary conditions were non-existent, and there was no end in sight. My complaining became more frequent. I literally cried out to God to bring a rescue and remove me from those circumstances, and end the frustration and turmoil in my spirit. Fortunately, He didn't answer my plea in that way. What He did was to break me and reveal to me that I had made it all about me, and not about His plan.

I will never forget the brokenness I felt in realizing my self-centeredness. Immediately, a blanket of peace and joy came over me. It changed everything! I was where I was supposed to be, because He had placed me there. Time no longer mattered. Conditions no longer mattered. What mattered were the people and His purpose.

I reflect on this often. I had lost sight of God, and His purpose, and had lost the joy and peace that He intends. As those verses in Matthew describe, being filled with joy and peace is the condition in which we can then overflow with Hope and be light for others.

PRAYER TARGET:
Those who are worn out by their circumstances.

PERSONAL PRAYER FOR KNOXVILLE:
Lord, there are many in our city who are weary from having to endure circumstances they did not choose, and problems they have no ability to control. I pray that You would reveal to them in the middle of those circumstances that You are the source of peace and joy. Show them that they have a purpose ordained by You. Sustain them with the reality of Your love, so that hope replaces desperation, and that Your peace comes through, even in the toughest of days. Amen.

WEEK THIRTY THREE: THURSDAY

AUTHOR: PAMELA NEU
FAMILY STRUCTURE: HUSBAND AND 3 CHILDREN
OCCUPATION: HIGH SCHOOL BIBLE TEACHER

GIVE IT UP! HEART ISSUES

"Those who wait upon the Lord will renew their strength. They will soar on wings like eagles; they will run and not grow weary, they will walk and not be faint." Isaiah 40:31

I have three adult children now. The youngest is eighteen, and or some reason the law deems him an "adult." I choke a bit when I say the words…so, I have three adult children now. This means that my daily life contains a lot of "Mom, remember when you….," followed by well-deserved laughter.

Recently one asked, "Mom, remember when you used to tell us to do something and we wouldn't and you would just say, 'I might as well do it myself' and then you would? (Said without comma or breath) How do you think that worked for you?"

Yeah, it really didn't. I spent a lot of time doing things FOR my children because I wanted so much for them to be eager to obey. I didn't want them to clean their rooms…I wanted them to WANT to clean their rooms! It was a heart issue for me!

Heart issues…they are for Jesus. Moms, let's pray for patience in waiting on the Lord to do HIS work in our children. His timing. His maturing. His plan is so much better than ours. If we find ourselves weary today, let's do our part in instruction, then simply take a breath and wait on the greatest Father of all. The process will not bring immediate gratification…and maybe not even a clean room…but we WILL soar on wings like eagles. And some day, so will they.

PRAYER TARGET:
Moms in Knoxville and the sacrifices they make.

PERSONAL PRAYER FOR KNOXVILLE:
Father, what a privilege it is to call You by that Name. What an honor it is to love our children and have just a glimpse of how much You love Yours. Open their hearts, open their ears, and when they hear our voices, let them hear Yours. Amen.

WEEK THIRTY THREE: FRIDAY

AUTHOR: BRYAN ROBERTSON
FAMILY STRUCTURE: WIFE, 3 CHILDREN, AND 1 FOSTER CHILD
OCCUPATION: FAMILY & ASSIMILATION PASTOR

LOOKING BEYOND YOURSELF TO PRAY AND CARE FOR OTHERS

> **"But if serving the LORD seems undesirable to you, then choose for yourselves this day whom you will serve, whether the gods your ancestors served beyond the Euphrates, or the gods of the Amorites, in whose land you are living. But as for me and my household, we will serve the LORD." Joshua 24:15**

I didn't get married until I was twenty-nine years old. Before marriage, I had graduated college at Mississippi State University and been a coach and teacher at Hernando High School in Mississippi for two years. God called me to the ministry at that point in my life. I went straight to seminary and got my masters at Mid-America Baptist Theological Seminary. So, for ten years after high school, I did what "I" wanted to do as a single man. And during those ten years I got very selfish.

But then, the Lord brought me a great wife. I realized quickly that I didn't need to just please "me" anymore, but I needed to please her. I learned I didn't need to meet my needs and wants alone, but hers as well. I needed to love her as Christ loves the church (Ephesians 5:25). I now had a spiritual and physical responsibility of another person. I had to not only look out for my interests but also for the interests of others (Philippians. 2:4). Therefore, I had to look beyond myself.

Now, after twenty years of marriage and three children I am still realizing, "It's not about me". It is about others. God wants to flow through me with His Spirit to influence others – my wife, my children, my in-laws, etc. And to take it to a whole new level, we've been foster parents to ten different children. Now that got me out of my comfort zone! If we as the church follow God's instructions, we find we are supposed to take care of orphans (James 1:27); therefore, we even adopted one of the ten and may adopt another one.

God has placed you where you are for a reason. He wants to shine through you so that others can know Him. We can either make a difference or not. Stop living for yourself and live for the kingdom of God. Johnny Hunt is noted for saying, *"I want to take as many people to heaven as I can."* Start with being a witness for Jesus in your family and watch how YOU can affect generations beyond you. Be dead to self and alive unto God (Romans 6:11).

PRAYER TARGET:
Families self-sacrifice and their legacies.

PERSONAL PRAYER FOR KNOXVILLE:
Father God, I pray that You would fortify families to grow and build the kingdom of God. Fill us with Your Spirit to overflowing. Please bind the devil from ripping families apart and use us as Your bride to help others be a part of the family of God. In Jesus' Name I pray. Amen.

WEEK THIRTY FOUR: MONDAY

AUTHOR: LEIGH M. LEDET
FAMILY STRUCTURE: HUSBAND AND 2 ADULT CHILDREN
OCCUPATION: ELEMENTARY SCHOOL PRINCIPAL

CHOOSE TO SHINE IN YOUR SCHOOL

"You are the light of the world. A town built on a hill cannot be hidden. Neither do people light a lamp and put it under a bowl. Instead they put it on its stand, and it gives light to everyone in the house. In the same way, let your light shine before others, that they may see your good deeds and glorify your Father in heaven." Matthew 5:14-16

"Choose." The dictionary defines the word as to *select freely and after consideration.* After a particularly challenging few months last school year I found myself in a funk. My general attitude was negative, it was a stretch to see the good around me, and I was constantly tired and disenchanted with everything. On the morning of field day, I was in a particularly bad mood. I dreaded the day. As I dug through my t-shirts to find something to wear, a shirt that I haven't worn in years fell out of the drawer. It said in bold letters across the front "Choose to Shine." It was like the Lord hit me square in the face. Immediately I thought about His scripture in Matthew that describes the lamp on a stand - giving light to everyone. I was reminded that each day we get to CHOOSE whether to hide under the bowl or whether we are going to climb up on the stand and shine. It is our choice. And when we choose to shine, scripture says that others will be led to glorify the Father. When you understand the impact of your choice it changes everything. I CHOOSE TO SHINE! Will you?

PRAYER TARGET:
Teachers; and all believers choosing to shine in school.

PERSONAL PRAYER FOR KNOXVILLE:

Father, I pray that our community will choose to shine. Let us wake up each day, recognizing the gifts and blessings that You, the Lord, have given to us. I pray that we will choose to focus on the positive, and run from evil, so that others can see our light. Let us shine so brightly that there is no doubt that the Lord is at work in our lives. May we be known for our good deeds through Christ; not for our own glory, but for the glory of the Lord. May our city see the light that only Jesus can ignite. Amen.

WEEK THIRTY FOUR: TUESDAY

AUTHOR: DIANE STEWART
FAMILY STRUCTURE: WIDOW
OCCUPATION: RETIRED

ONLY THE LONELY

> **"Fear not, for I am with you; be not dismayed, for I am your God; I will strengthen you, I will help you, I will uphold you with my righteous right hand." Isaiah 41:10 "... for he has said, 'I will never leave you nor forsake you.'"**
> **Hebrews 13:5b**

Close your eyes. Imagine you are at a large sporting event or concert. Have you ever felt lonely in the middle of a crowd? I dare say most of us could answer, "Yes," to that question. My answer was "Yes" when I saw lights blinking and sirens blaring. The bedroom was full of police and paramedics. They were trying to save my husband's life after he had a massive heart attack. They were not able to start his heart; the Lord had called him home. After forty-five years of marriage, I can't begin to describe the depths of loneliness I felt. Others experience the same feeling. Think about a mother and her young children living in their car. They are homeless and are trying to stay away from an abusive spouse. She feels loneliness and doesn't know where to turn. What despair and loneliness would cause a teenager to take his or her life when he or she has so much of life ahead? These and many more scenarios of loneliness are what people face on a daily basis.

Is there a time when you have faced loneliness? Those who are Christians just may need to be reminded that you are not alone. God has promised He is with us and will never leave us. A strong relationship with Him through prayer and Bible study will get each of us through times of loneliness. But what about non-believers? They don't have the hope of God's presence to see them through their desperate times. As Christians who have experienced the same sense of loneliness, shouldn't we have a deep concern to help those people who don't know Jesus as their personal Savior? We have the answer to their loneliness. Shouldn't we share the Good News?

Don't we want them to have God's presence so they no longer feel alone? Reach out to those in need today. Serve God through caring for others.

PRAYER TARGET:
Believers and non-believers facing loneliness.

PERSONAL PRAYER FOR KNOXVILLE:
Lord, God, I have felt loneliness as have most people. Thank You that I know You. I trust Your promise when You say You will be with me and will never leave me. Help all of us to be aware of people around us who are lonely. If they are Christians, may we remind them of Your promise to be with them and to help them. If they are non-believers, help us share Jesus with them so they, too, may claim God's promises. In Jesus' precious Name I pray. Amen.

WEEK THIRTY FOUR: WEDNESDAY

AUTHOR: DERICK AND EMILY RADCLIFFE
FAMILY STRUCTURE: MARRIED
OCCUPATION: NP AND CASE MANAGER

KINGDOM OF GOD AND HEAVEN

> "Another parable put he forth unto them, saying, the kingdom of heaven is like to a grain of mustard seed, which a man took, and sowed in his field: Which indeed is the least of all seeds: but when it is grown, it is the greatest among herbs, and becometh a tree, so that the birds of the air come and lodge in the branches thereof. Another parable spake he unto them; The kingdom of heaven is like unto leaven, which a woman took, and hid in three measures of meal, till the whole was leavened."
> **Matthew 13:31-33**

Dallas Willard describes the Kingdom of God as "the range of God's effective will… and it is present where what God wants done is done."

We, who believe, must do away with this underlying notion that we are somewhere we aren't supposed to be. We must eliminate the idea that being on earth somehow limits us, and we are just biding our time here until we get to Heaven. To abandon this and realize that God created this world for us is the beginning of the fact that we can have the life of Heaven in us now; and we have immediate access to this life, but only through Christ. I am exactly where I am supposed to be. Believe this and you can begin to let the power of God's Kingdom manifest itself freely to bless us those around us.

Yes, this is a broken world. But it is a broken world that God loves. The Almighty is right now at work caring for and creating new wonderful things for us in this world. Let us join our Creator in this work by throwing off all that hinders and be born again.

This day be born again: Born again to the beauty that is all around the great city of Knoxville and surrounding areas to the recognition of all of God's creatures. This includes us as glorious and excellent things. Be born again to the fact that our preparation for eternity is now in process. Be born again to the fact that God cares about our work and it is immensely important to Him who loves us.

PRAYER TARGET:
People of Knoxville and surrounding areas, born again in a broken world.

PERSONAL PRAYER FOR KNOXVILLE:
Oh Abundant King, Mysterious Gardner, Brilliant Creator, we affirm Your goodness and Your greatness. Not because we can understand it, but we affirm it because we have seen and tasted of it. As for us, we know it is good to be near the Lord. Cement on our hearts the fact that even though we are but brute beasts before Thee with hearts prone to wonder, You are always with us. Your Love is ever before us. Please, Holy Lord, grant us the grace needed to consume more. More of You, of your light, of your breathtaking beauty, of your sustaining truth. Allow us to open our minds to the presence of the eternal in our lives right now, and let us wait no longer to begin to gaze upon the beauty of the You, Lord. Father, tolerate nothing less from us than complete surrender. And so, it is to Him who literally holds the universe in existence that we give all glory, thanks, honor, and praise. Let it be so. Amen and amen.

WEEK THIRTY FOUR: THURSDAY

AUTHOR: SUSANNE HUFF
FAMILY STRUCTURE: HUSBAND AND 2 CHILDREN
OCCUPATION: CHURCH ADMINISTRATION

ONE BRIDGE AT A TIME

> **"Therefore, do not worry about tomorrow, for tomorrow will worry about itself. Each day has enough trouble of its own." Matthew 6:34**

We'll cross that bridge when we get there." My mother used to say that to me in different seasons of my life when I would worry about things of which I had no control. My mother was the strongest women I've ever known. She raised nine kids, was very active in her local church, ran an accounting business from home, rarely got more than four hours of sleep a night, and yet she still always had an unwavering faith and positive outlook on life. She walked out the instruction given by Jesus in Matthew 6:34.

Are you a "glass half empty or glass have full" kind of believer? It can be exhausting having a worry free, positive attitude all the time. Only by taking our eyes off self and putting them on to Jesus can you hope to obtain this, through the power of the Holy Spirit.

What does it gain us to worry about the future, things that are out of our control? Jesus tells us in Matthew not to worry about what we will eat, drink, wear…not to worry about tomorrow. We have enough through Jesus to sustain us today, and tomorrow is a whole new day for Him to help us "cross that bridge."

PRAYER TARGET:
Believers in our city seeking to maintain freedom from despair and worry.

PERSONAL PRAYER FOR KNOXVILLE:

Precious, heavenly Father, who knows all things and desires only the best for His children, help us to give all our worries and fears to You. Help us to be anxious for nothing, and in everything by prayer and petition, with thanksgiving, present our requests to You. We lift our city to You, Father. We find peace in knowing You are in control. Let the peace that passes all understanding, cover Your people in our city and be a beckon, drawing those that are lost to a personal relationship with You. Let them see something so different and desirable in Your children that it can be nothing short of Jesus Christ. Amen.

WEEK THIRTY FOUR: FRIDAY

AUTHOR: ASHLEY DAVIS
FAMILY STRUCTURE: HUSBAND AND BLENDED FAMILY, 2 BOYS, 2 GIRLS AND 1 SON-IN-LAW
OCCUPATION: MEDICAL

USING GOD TO ESTABLISH BLENDED FAMILIES

"Therefore, let us no longer criticize one another. Instead decide never to put a stumbling block or pitfall in your brother's way." Romans 14:13

Through the trial of blending a family, I have used these words as a reminder of my calling. My children are my greatest joy in life. My oldest, did not choose his circumstances, of being from a broken home. As long as he remembers his father and I have been divorced we are okay. With the strain of blending families, there are times when taking the high road can be challenging. However, my goals for my children are to be safe and loved. At the core of this, I want to cultivate the healthiest environment that is positive for the children. I want my children to see a united front between my son's father and me.

Through the struggle of legal battles, when one cannot control the other party, this can become difficult. I must remind myself of this commandment. It keeps me focused on God and His goodness. It reminds me that with each day I have the choice to cultivate this relationship with my son and my step-son. All they deserve is a relationship of pure joy and love with their other parent. To provide that, I must continue to have my son give that call to his dad and encourage that relationship with each passing day.

We are biblically commanded to not criticize one another and not cause unnecessary stress to others. I am using this focus and I have found peace. The peace that only God can provide.

PRAYER TARGET:
Blended families.

PERSONAL PRAYER FOR KNOXVILLE:
Father, I pray that every man or woman in this city will be filled with Your Spirit. If they are married and in blended families, help the parents learn to co-parent. Let families become one. Allow these families to have peace and not use children as pawns in their lives, but see those children as children of God.

Father, I ask that You work with this community's hearts and work towards unity and healing of blended families. May you mend relationships. Help us to allow ourselves and our pride to be put aside. God, help us to create relationships, teach our children the strength of positive communication, and encourage our children to love fully their other parent. Amen.

WEEK THIRTY FIVE: MONDAY

AUTHOR: JASON ZACHARY
FAMILY STRUCTURE: WIFE AND 1 SON
OCCUPATION: STATE REPRESENTATIVE AND BUSINESS OWNER

THE ANCHOR FOR TRIALS

"We have this hope as an anchor for the soul, firm and secure...." Hebrews 6:19

The world we live in today is unlike anything I thought I'd see in my lifetime. Culture has changed so rapidly over the last few years that I can't even imagine what this world will look like when my son is my age. There are times when, as believers, we look at the storm around us culturally or personally, and we lose focus on where our hope should rest.

One of the many blessings of walking with Christ is that we know our hope is in Him. The hope is not in any politician, thankfully, our family, business or even our church community. Our hope is in Christ! As Hebrews 6:19 tells us, *"He is an anchor for our soul. He holds firm and secure!"* When life rages around you and the wind lifts you off the ground, claim the promises of His word and remember that He is your anchor, holding you firm and secure, no matter how large the storm, how high the waves, or how strong the wind.

A faith in Christ guarantees the hope for your soul and He will not let go! So, not matter what happens in culture, relationships or the economy, rely on the fact that our anchor is firm and secure when placed in Christ.

PRAYER TARGET:
Those of us walking into, through, or out of a trial.

PERSONAL PRAYER FOR KNOXVILLE:
Lord Jesus, thank You that no matter what happens around us or what the enemy might do to try and deceive, Your word tells us that You are the anchor for our soul. We pray, Lord, that You would remind us that You love us more than we could ever imagine and You will never let go. Even when we pull away, You hold firm and secure. Allow us to recognize those around us who need this encouragement. As we walk in and out of challenges and trials, strengthen our faith and equip us to minister to those who may soon be, or currently going through, the same trial. We love You and place our hope in You. Amen!

WEEK THIRTY FIVE: TUESDAY

AUTHOR: LUCAS HUNTER
FAMILY STRUCTURE: PARENTS
OCCUPATION: STUDENT AND INTERN

TO SHARE YOUR SALVATION IS TO LOVE YOUR NEIGHBOR AS YOURSELF

> "For there is no distinction between Jew and Greek, for the same Lord over all is rich to all who call upon Him. For 'whoever calls on the name of the LORD shall be saved.' How then shall they call on Him in whom they have not believed? And how shall they believe in Him of whom they have not heard? And how shall they hear without a preacher? And how shall they preach unless they are sent? As it is written: 'How beautiful are the feet of those who preach the gospel of peace, Who bring glad tidings of good things!'" Romans 10:12-15

A biblical command to spread the gospel trumps the fleshly desire to be comfortable, content, and happy to sit back and watch many people around us walk the broad path that leads to destruction. See here, that all you've been commanded to do is help your neighbor call upon the one true God, who saves those whom call on His name. Would you help your neighbor call upon Him? You have been sent, you are the one who brings glad tidings.

God is not a respecter of man. He sees no difference between the Jew and the Greek. God sees souls, lost or saved, all sinners. I implore those who know Christ to spread His word, His good news and glorious gospel.

In Matthew 9:36-37, Jesus' desire is that more workers would be sent out. In Romans 10:14-15, Paul's plea is that more would go to tell the good news of Christ. Follow the command, be

349

obedient to the Bible, which tells us to follow the Great Commission and "Go therefore and make disciples of all nations, baptizing them in the name of the Father and of the Son and of the Holy Spirit, teaching them to observe all things I have commanded you; and lo, I am with you always, even to the end of the age." Matt. 28:19-20

PRAYER TARGET:
The unreached people of Knoxville, and those who can reach them

PERSONAL PRAYER FOR KNOXVILLE:
Father, I thank You so much for Your Word, and that is has authority over my life. I pray I would be obedient to the commands You have given me, no matter if it makes me uncomfortable. Father, I pray for the city of Knoxville, for there are many here who do not know Your name and who have not called upon it to receive eternal life. I pray their hearts would be tilled to receive the Gospel. Father, add more workers to the harvest, and send those who know and believe in Knoxville to take Your name to the unreached. I pray our desires would become Your desires, and we would seek to glorify You in Your glorification. I pray Your will would be done on Earth as it is in heaven. I thank You, Jesus, for being the author of our faith. You are with us always, even to the end of the age. I pray we would be emboldened by Your Holy Spirit, and we would seek to spread your name to the ends of the Earth, starting here in Knoxville, Tennessee. I pray these things in the Name of Jesus Christ. Amen.

WEEK THIRTY FIVE: WEDNESDAY

AUTHOR: HEATHER DUNCAN
FAMILY STRUCTURE: HUSBAND AND 3 CHILDREN
OCCUPATION: MIDDLE AND HIGH SCHOOL MUSIC EDUCATOR

A GODLY FUTURE: A DELIGHTFUL INHERITANCE

> **"LORD, you alone are my portion and my cup; you make my lot secure. The boundary lines have fallen for me in pleasant places; surely I have a delightful inheritance." Psalm 16:5-6**

I discovered this verse during college, at a time when I was having difficulty waiting for my future to unfold. Like so many young people, I was worried about my path: would I meet "the one;" would I get into grad school; or would I travel to another country? Fast forward twenty-five years, and times haven't changed much. There are still things I am longing and waiting for, and I still wonder not only about my future, but my children's futures.

The thing that I've learned, however, is not that God doesn't want us to pray about these things, or have faith for the impossible; but He wants us to know that our futures are "secure" in Him. This verse tells me two things: First, I have a promise of relationship with Him. He is my "portion and cup," and second, I can trust Him with the direction my path takes, and the "boundary lines" I'm given.

So, regardless of whether I am facing hardship or an uncertain future, I need not fear. I have the assurance of His presence, and since I am a child of Yahweh, I'm promised a "delightful inheritance."

PRAYER TARGET:
The immigrants and refugees in this city and the future they will have.

PERSONAL PRAYER FOR KNOXVILLE:
Father, I pray that the immigrants, who are seeking a new home in Knoxville, would know that they are not here by accident. May they know that there is One who has called them here for a purpose greater than education, opportunity, or physical freedom. Lord, please surround them with people who can love on them and meet their physical as well as spiritual and emotional needs. I ask that the spiritual and emotional chains that bind them be broken, and the freedom that only comes through faith in Christ and the Spirit's presence would envelop them. Lord, give them an inheritance in this city, so they can stand side-by-side with us, clothed in dignity and honor. Father, give them a spiritual inheritance as well - a spiritual inheritance that can never be taken away from them because it comes from You. Amen.

WEEK THIRTY FIVE: THURSDAY

AUTHOR: ANITA VOORHEES
FAMILY STRUCTURE: SINGLE
OCCUPATION: STUDENT

IDOLS OF THE HEART

"Come, all you who are thirsty, come to the waters; and you who have no money, come, buy and eat! Come, buy wine and milk without money and without cost. Why spend money on what is not bread, and your labor on what does not satisfy? Listen, listen to me, and eat what is good, and you will delight in the richest of fare."
Isaiah 55:1-2

A pagan is a person who does not worship God. That includes a person who worships idols. We often think of idols as little gold statues, but idols come in all different shapes and sizes. It is a sin to value an idol above the Lord. What do you value more than the Lord? What gives you more satisfaction that the Lord? If it is your friendships, relationships, school, hobbies, and other interesting items that you turn to for satisfaction, then you are worshipping an idol of your own making. Anything that keeps your eyes steadily turned away from Jesus can be an idol.

The Lord makes it clear in the Bible. He is ultimately the only One who can satisfy and quench our thirst, not an idol. He beckons all who are thirsty to come to Him because He is the wellspring of life. Isaiah 44:9 states, *"All who make idols are nothing, and the things they treasure are worthless. Those who would speak up for them are blind; they are ignorant to their own shame."* God makes it clear that He is a jealous God who desires our attention. Are you putting anything before God today? If so, confess your idols and ask Him to prune you and strike down any idol in your heart. Change. Serve the One True God!

PRAYER TARGET:
Those who have idols in their lives.

PERSONAL PRAYER FOR KNOXVILLE:
Father, search us and reveal to us the idols in our lives. Strike down those idols so that we may find total satisfaction in You. Soften our hearts to the true gospel. Father, we desire communion with You alone, and we pray now that the people in this city will always make You first in their lives. Amen.

WEEK THIRTY FIVE: FRIDAY

AUTHOR: ROBBY MARTIN
FAMILY STRUCTURE: MARRIED WITH 8 CHILDREN AND STEPCHILDREN
OCCUPATION: COMMERCIALIZATION MANAGER

WILL WE STAND?

> "...they all held the torches in their left hands, the trumpets in their right, and shouted, 'A sword for the Lord and for Gideon!' Every man stood in his place around the camp, and the whole enemy army ran away yelling. While Gideon's men were blowing their trumpets, the Lord made the enemy troops attack each other with their swords."
> **Judges 7:20-22**

After all of his testing, all of his denying that he was the one, Gideon still found himself struggling to fully believe what God was about to do. So, after God sent Gideon on a spying mission to the enemy camp, he came back worshipping the Lord for the discussion he was allowed to overhear.

Finally, he set his men in place to carry out a pot-breaking, horn-blowing calamity upon the enemy. The plan was crazy! And yet, because it was God's plan, it worked so well that the enemy began destroying themselves! But, even with all God had done, the author of Judges was inspired to include the phrase, *"Every man stood in his place..."*

How can we expect that any less is called of us? Yes, God is in control. Yes, His will is going to be seen and carried out. And, no, God does not need us to be in place to see this happen! But, I wonder... What if we each were to stand where God has put us? What if we were to be in place where He intends for us to be? Will you find your place, and then, stand with us?

PRAYER TARGET:
Every believer in our city that will stand for God.

PERSONAL PRAYER FOR KNOXVILLE:
Oh, Lord, and maker of us all, may we come to fully understand that you have a place for each of us to stand. Some may stand in a place of encouragement in uncertain times in their church. Some may stand in places where mercy is needed to ease the pain or burden due to illness and physical death. But, Lord, You have put within each and every one of us, a place in which we are to stand. May we purposely arrange our lives to allow Your place for us to take a high priority. And, having prepared in such a way, may we stand for the Kingdom, stand for our City, stand for The Church, and stand for our families! May Your victory, no matter how crazy the plan may seem, be unbelievably complete and whole! We look forward to all you will do, as we simply stand in our place! In Jesus' precious Name we pray this. Amen!

AUTHOR: THERESE ANNE MATTHEWS
FAMILY STRUCTURE: HUSBAND, 6 CHILDREN, 4 SONS-IN-LAW, AND 12 GRANDCHILDREN
OCCUPATION: HOMEMAKER

JUST TRUST AND OBEY

> **"My son, do not forget My teaching, but keep My commands in your heart ... Let love and faithfulness never leave you; bind them around your neck, write them on the tablet of your heart ... Trust in the Lord with all your heart and lean not on your own understanding; in all your ways acknowledge Him, and He will make your paths straight."**
> **Proverbs 3:1,3, 5-6**

One thing that amazes me when I read Scripture is the constant cycle -- sin, repentance, God's forgiveness and blessing, then sin, ... Why don't they "get it" I ask myself? Wandering in the wilderness, how do Almighty God's chosen people forget everything He has done for them? Why do they question His plan, protection, and provision and not trust Him? Why do they choose to disobey Him?

And then I think of myself ... why don't I "get it?" How can I ever question God's perfect love and provision for my life and choose to lock myself in a prison of fear, insecurity, pride, or any sin?

God's Word makes it very clear. That clarity has distilled my walk with Him into two simple directives: Trust and Obey. In completely trusting in Him and His promises – knowing from the core of my being that His Words are true – I am liberated to simply obey Him. So, my challenge is to obey: to love an adversary when I've been wounded by them; to honor a parent though behavior is dishonorable; to follow my husband's lead, even when I'd rather not; and to act upon the prompting of the

Holy Spirit, though I have no clue where He is leading. When I am able to do that in any circumstance – just trust and obey – I experience profound joy and blessings.

PRAYER TARGET:
Families seeking to trust and obey our Lord.

PERSONAL PRAYER FOR KNOXVILLE:
Father, I pray that every person and family in this city know how much they are loved and treasured by God. You created us in Your image, desiring to have a perfect relationship with us, and when sin entered our world, You redeemed us so that we can have eternal life with You. How I pray for each of us to bask in that Truth! We are loved. We are treasured. Dear God, You sent Your Son to die so that we can be His heirs in His kingdom. There is nothing we can or cannot do to change that.

I pray this truth is so real that each of us can surrender ourselves to His Sovereignty; to die to ourselves so He can live through us. May we trust and obey Him so that our lives on this earth will be filled with His abundant love, peace and joy. Amen.

WEEK THIRTY SIX: TUESDAY

AUTHOR: SANDY EDDINS
FAMILY STRUCTURE: HUSBAND, 2 MARRIED CHILDREN, AND
5 GRANDCHILDREN
OCCUPATION: RETIRED TEACHER

MY HELP COMES FROM THE LORD

"I will lift up my eyes to the hills, from where does my help come? My help comes from the LORD, who made heaven and earth. He will not let my foot be moved; He who keeps me will not slumber. The LORD is my keeper, He gives me shade, the sun will not strike me, nor will the moon by night. The LORD will keep me from evil, and preserve my soul. The Lord will protect me forever, and even forevermore." Psalm 121

When I learned to read this Psalm, it became mine. I was bedridden for two years, and I memorized it while I was unable to go to school. My best friend brought my school work to my home each day, and as the impact of the Psalmist's words came to me more and more, I realized that I could pray this Psalm, not only for me, but for others. It still is what I pray for myself, family, and friends, and the many homeless people in his city.

Our Keeper is on a throne looking down on each of us, yet He is at our side to shield us from harm. Does this mean that we will never find ourselves in difficulty or danger, or that we will never feel physical or emotional pain? No. Many in our city experience each of these, especially the homeless and street people. Through the trials of life, we need not fear life or death, today or tomorrow, or time or eternity. We are in His loving care. We should never trust a lesser power than God Himself. Nothing deters or diverts Him. We are safe and we never outgrow our need for God's untiring watch over our lives.

PRAYER TARGET:
Families, friends, of the homeless of Knoxville and surrounding areas.

PERSONAL PRAYER FOR KNOXVILLE:
Father, may my city be protected by You, Lord, who does not slumber. You are the Keeper of all who live here. Many do not know You and many in this city do not have safe places to sleep or good food to eat. Help us lift them to You daily. I pray for those who place their lives in unsafe places and for those that eat and drink things they think will bring them joy. Thank You for the churches and organizations who love them, bring them in for fellowship and warmth, feed them, and show them the love of Christ. Help each person who receives that gift of local love to feel the true eternal joy that will come from knowing You personally and worshipping You. Amen.

WEEK THIRTY SIX: WEDNESDAY

AUTHOR: EMILY HALL
FAMILY STRUCTURE: HUSBAND AND 3 YOUNG CHILDREN
OCCUPATION: HOMEMAKER AND HOMESCHOOLING MOM

LOVING OUR NEIGHBORS

> **"How beautiful on the mountains are the feet of those who bring good news, who proclaim peace, who bring good tidings, who proclaim salvation, who say to Zion, 'Your God reigns!'" Isaiah 52:7**

Do you know your neighbors? Do you pray for them? Do you pray for opportunities to know them and to speak the good news and peace to them? Take a few moments to think of those who live closest in proximity to you. Who are they? What do you know about them? How can you love and serve them today or in the near future? If it is true that within all of us is a great thirst for the living waters that only God can provide (John 7:37-38), are we as believers in relationships with our neighbors in such a way that we can point them to the One for whom they thirst?

We live in an age of great distraction, busyness, travel, independence, and isolation. Preaching to strangers only earns us titles of intolerance and judgment. How can we still obey God's greatest commands to love Him and love our neighbors as ourselves? What would it look like to cross the divides that separate us from those who live around us? He who knows every hair on our heads, knows where we live and who lives beside us. Call out to Him for wisdom and courage to build relationships with those who do not know and believe the One we call Lord and Savior. He will not fail to open doors and pave ways for His salvation to reach to the end of the earth, and to the ends of our streets.

PRAYER TARGET:
Our neighbors of us all, near and far.

PERSONAL PRAYER FOR KNOXVILLE:
O God, empower and embolden your children to reach out
to their neighbors with words and actions that point to Your
great love. Build Your church here in Knoxville through the
relationships of those who live next door. Help us to remember
our neighbors who do not know You in our prayers and give
us opportunities to reveal who You truly are to them. Not the
picture they may see on TV or Facebook, but the real You who
lives by Your Spirit in the hearts of believers. Help us to love our
neighbors as ourselves, and give us courage to speak into the
windows You give us, words of life, hope, and peace. Amen.

WEEK THIRTY SIX: THURSDAY

AUTHOR: BOB SCHMID
FAMILY STRUCTURE: WIFE
OCCUPATION: BUSINESS OWNER AND CENTER PRAYER MINISTRY

CHERISH

> **"The Kingdom of Heaven is like a treasure hidden in a field. When a man found it, He hid it again, and then is his joy went and sold all that he had and bought that field."**
> **Matthew 13:44**

Home alone, quiet, still, on a Sunday morning (thanks, Saturday church) I begin doing chores around my greatly neglected house. I feel the presence of the Father really close to me. This is not uncommon. It is often in these moments that we have had some our greatest conversations, when He used what I am doing to teach me, chasten me, guide me. Often, they are simple questions that cut to the heart of a matter.

Today is not different. In my Spirit He asks, *"What do you cherish?"* Quickly I begin to compile a list: my home, these moments, my wife and child, my city, and friends. But then I asked back, *"What does it mean to cherish?"* Immediately today's scripture came to mind. I think it cuts to the heart of what to cherish is all about: those things in our lives that we would with joy sell all that we have to obtain. Gently, lovingly, with no condemnation He pushes me further into His Truth as He leaves me contemplating His final words. He says, *"Take stock of what you cherish."*

The realization that things we cherish require time and effort to maintain give plenty of room for contemplation. East Tennessee, what do you cherish today? Who do you cherish? Why do you cherish each?

PRAYER TARGET:

People learning how to cherish what is important .

PERSONAL PRAYER FOR KNOXVILLE:

: Father, I am guilty of forgetting how to cherish well. Those things on my list that I say that I cherish are not supported by my actions. That includes my home, my relationship with You , my family relationships, my health, and on and on. I pray that this moment, Lord, that You would create the space and time for every reader today to physically create a list of the things they cherish. Give them time and the know-how to evaluate how they are doing with each item on their list. I pray for new strategies to give the things we cherish the priority they deserve. Father, we are so blessed to live in the East Tennessee area. I pray that our community and region will be listed among those things that we cherish, that we will unite our prayers for our city, and that each of us will cry out for a mighty move of Your hand over our region.

In Christ's Holy Name I pray. Amen

WEEK THIRTY SIX: FRIDAY

AUTHOR: RUTH GEIGER
FAMILY STRUCTURE: HUSBAND, 2 SONS AND DAUGHTERS-IN-LOVE, AND 5 GRANDCHILDREN
OCCUPATION: WOMEN'S BIBLE STUDY LAY LEADER

GOD REMEMBERS YOU!

> **"But God remembered Noah and all the beasts and all the cattle that were with him in the ark; and God caused a wind to pass over the earth, and the water subsided." Genesis 8:1**

Has someone close to you seemingly forgotten you? Not so with our God! He remembers you!

In the midst of wickedness and judgment, God's grace burst forth to Noah! God established a covenant with him and gave him specific instructions on how to build the ark and how to fill it. And Noah did all that God said!

Do you think that possibly in all those years while building the ark that Noah sensed rejection, loneliness, fear, despondency, weariness, and thought, "God, have You forgotten me?"

But God remembered Noah . . . the word "remembered" means "paying attention to, to print upon the memory." It represents the activity of God on behalf of those He remembers. His remembrance leads to action on behalf of that person's welfare.

Note the second part of Gen. 8:1 – God caused . . . winds and waves are under God's control. God can use anything, including wind and water, to do His bidding and accomplish His purposes. *Do loneliness, fear, and uncertainty leave you feeling forgotten? Dear struggling saint, God can dry them up.*

God's remembrance of Noah brought an end to the flood, deliverance to Noah and his family, and a new creation. Child of God, let those words, "God remembered" wash over you and trust Him to take action on your behalf. God remembers you!

PRAYER TARGET:
Those who see themselves as forgotten by God and others.

PERSONAL PRAYER FOR KNOXVILLE:
LORD God, I ask You to declare "I remember you!" to those who believe they are forgotten. Please fill their hearts and minds continually with the Truth that Your remembrance of them leads to action on their behalf. By Your grace, give each one the faith to look expectantly for Your activity in the wow moments and also in the mundane moments of daily living. All for Your glory, LORD, and in the powerful name of Jesus Christ. Amen.

WEEK THIRTY SEVEN: MONDAY

AUTHOR: KAY STOKELY
FAMILY STRUCTURE: HUSBAND, 4 CHILDREN, AND 13 GRANDCHILDREN
OCCUPATION: HOUSEWIFE

ONLY GOD CAN SATISFY THE LONGING HE HAS PLACED IN OUR HEARTS

"Trust in the Lord with all your heart and lean not unto your own understanding." Proverbs 3:6

I was blessed to have been born into a loving, supportive family. We went to church when the doors were open. There was very little money to spare. I never went hungry but I had a roof over my head and hand-me-down clothes from my cousins. I worked my way through college where I met my future husband. My husband's background was totally different from mine. It was comfortable and prepared him for a life as a business man. His career as a businessman has provided our family a comfortable lifestyle. We had four healthy children, cars, clothes, and a nice home. We often traveled. Some would say we had the perfect life, but I knew something wasn't right with me. Though I attended church, I was spiritually dead. God hadn't moved away from me, but I had moved away from Him.

One day, a friend asked me to Bible Study Fellowship. I filled out a card that asked why I wanted to attend, and I answered honestly, "Because I think I've lost my faith." During that year of study, the Holy Spirit removed the veil from my eyes that had clouded my understanding of the Word of God. The Gospel for the first time made sense to me. I asked Jesus to come into my heart and my life.

A comfortable life does not give a person joy and contentment…only God can do that! Jesus fulfills us and prepares us to do His work.

PRAYER TARGET:
All who feel dissatisfied with their lives.

PERSONAL PRAYER FOR KNOXVILLE:
Father God, let us recognize and confess our need for You. When we feel empty, we look around to fill ourselves with something… anything! Our choices are usually wrong and often hurtful to us and others. Prompt us to desire You and accept no substitutes. Give us a hunger for You. And, then Lord, fill us with your Holy Spirit. In the name of your Son, Jesus, our Savior, Amen.

WEEK THIRTY SEVEN: TUESDAY

AUTHOR: CAROL JORDAN
FAMILY STRUCTURE: HUSBAND AND 3 CHILDREN
OCCUPATION: CAMPUS MINISTRY

GROWING STRONGER BY NOT WAVERING IN OUR FAITH IN GOD

> "Yet, with respect to the promise of God, he (Abraham) did not waver in unbelief but grew strong in faith, giving glory to God, and being fully assured that what God had promised, He was able also to perform. Therefore, it was also credited to him as righteousness. Now not for his sake only was it written that it was credited to him, but for our sake also, to whom it will be credited, as those who believe in Him who raised Jesus our Lord from the dead, He who was delivered over because of our transgressions, and was raised because of our justification." Romans 4:20-25

Oh friend, do you long to bring glory to God and point others to Him? Abraham accomplished giving glory to God by taking God at His Word and not wavering in unbelief. Abraham knew that God had promised him that the Savior of the world would come through his descendants. He was able to trust God even as he and his wife grew older and eventually passed the natural ability to have a child. Because Abraham kept his focus on God and His ability and off his ability (inability), the Bible teaches that he grew strong in his faith and gave great glory to God.

Let's think about this truth. As it became impossible in Abraham's body for the promise of God to be fulfilled, Abraham grew in his belief that God would accomplish His promise of a child. Abraham moved his trust from any ability in himself to sole trust in God and His ability.

As believers let's do the same. Let us allow God's indwelling Spirit to reveal Himself and His promises, and let us not waver in our faith in Him

PRAYER TARGET:
College students growing stronger and not wavering in faith.

PERSONAL PRAYER FOR KNOXVILLE:
Heavenly Father, I come to Your throne of grace and ask for You to draw the college students of Knoxville to Yourself. I ask for the students who do not have a personal relationship with You to meet You, their trustworthy Savior. For students who are Your children, I ask that they walk intimately with You day by day, fully surrendered to You and Your plan for them, empowered by Your Holy Spirit, hungry for Your Word, and living lives of purity that are honoring to You. Ground them in their identity in You and show them that in You alone is joy, hope, peace, freedom and purpose. Free them from the lure and traps of this world and prepare them for a lifetime of service to You. And… may they be unwavering in their faith in You. Amen.

WEEK THIRTY SEVEN: WEDNESDAY

AUTHOR: CHRIS BLUE
FAMILY STRUCTURE: WIFE
OCCUPATION: MUSICIAN AND LOVER OF PEOPLE

LOVE THY NEIGHBORS

> **"There is one body, but it has many parts. But all its many parts make up one body. It is the same with Christ."**
> **1 Corinthians 12:12**

In our society, it's hard to stomach the man next to you having more than you. We want ours, yours, theirs, and everybody's. We have been victims to the notion that having more things than my brother establishes me as one greater than my brother, when the reality of that is not the case. *Love thy neighbor as thyself* means simply what I have is what you have. Where you lack, I lack because although we make-up of distinct parts we are all one body!! That's why I love John 3:16. The verse shows us the epitome of God's love. Love is about consistency and commitment These two words are the core words of doing and saying what you we going to do. The world is missing many people today that do and take action on what they say they are going to do!

God's love says, *"I believe in you!"* It forgives before we commit. It bares patience before habitualness. I'm grateful that God loves me the way that he does.

Before I could ever fall or even make my first mistake, not only did He already know what I would do but He already had decided to stay with me through all endeavors.

God's love is perfect and boundless.

PRAYER TARGET:

All people to realize we are all neighbors.

PERSONAL PRAYER FOR KNOXVILLE:

God, thank You for loving all of mankind. Thank You for Your sacrifice to us that we might follow the example You set for us in our lives. Father, let us consider Your example to love so much that we consider our neighbors in all we do. Help us to be selfless and to simply care for every person as we do for ourselves. Father, I pray that You will touch the hearts of every person that is reading this right now. Our world is in so much trouble with a lot of violence, but Your love can touch all and change the violence to love. I pray for every person and family, of any race, ethnicity, belief, or creed!! Let each love You. God, I thank you for being the "All" that life needs; and that's love!! Amen.

WEEK THIRTY SEVEN: THURSDAY

AUTHOR: BRENDA FOLZ
FAMILY STRUCTURE: HUSBAND
OCCUPATION: VOLUNTEER BIBLE STUDY LEADER

TUNING IN TO GOD'S LOVE AND LEADERSHIP

"Let the morning bring me word of Your unfailing love for I put my trust in You. Show me the way I should go for to You I lift up my soul." Psalm 143:8

One early morning while visiting in Jerusalem, I was desperate to hear the Lord's voice and feel His presence. All I could hear was traffic, vendors shouting, camels braying and others talking. As disappointment filled my heart, I heard that still, small voice saying, "I am here just listen." Over the years, the LORD has taught me to tune my ears and heart to a word from Him.

God loves with an unconditional love that cannot be earned nor is it deserved. Trust in Him and His faithfulness and He will delight and satisfy with the promise of His unfailing love.

Listen for that still, quiet voice over the noise of this world.

Seek Him daily and early and He will direct your day.

Surrender to His will and way no matter the trials or circumstances and you will find peace and wellness in your soul.

PRAYER TARGET:
Brothers and sisters across Knoville and surrounding areas in Christ learning to seek His Love.

PERSONAL PRAYER FOR KNOXVILLE:

Father, I pray for the Lord's love to fill every brother and sister in this city. May we tune our ears and hearts to hear His voice and may He guide and direct our way. As we surrender to Him, may we go where He tells us to go, do what He tells us to do, and say what He tells us to say. Lord Jesus, please quiet our hearts and minds to hear Your voice, to seek Your will, and follow Your lead in this noisy, demanding world. Amen

AUTHOR: RILEY LOVINGOOD
FAMILY STRUCTURE: SINGLE
OCCUPATION: COLLEGE FOOTBALL PLAYER

LIVING WITH A VICTORIOUS MINDSET

> "Who then will condemn us? No one—for Christ Jesus died for us and was raised to life for us, and he is sitting in the place of honor at God's right hand, pleading for us. Can anything ever separate us from Christ's love? Does it mean he no longer loves us if we have trouble or calamity, or are persecuted, or hungry, or destitute, or in danger, or threatened with death? As the Scriptures say, 'For your sake we are killed every day; we are being slaughtered like sheep.' No, despite all these things, overwhelming victory is ours through Christ, who loved us. And I am convinced that nothing can ever separate us from God's love. Neither death nor life, neither angels nor demons, neither our fears for today nor our worries about tomorrow—not even the powers of hell can separate us from God's love. No power in the sky above or in the earth below—indeed, nothing in all creation will ever be able to separate us from the love of God that is revealed in Christ Jesus our Lord."
> **Romans 8:34-39**

So often in this world we see people putting Christianity and Christians down. As Christians, many times we feel defeated because of this. We need to change our mindset on how we view our everyday life as believers. God did not make us to be timid and afraid, but bold and courageous in our efforts to show his love in everyday life.

In this section of Romans 8, we can actually see that we have Jesus sitting on the throne fighting in our behalf. Because He has already won the war in the end, then why should we act so defeated and scared about how we go about being a Christian?

Living with a victorious mindset everyday will change how you see everything in your day, and the people around you will easily notice something different about you. If we just take chances that we usually wouldn't have, and get outside of our comfort zone, then we will realize that we will be used in a mightier way! I have been blessed to play college football right now and in that there have been a lot of struggles with being in this role, but ever since the Lord has taught me this, my life has changed on how I think about every situation or person with which I am faced.

PRAYER TARGET:
Everyone who wants to be used by Christ.

PERSONAL PRAYER FOR KNOXVILLE:
Father, I pray for this city, that every person will be able to see the love of Christ because it is absolutely life changing. I pray that everyone will be able to have the crazy love that can heal, fix, and save anything or anyone. Father, bring everyone together as one body of Christ and help us to live boldly. With Your help and our submission our whole city can be blown away by the power of Christ! So, my prayer is that every Christian's heart in this city will be broken for the people they know that do know Christ yet. Help us lead them to You. I pray boldly that we let You use us in the mighty way that only You can do! Amen.

WEEK THIRTY EIGHT: MONDAY

AUTHOR: ANA DYKES
FAMILY STRUCTURE: HUSBAND AND 3 CHILDREN
OCCUPATION: SCHOOL CROSSING GUARD

WITH GOD ALL THINGS ARE POSSIBLE

"...... Let the weak, say I am strong!" Joel 3:10b

I was born in Colombia, South America, the youngest of three girls. Times were tough and it was a struggle for my parents to feed us. My father left us to go to Panama to find work. During this time, my mother was sponsored to become a nanny for an American family in the U.S. Unfortunately, while left in my father's care we were emotionally, physically, and sexually abused. A few years later my mother brought my sisters and me to live with her in America.

When I was in third grade the specialist at my school told my mother that I had a learning disability and that they were going to send me to a special school. While attending this special school I learned many of the children had severe emotional and physical problems. After three months, I was removed and placed back into public school. Through my early difficulties in life I learned how to pray. I prayed when I went to school and every time something happened to me. As young as I was I still felt a need to talk to God. He was my friend and my helper in times of need!

Do you ever feel unworthy? Do you have anxiety and fear? I did. I felt all those things in my life. I felt so much insecurity that it just consumed me. I felt hopeless. I knew about God but I didn't grasp how much Jesus loved me. Jesus says, *"Come to me all of you who are weary and burdened, and I will give you rest"* (Mathew 11:28).

So, you see, we don't have to continue living with your pain and insecurity. Jesus wants to take it from us and give us a new life. Jesus said, *"Here I am! I stand at the door and knock. If anyone hears my voice and opens the door, I will come in and eat with that person, and they with me"* (Revelation 3:20). Sharing a meal with the one who loves me so much that he died for me is amazing! The most incredible thing is that we all can share a meal with Jesus daily. Let Him be your dinner date!

PRAYER TARGET:
People who feel weary and burdened.

PERSONAL PRAYER FOR KNOXVILLE:
Father, today we lift to You the orphans, the widows, the children, the poor, and the meek. We ask You, Father God, for mercy and deliverance. We pray that we will find hope in Jesus and salvation for lost souls. Lord Jesus, take away the shackles of being a victim and replace it with a crown of victory. Take away any pain that has been carried throughout the years and replace it with Your love. Let the weak say I am strong because of what the Lord has done for us. In Jesus' Name, I pray. Amen.

WEEK THIRTY EIGHT: TUESDAY

AUTHOR: CARMEISHA ARNOLD
FAMILY STRUCTURE: HUSBAND AND 4 CHILDREN
OCCUPATION: MARRIAGE AND FAMILY COUNSELING, MOTIVATOR

WITH EVERY BREATH

"Sustain me according to Your word, that I may live; And do not let me be ashamed of my hope." Psalm 119:116

A few years ago, as I lay in a hospital bed, the doctor shared the revelation that I was experiencing a Pulmonary Embolism - a blood clot in my lung. As each little breath became more difficult to grasp because of the pain, I started to appreciate the exhale. At that point though, I didn't calculate the cost - financially, spiritually, physically, or mentally. Daily I'd have to practice taking long deep breaths to help increase my blood's oxygen levels. I couldn't do everything the same or as quickly as before...and for me, it was discouraging.

Over the course of time, I realize that what I gained outweighed the costs. Through this, I've learned to trust, depend, and expect God to be present in difficult situations.

As I look at our nation and the discomfort we're experiencing, I take notice of the things in life that shock me and leave me gasping for comforting words. I acknowledge the pain that so many around me are experiencing, and I am reminded, once again, of a God who will sustain.

PRAYER TARGET:
Leaders in the city experiencing discomfort, that they will be sustained.

PERSONAL PRAYER FOR KNOXVILLE:

Heavenly Father, I ask that You breathe Your breath of love on the city of Knoxville. My prayer is that you would cause every born-again believer to rise and declare You to be the only true and living God. Help each of us to exhale hate and inhale love; exhale misunderstanding and inhale compassion; and exhale division and inhale comm'unity'. I pray that we might learn to extend grace as much as we've received it. Where there is unrest within us: our homes, our communities, our nation… Give us peace. Remind us, God, that this too shall pass and that we will recover! Help us to trust You again to heal our dis-ease, as You strengthen our dependence on You. Rid us of the things that prevent us from having unobstructed communication with You. Lead us, for YOU are our hope! It is so and so it is, in Jesus' Name, Amen.

WEEK THIRTY EIGHT: WEDNESDAY

AUTHOR: JIMMY HARPER
FAMILY STRUCTURE: WIFE, 2 MARRIED CHILDREN, AND 1 GRANDCHILD
OCCUPATION: CAMPUS PASTOR AND FACULTY MEMBER

FINDING THE SECRET PLACE

> **"He who dwells in the secret place of the Most High shall abide under the shadow of the Almighty. I will say of the Lord, He is my refuge and my fortress; My God in Him will I trust." Psalm 91:1-2**

For Christ followers to be who we are supposed to be and for the church to be what it's supposed to be, God's people must learn to know Him in a deep, intimate, powerful way. In Psalm 91, two words really jump out and give insight into what our relationship needs to be with God: those words are secret and shadow. These words give us insight into prayer.

When we enter the secret place, it is not something about which we tell others It is a deeply spiritual experience. It is a place we meet with God. It creates in us a desire to move our relationship with God to a deeper level. It is a place we go to regularly.

We pray in the shadow. We maintain a closeness in proximity to God. We follow Him securely to allow nothing to separate us from His presence, His power or His anointing. In prayer, we allow God to sanctify us, or set us apart for His work and His service. We spend with God to cause us to see what He sees, say what He says, do what He does and be The People of God He wants us to be.

When we draw close to God through prayer, we will begin to understand what it means to abide, rest or lodge in His presence. Let us daily put aside time to spend with our Savior.

PRAYER TARGET:
Understanding the comfort of the secret place of the Lord.

PERSONAL PRAYER FOR KNOXVILLE:
God, life is sometimes difficult and troublesome, but You are the abundant life we need to survive and thrive in a sometimes crazy, mixed up world. Help us to learn to spend quality time with You! We need to develop intimacy with You to learn more about Your ways. We need to follow You closely enough to stay focused on Your will and Your plan for our lives. Give us depth in our relationship with You, Almighty God! Allow us to trust in Your ways, Your thoughts, Your design and not our own. Help us give ourselves to You afresh and anew every day as we commune with You. Teach us Your ways, oh Lord, and consecrate our hearts to You. Amen.

WEEK THIRTY EIGHT: THURSDAY

AUTHOR: ASHLEY OSAKUE
FAMILY STRUCTURE: HUSBAND AND 1 DAUGHTER
OCCUPATION: MINISTER'S WIFE AND STAY AT HOME MOM

SLEEPLESS

"Take my yoke upon you and learn from me, for I am gentle and humble in heart, and you will find rest for your souls."
Matthew 11:29

My husband and I recently welcomed our precious baby girl, Autumn, into the world. Autumn's arrival has changed everything. She has added to our joy in ways unimaginable. Prior to and during pregnancy I was always on the go. A dinner here, a lunch there, and just being a preacher's wife and working in the Ministry kept me on the move. However, once I had Autumn everyone said, "You must rest," and "Give your body the chance to heal," or "Sleep when the baby sleeps." After these suggestions I was thinking, "Okay. Let me try each of these."

Neither worked for me! Sleep seemed impossible. My mind and body did not understand what was happening. It took several weeks of adjusting, wise counsel, support from my husband and family, and much prayer and meditation on the Word for me to close my eyes without waking up in a chaotic state. What was the problem? Yes, I know hormones played a huge role, but what else had my heart and mind racing? Fear! Fear of the unknown. Fear of inadequacy. Fear of failing as a mother. Fear of change. Fear was crippling me. It caused me to see life in an obscured way. 2 Timothy 1:7 tells us, "God hasn't given us the spirit of fear, but He's given power, love, and a sound mind." God also tells us, "Do not be anxious about anything, but in everything by prayer and supplication with thanksgiving let your requests be made known to God. And the peace of God, which surpasses all understanding, will guard your hearts and your minds in Christ

Jesus" (Philippians 4:6-7)

PRAYER TARGET:
Those in need of rest.

PERSONAL PRAYER FOR KNOXVILLE:
Father, I pray for everyone who is battling fear. Lord, break the power of fear in their lives. Let them walk in Your truth. Give them a knowing that You are with them and will never leave. Give them wisdom to cast their cares on You. I pray that You will help them to rise above fear and find rest in You.
In Jesus name. Amen.

WEEK THIRTY EIGHT: FRIDAY

AUTHOR: DAVID CRUTCHLEY
FAMILY STRUCTURE: WIFE AND 4 CHILDREN
OCCUPATION: CHAIR OF RELIGION

WHAT DO YOU WANT ME TO DO FOR YOU?

"And as He was leaving Jericho with His disciples and a large crowd, a blind beggar named Bartimaeus, the son of Timaeus, was sitting by the road. When he heard that it was Jesus the Nazarene, he began to cry out and say, 'Jesus, Son of David, have mercy on me!' Throwing aside his cloak he jumped us and came to Jesus. And answering him, Jesus said, 'What do you want Me to do for you?' And the blind man said to Him, 'Rabboni, I want to regain my sight!' And Jesus said to him, 'Go, your faith has made you well.'" Mark 10:46-47, 51-52

The Bartimaeus story in the Gospel of Mark pivots around the theme of blindness. Jesus is at the sunset of his life on his way to Jerusalem and the cross. He is on the outskirts of the city of Jericho when he hears a disruptive cry, "Jesus, Son of David have mercy on me."

Bartimaeus is the author of the cry. He is a victim of a common disease in that day, blindness. Jesus reacts to the cry for help -- He stops. Jesus stood still. The destiny of the beggar hinges on Jesus stopping.

Jesus summons the beggar and asks Bartimaeus a single, open-ended question, "What do you want me to do for you." This is not an idle question. Jesus gives the beggar the opportunity to define the substance of his faith. The beggar responds to the question "Rabonni, I want to regain my sight." Jesus answers the beggar with the assurance, "Go your faith has made you well."

Out of the simple vignette and cameo we hear Jesus' haunting existential question that confronts each one of us on this short journey called life, "What do you want me to do for you?"

PRAYER TARGET:
Learning to ask Him what is needed.

PERSONAL PRAYER FOR KNOXVILLE:
Lord, make us restless for You as a city and its people. Help us as we set sail on the sea of life to examine the manifest we carry and the motives that drive our sails. Guard us from the acids of modernity and worship at the temple of modern idols. Give us the will to travel with honor, compassion, and kindness for others. Awaken us to the offer of serving others and touching the lives of our city with Your fingerprints of mercy, love, and grace. Help us to stop and hear people's questions. Remind us today of life's fundamental question, "What do you want Me to do for you?"

WEEK THIRTY NINE: MONDAY

AUTHOR: NIRSSA C. DEARINGER
FAMILY STRUCTURE: HUSBAND AND 2 GIRLS
OCCUPATION: CUSTOMER SERVICE REPRESENTATIVE

BE STRONG IN THE LORD AND HIS MIGHTY EVERLASTING POWER

> "Finally, my brethren, be strong in the Lord and in the power of his might. Put on the whole armor of God, that ye may be able to stand against the wiles of the devil. For we wrestle not against flesh or blood, but against principalities, against powers, against rulers of the darkness of this world, against spiritual wickedness in high places." Ephesians 6:10-12

Because of his Mercy and his Grace, we continue to be forgiven. The Lord loved us All enough to die on the cross for our inequities. Our Heavenly Father, that created us in his image, has equipped us all with the same spirit, body and freewill to love or not to love. We sometimes feel weak but He makes us strong. The least we can do is to follow His lead, obey His word and spread His love to others.

PRAYER TARGET:
Those who are weary and need strength in Him .

PERSONAL PRAYER FOR KNOXVILLE:
Father, I pray for all cities that house so many broken people and many lost souls. Father, there are many that do not know about You or how to wake up to the scents of Glory. Help us teach others of You by sharing the same love You taught us to give. Your promises were marked with Your blood, Father. Therefore, help us to trust You by faith and know that You are always there for us, even when we do not see You, feel You, or know that we

can touch you. We trust ourselves to You – the Son, Father, and Holy Spirit. Amen!

WEEK THIRTY NINE: TUESDAY

AUTHOR: XAVIER HARMON
FAMILY STRUCTURE: SINGLE
OCCUPATION: AGRICULTURE AND DATA ANALYST

ABIDING

> **"If you abide in Me, and My words abide in you, you will ask what you desire, and it shall be done for you. By this My Father is glorified that you bear much fruit; so you will be my disciples." John 15:7-8**

A doctorate degree had been my goal for several years until my last semester of master's work. I had already signed an offer with a school, but something wasn't sitting right in my spirit. God was beginning to work in my heart. One day, I was asked what I would do with a doctorate degree. For the first time in three years I could not answer that question. What previously had been my goal now left me heartbroken. I had let pride and selfishness become my drive. I had wanted to get the degree for myself, for attention and pride, instead of bringing God glory.

Jesus calls us to abide in Him, and let His word abide in us, so that the desires of our hearts are transformed from selfish desires into alignment with God's will. This is His amazing promise; if we abide in Him, we can ask what we desire and it shall be done, all to the glory of God. As I drew closer to God through prayer and obedience, my desires changed. I felt God calling me to stay in Knoxville. While it was a huge step to give up my goal, He has blessed me with immeasurably more than I could have imagined.

PRAYER TARGET:
Young people of the city, learning to abide in Him and trust in His will.

PERSONAL PRAYER FOR KNOXVILLE:

Father, my prayer is that everyone in the city would abide in You so that their desires are aligned with Yours. In particular, Father, I pray for the young people in the city. You are the vine and we are the branches who desire to bear fruit, but man by nature is selfish and broken. We may place our job, school, sports, or a significant other above abiding in Your word and desiring to bear fruit. Help us to see our world through Your eyes, that we may recognize the areas in our lives that need pruning, where selfishness and pride have taken over. Remove these desires from us and help us to abide in You, LORD. Make our desires aligned to Yours. Even when the pruning may not be easy, give us the strength to abide. Every day draw us closer to You through prayer and obedience that we may bear much fruit all to Your glory. We ask this in the name of Jesus. Amen.

WEEK THIRTY NINE: WEDNESDAY

AUTHOR: VERETTA E. AVERY
FAMILY STRUCTURE: 2 CHILDREN
OCCUPATION: RETIRED EDUCATOR

PRAY, LISTEN, AND LEAN

"Trust in the Lord with all thine heart; and lean not unto thine own understanding. In all thy ways acknowledge Him, and He shall direct thy path." Proverbs 3:5-6

As I think back through my life, I have seen many time when You, God, have stepped in to "make things happen," ordered my steps, and revealed my path when I didn't know how or what I was going to do. During my first bout of cancer, I was frightened, afraid, and did not know how I was going to get through this terrifying diagnosis. It was then I heard Your voice… "Trust me, I have this." But how? I needed to learn that it was not up to my understanding and that I should listen to You. Throughout treatments and therapies, You indeed had it as my body healed. I thank You for the care I received I as I learned to lean into You. But, I missed that listening part.

A physical crisis struck again several years later when I had a stroke. "Lord," I said, "Why is this happening?" Again, fear gripped me. I didn't know if I was going to survive this. If I did, what would my condition be? Then I heard Your voice: "Veretta, remember to trust me. I've got this."

"But, Lord, this is hard," I said. I prayed and I listened and then I started to lean on Him again. In leaning, I learned to relinquish what I thought I could do and trust in the Lord. He continued to reveal to me that I can't depend on my ways. My ways were not always His ways; my thoughts were not His thoughts. I need to lean into Him. When I did, I became stronger.

Trouble came my way again - divorce after thirty plus years of marriage and a second diagnosis of cancer. It was brutal but I listened to the Lord. Again He said, "Veretta, trust me, I've got this." I replied, "Yes, Lord I know you do." Now I am praying, listening and leaning. I know that He has always been there orchestrating events and catching me when I'm falling. I am thankful I am a child of the King, His daughter. He gave me the courage to do what needed to be done. He loves me. I don't look like I used tom but I am better because I learned to pray, listen, and learn. The scripture above has become very personal to me.

PRAYER TARGET:
That women in Knoxville will remember that they are daughters of the King!

PERSONAL PRAYER FOR KNOXVILLE:
Father, I pray for each and every woman of Knoxville to learn to trust in the Lord. There are so many challenges that we face each and every day, but we can face everything with You, God. If we knit together as daughters of the King and sisters in Christ, there is nothing we can't face. I pray for all of the mothers, daughters, sisters, friends, workers, retirees, and students. I pray for women of all races and ethnicities. It is our duty, Father, to stand together for our city, its reconciliation, and to fight the pervasive enemy. With You, God, all things are possible! I pray that any woman that is in an abusive relationship, whether emotional or physical, has the courage to break those chains. Help her seek refuge, cling to hope, and always believe. God, You are speaking to us all the time. Help us listen and allow the Holy Spirit to love us. Make our city great. Thank You, Father. Amen.

WEEK THIRTY NINE: THURSDAY

AUTHOR: JEANNE BARKER
FAMILY STRUCTURE: HUSBAND, GROWN CHILDREN, AND GRANDCHILDREN
OCCUPATION: EDUCATOR

THE GREAT I AM

> **"So Samuel told him everything, hiding nothing from him. Then Eli said, 'He is the LORD; let him do what is good in his eyes.'" 1 Samuel 3:18**

This verse goes to the heart of the matter both literally and figuratively in living the Christian life and experiencing the fullness promised in God's Word. I love a statement by E. Glyn Evans in Daily with The King, *"Christianity is not me using God, but God using me."*

I saw a great example of the sovereignty of God in the modern story of All Saint's church in Smyrna, Tennessee as portrayed in the movie, *All Saints*. God gets to decide how and when and to what extent my hopes and dreams are filled. In my life, I know that God desires to fulfill His Will and when I align with that, I experience joy beyond comprehension.

PRAYER TARGET:
Anyone who wants to keep control of their circumstances.

PERSONAL PRAYER FOR KNOXVILLE:
Father, You are I AM. You have always been in control and will continue to be in control. Help us surrender to You and Your plan for life. You are the only true way to joy. Help each person know that You are sovereign. Let us rest in the knowledge that you give in John 13:7 where You tell us, "I may not know what You are doing now, but you shall understand afterward." I pray this in Your Name, Father. Amen.

WEEK THIRTY NINE: FRIDAY

AUTHOR: BOBBI BARRON
FAMILY STRUCTURE: WIDOW
OCCUPATION: PATIENT ACCESS

BLIND FAITH

"For I know the thoughts that I think toward you, saith the Lord, thoughts of peace, and not of evil, to give you an expected end." Jeremiah 29:11

After the sudden death of my husband I found myself alone for the first time in my life. Mitchell and I married when I was thirty years old and for the next twenty-six years we were together constantly. Being alone was just not in my nature. I lived with my parents until I married so this was a whole new experience. People told me that I should not make any major decisions for a year after losing my spouse, so I began this new phase of my life.

After a year I made the decision to move to Knoxville, TN where my brother and two sisters were living. My family has always been my ROCK. I could never do life without them. With their help and support I quit my job that I loved and left my many friends. The Lord was definitely working in my life because even before I moved I had a new job, and my brother and sister-in-law had made a place for me in their home. This was a very hard decision for me because I never thought I would live any place other than Oxford, Alabama. The Lord continued to open doors for me and to this day I am constantly reminded that He is still working and opening new doors.

Since moving to Knoxville, I have had the privilege of being a part of the "Survivors and Thrivers" group in my church. This group of widows have become some of my best friends and support. These ladies have all experienced the same loss and, therefore, have an understanding on ways to help each other.

Through our monthly dinners and activities, we have developed a special bond.

I am reminded daily that God knew all along what was best for me. I just needed to trust Him and remember that He has my best interest.

PRAYER TARGET:
Widows learning to seek comfort and friendship in the body of Christ.

PERSONAL PRAYER FOR KNOXVILLE:
Father, I pray for this city. I pray that everyone in it that is alone will find comfort in You and follow Your lead in their lives. Bring support and guidance to each and help all to realize that they are never alone with You by their sides. Amen.

WEEK FORTY: MONDAY

AUTHOR: TINA HULBERT
FAMILY STRUCTURE: HUSBAND AND 2 CHILDREN
OCCUPATION: FULL-TIME WIFE AND MOM, PART-TIME ENGINEER

FROM DEFEAT TO VICTORY!

> **"I keep asking that the God of our Lord Jesus Christ, the glorious Father, may give you the Spirit of wisdom and revelation, so that you may know him better. I pray that the eyes of your heart may be enlightened in order that you may know the hope to which he has called you, the riches of his glorious inheritance in his holy people, and his incomparably great power for us who believe."**
> **Ephesians 1:17-19a**

Most of my life I have known of God, but not really known God. My happiness depended upon my circumstances, and I felt isolated and lonely. In addition, I added guilty to the list of my frequent feelings as I let the enemy bring up my past to me over and over and over again. I lived life defeated. That is until I had children and decided that I wanted them to make better decisions than I had in my life. I really started studying God's word and praying to know Him more. The Bible says that I can do all things through Christ (Philippians 4:13) and that if I need wisdom I should ask God and He will give it to me (James 1:5). But the power in those promises is only fully received by knowing the Giver. Spending time with Him. Asking Him to give me the Spirit of wisdom and revelation. I don't need to know how to be happy, but to KNOW HIM BETTER! That was the key to finding joy in the midst of my everyday life. That was the key to knowing the hope that I have in Him and the power that He has given me to live this life joyfully, boldly, and victoriously.

PRAYER TARGET:
Mothers of the city who live defeated.

PERSONAL PRAYER FOR KNOXVILLE:
Father, my prayer is that no mom in the city of Knoxville would live life feeling defeated or lonely! I ask You, God, to give every mother the Spirit of wisdom and revelation to know You better! I pray in Jesus' Name that you would open the eyes of their hearts to know the Hope that they have in Jesus, and the great and mighty power that He graciously pours out on all believers to live their lives victoriously, no matter what their circumstances! I pray that every mother would have at least one other woman in her life to speak Truth to her and to link arms to walk together through the season of motherhood. I pray that we would build each other up instead of tearing each other down!!

Father, I pray that every mother would claim Proverbs 16:3 over her children which says, "Commit to the Lord whatever you do, and your plans will succeed." I pray that they will commit their children to You and that You will help them raise their children to be mighty warriors for Your Kingdom. I pray for their husbands to commit to You as well, Lord. Where there is not a husband in the home I pray that You would raise up Godly men to stand in the gap for these children! I pray that these men would be supportive and Christ-like in their relationships with these mothers and their children!

And most of all, Lord, I pray that each person reading this would know how wide and long and high and deep is Your love for them. Thank You for all You are doing in our city! Amen

WEEK FORTY: TUESDAY

AUTHOR: KIM MCFALL
FAMILY STRUCTURE: HUSBAND AND 2 CHILDREN
OCCUPATION: TEACHER

FREEDOM FROM BITTERNESS

"But to those of you who will listen, I say: Love your enemies, do good to those who hate you, bless those who curse you, pray for those who mistreat you." Luke 6:27-28

Oh, friends... how difficult it is to truly LOVE our enemies. Especially those enemies who mistreat us over and over again, or mistreat our spouse or our children. God calls us to not only love our enemies, not only to forgive our enemies, but to "BLESS those who curse us." *Bless* them?? Yes. He calls us to *"Pray for those who mistreat us."* Ouch. When the hurt is deep and the enemy is relentless, it sure seems impossible to genuinely lift our enemies in prayer, on our knees, to our Heavenly Father... but it's not impossible. Nothing is impossible with God. Being obedient to God brings blessings, and one of those blessings is freedom from the bitterness we harbor when we don't fully forgive our enemies, pray for them, and bless them, as we are called to do. The peace that comes from true forgiveness brings healing and joy.

Is there someone who comes to mind when you hear the word "enemy?" Who is God calling you to forgive? To bless? To pray for? Lift them up now, friends. Pray for them. Pray for their families. Ask God to reveal to you ways that you can bless them. Ask God to forgive you for your bitterness, resentment, anger, and keeping a record of wrongs. Only then will you experience His peace in your heart.

PRAYER TARGET:
Everyone who holds on to bitterness and unforgiveness.

PERSONAL PRAYER FOR KNOXVILLE:
Father, I pray that the chains of bitterness will be broken among us. Send Your peace and fill the hearts of men and women throughout our city who kneel in prayer and lift their enemies to You, Heavenly Father.

Oh God, hear every cry and heal every broken heart. Take us from bitter to better and allow us to experience freedom and a peace that passes all understanding. God as we come to You, broken, we ask You to bring restoration and healing to our relationships that are being hurt by our own pride or anger. Bless our enemies, Lord. Shower them with Your grace and give them mercy. Father, draw them close to You. We pray all this in the name of Jesus. Amen.

WEEK FORTY: WEDNESDAY

AUTHOR: RACHEL LOVINGOOD
FAMILY STRUCTURE: HUSBAND, 2 MARRIED CHILDREN, AND
1 COLLEGE STUDENT
OCCUPATION: AUTHOR AND SPEAKER

REAL STRENGTH FOR LIVING

> **"And David was greatly distressed, for the people spoke of stoning him, because all the people were bitter in soul, each for his sons and daughters. But David strengthened himself in the LORD his God." 1 Samuel 30:6**

When was the last time you were distressed? Probably not that long ago. So many things happen to cause us distress. Our kids may get hurt. There's a bad report from the doctor. A marriage gets in trouble. We receive a bad grade on a test or lose a ball game… you get the picture. These can all feel overwhelming and we wonder how we will get through it.

The world we live in offers us plenty of options to escape from our stress and even some false ideas on where we can find strength. What is your go to response to feeling distressed? Do you reach for a drink, go shopping, grab some chocolate, exercise, or call someone to vent? Although any of these might take our minds off of the issues they will only leave us feeling weaker and emptier.

I love what David did when he was faced with opposition. When the people around him were bitter in their souls (sound like anyone you know?), David chose to find his strength in the Lord. Instead of wasting his time with collecting more stuff, with complaining to his friends, with shopping online, with stuffing his face with junk food - David turned to the Lord and found strength.

How cool is that? And smart because when we learn to find our strength in the Lord, He will never let us down. Let's start turning to God first. Lay your burden at His feet. Ask Him for what you need. Confess where you feel weak and offer yourself as a vessel for Him to fill with His Spirit and use even in the midst of difficult times. That will make us strong.

PRAYER TARGET:
All who have stress that is gripping their lives.

PERSONAL PRAYER FOR KNOXVILLE:
Father, let Your people recognize that You alone are the strength we need. Forgive us for turning to other things or trying to handle life on our own power when we have Your unbelievably great power that we can access if we surrender our lives to You. Help us to never settle for less than living in victory and power because we have been strengthened by You! Amen.

AUTHOR: BRENT EDWARDS
FAMILY STRUCTURE: WIFE AND CHILDREN
OCCUPATION: SALES SUPPORT

FROM SHAME TO HONOR

"Let the redeemed of the LORD tell their story—those he redeemed from the hand of the foe. Some wandered in desert wastelands. Some sat in utter darkness. Some became fools through their rebellious ways. Some went out on the sea in ships; and went down to the depths; in their peril their courage melted away. Then they cried out to the LORD in their trouble, and he brought them out of their distress. Let them give thanks to the LORD for his unfailing love and his wonderful deeds for mankind."
Psalm 107: 2, 4, 10, 17, 23, 28, 51

I remember hearing Sunday school stories of the valiant men and women of God. There was Moses, bravely calling on Pharaoh to let God's people go. There was David, fending off lions and slaying the bully Goliath. And Rahab, instrumental in the fall of Jericho as the Hebrews took the Promised Land. I wished I could be one of those people of faith!

But there was more to the story. The Moses that took matters in his own hands by killing an Egyptian. The David who betrayed his wife and coldly arranged the death of his army captain and other valiant men. And Rahab who had a questionable occupation.

These verses from Psalm 107 illustrate the different experiences that bring people to the point of calling out to the Lord. Some are lost in the desert, others tossed around in a boat on rocky waters, and others suffering shame from their own foolish decisions. Though the experiences were varied, brokenness is what brought them to the pointing of crying out for salvation.

We're all broken vessels in need of repair – from illness, tragedy, or foolish mistakes. But God's love and grace transcends all of our life circumstances. It is God who makes beauty from ashes. Let the redeemed of the Lord say so!

PRAYER TARGET:
People struggling with regrets.

PERSONAL PRAYER FOR KNOXVILLE:
Oh Lord, thank You for Your grace. Thank You that from brokenness You bring healing and restoration. Give us courage to lay our regrets at Your feet and live each day for Your glory. Amen.

WEEK FORTY: FRIDAY

AUTHOR: DAMETRAUS JAGGERS
FAMILY STRUCTURE: WIFE AND 2 CHILDREN
OCCUPATION: ADMINISTRATOR

WHY ARE WE ANGRY?

> "Know this, my beloved brothers: let every person be quick to hear, slow to speak, slow to anger; for the anger of man does not produce the righteousness of God." James 1:19-20 Be angry, and do not sin; ponder in your own hearts on your beds, and be silent." Psalm 4:4

In this passage of scripture, James challenges us to examine our anger. There is a misnomer in some circles that Christ followers are not allowed to be angry. Unfortunately, that is not what James means in verse 20 and it's not what the Psalmist means in the fourth chapter of Psalm when he says, "be angry, and do not sin." The expectation is not that we don't get angry. It's not that we remain silent, in the sense that we don't give voice to the issues and challenges around us. It's not that Christ followers are not allowed to be angry? It's not that Christ followers should remain silent and passive about the personal, community, and global issues around us. It's okay for Christ followers to be angry... it's okay that we are bothered and uncomfortable with the injustice and lack of humanity around us... if that's what we're truly angry about. The real question for us is... exactly, about what are we angry?

You see, James emphasizes that "the anger of man" does not produce the righteousness of God. So, the question may be asked again, about what are we upset or angry? Are we upset about those things that are important to us but are not Christ-centered? Are we angered about the treatment of those who are vulnerable? Or is our anger motivated by the potential threat to our livelihood and comfortable lifestyles? Christ followers, believers, beloved... where are we directing our anger? We should be selective about things that make us angry. If we're going to be irritated, let's direct that irritation toward things that are righteous in the eyesight of God. Should we be mindful of our anger? Yes, we should. Should we be careful about our use of words? Yes, we should. Do we have to be silent, voiceless, or inactive about the challenges and issues we see in our world? Absolutely not. What we must do is listen to hear and understand. We must be thoughtful and biblically grounded. We must seek God for discernment and guidance. And then we must move forward in seeking God's righteousness and move away from our anger.

PRAYER TARGET:
Adults ages thirty and up who struggle with anger.

PERSONAL PRAYER FOR KNOXVILLE:
God, grant us discernment in our daily affairs that we may seek Your heart. God, break our heart for the things that break Your heart. Helps us to seek Your righteousness regarding the issues of justice, morality and humanity, so that when we feel hopeless about the world around us, we will be bound to act from Your righteousness. Give us wisdom to examine our anger and guide us to a place that compels us to respond to Your "righteous anger." And in our response, let Your light so shine in us that people will be drawn to Your son, Jesus. Give us boldness in the face of injustice. Give us peace in the midst of hostility and give us rest when we become weary. In Jesus' Name. Amen.

WEEK FORTY ONE: MONDAY

AUTHOR: BETSIE HUGHES
FAMILY STRUCTURE: HUSBAND, 5 CHILDREN, AND 5 GRANDCHILDREN
OCCUPATION: MORTGAGE CONSULTANT

WHOSE BATTLE IS IT ANYWAY?

> **"Finally, be strong in the Lord and in the strength of His might. Put on the whole armor of God, trust that you may be able to stand against the schemes of the devil. For we do not wrestle against flesh and blood, but against the rulers, against the cosmic powers over this present darkness, against the spiritual forces of evil in the heavenly places." Ephesians 6:10-12**

She fell to her knees and cried out in desperation, "I cannot do this anymore, Lord!!!!!"
God whispered in a clear, firm voice as if He was standing right beside her…. "YOU don't have to do anything."
We struggle every day in our relationships to try and figure them out in our own flesh and it leaves us weary and bitter. The doors of our hearts are closed to the miracle of what God can do if only we would stop trying in our own strength and let Him go to battle for us.

One of the hardest things we will ever do is to lay our lives down and sacrifice everything we think we want or deserve for what God has planned for us. This is especially true in our closest and most intimate relationships. We risk being hurt….again. We have to forgive…..again. But God can work in miraculous ways if we allow Him to go to battle on behalf of our families and marriages!! One small sacrifice of mindset can open the door just enough to let His light flood in and change everything. Our families and marriages are worth fighting for on our knees. Let's let God lead the charge! He will do it if we get out of the way.

PRAYER TARGET:

Husband and wives and strength for their marriages.

PERSONAL PRAYER FOR KNOXVILLE:

Lord, in desperation I ask that we will see the spiritual battle that is ongoing for our families and marriages. Give us spiritual fortitude to rely on Your Word to guide us in our marriages, not our emotions and worldly desires. I pray for our city, Knoxville and surrounding areas, that You will rise up an army of believers who will fight for their marriages by laying down their lives for the sake of their spouse. Help us learn to love like You love us, Lord. Help us to see clearly that our relationships are not so much about us and what we want or need, but they are a reflection of Your love and grace and the sacrifice of Jesus Christ. And then Lord, may You bless our homes with overflowing, abundant peace and love that we may be Your light to the world around us. Amen.

WEEK FORTY ONE: TUESDAY

AUTHOR: NATHAN VAN GUNDY
FAMILY STRUCTURE: WIFE, 2 SONS AT HOME, 1 SON IN NAVY, 1 FOSTER
DAUGHTER, AND 2 ADOPTIVE DAUGHTERS (ONE OF WHICH HAS SPECIAL
NEEDS)
OCCUPATION: GRAPHIC DESIGN

A BEAUTIFUL DISPLAY

> **"As he went along, he saw a man blind from birth. His disciples asked him, 'Rabbi, who sinned, this man or his parents, that he was born blind?'**
> **'Neither this man nor his parents sinned,' said Jesus, 'but this happened so that the works of God might be displayed in him.'" John 9:1-3**

Special needs individuals are just that: *individuals.* You may have expected the italicized word in that sentence to be "special" instead of "individuals." Not to diminish their specialness, but above all else, they are individuals, uniquely created in the image of God. They don't view themselves as different like the world does, and they don't want to be viewed with that narrow mindset. They want to be openly accepted for who they are, and that is a very biblical principle. Jesus was willing to accept you (and your sin) to the point of death. Talk about a beautiful display!

This passage in John is a great example of the compassion Jesus showed to those with special needs. This man could very well have been born blind because of his parents' sin. But instead of focusing on the temporal, he wanted his disciples to see the eternal. The man was viewed as an outcast because of his condition, but Jesus was going to use the man's shortcomings to show His glory where society least expected it.

Individuals with special needs serve a great and mighty purpose, and God WANTS to use them to glorify himself. They are a beautiful display of His love and mercy waiting to be revealed to the world. Don't use the dreaded "R" word to label them; instead, remove the label and see that God has a special plan for each one of them.

PRAYER TARGET:
Acceptance and connection from others for individuals with special needs.

PERSONAL PRAYER FOR KNOXVILLE:
Father, may the eyes and hearts of our city be open to the idea of bonding with individuals with special needs. They are not always easy to deal with, and they may not reciprocate the love and attention poured into them, but they deserve to feel loved and valued. Help us view them the same way You view us: as sons and daughters. You, God, sent Your one and only Son to die for us knowing full well how messed up we would become. That's what true love looks like. God, put a desire in our hearts to remove the labels we've grown accustomed to with regard to these wonderful creations of Yours. Help us make an effort to engage with them, because they deserve it. Allow Your light to shine through us and let Your love be so abundant in us that it overflows all over our city. Forgive us of our sins for not investing in these individuals because it's not easy or convenient. Father, we thank You in advance for answering our prayer and wait with anticipation to see what You're going to do through them to change their lives and ours! Amen.

WEEK FORTY ONE: WEDNESDAY

AUTHOR: JEREMY GRAHAM
FAMILY STRUCTURE: WIFE AND 5 CHILDREN
OCCUPATION: MINISTRY PRESIDENT AND FOUNDER

THE POWER OF A FATHER AND SON RELATIONSHIP

> **"I write not these things to shame you, but as my beloved sons I warn you. For though ye have ten thousand instructors in Christ, yet have ye not many fathers: for in Christ Jesus I have begotten you through the gospel. Wherefore I beseech you, be ye followers of me."**
> **1 Corinthians 4:14-16**

In my life, there is one revelation that I would like to share for today that truly changed my life. In the scripture above Paul gives two types of mentors in the Body of Christ: Instructors (translated school master) and Fathers. He is giving us the understanding that the Body of Christ is full of these school masters that only have the shallow relationship with the people he or she serves. These are those who "have a job" to teach, preach, lead bible studies, etc. However, Paul places the emphasis on the relationship between the Father and the Son. A hired servant will only do so much for the novice believer because there is no relationship. But the Father will wipe noses, change diapers, pray earnestly, and will invest in the Son because he is his own.

Every Paul should have a Timothy, and Timothy a Paul. Elijah had an Elisha and Jesus had His disciples. We are supposed to invest in the next generation to carry the mantle through the ages. Do you have a "son" or "daughter" to whom you can be a Spiritual Father and have a life devoted to him or her? What are you doing with the talents that God gave you? Are you investing them in other sons or daughters of God or holding onto them till the day you die?

Men, we should have spiritual sons! Women, you should have younger daughters in the faith! We cannot take our mantles of anointing with us when we die, so please invest them in the next generation.

PRAYER TARGET:

Christian men and women that will reach out to mentor younger men and women in the faith.

PERSONAL PRAYER FOR KNOXVILLE:

Father, we pray for the Body of Christ to understand this revelation of discipleship. We pray for the fatherless and the motherless in the churches today that have no one with which to have an intimate or personal relationship. We pray that Fathers and Mothers will come along to instill those attributes and characteristics only found in You, the true Father from Heaven. Let us imitate Jesus who imitated You, Father, and please give us the grace to take the time to invest into the generations of the future. In closing, I ask for the double portion to be released in the body of Christ as this revelation is received and implemented into the lives of many. In the wonderful name of Your dear Son, Jesus. Amen.

WEEK FORTY ONE: THURSDAY

AUTHOR: ROSE EDWARDS
FAMILY STRUCTURE: HUSBAND AND BEAUTIFUL STEP-CHILDREN
OCCUPATION: WOMEN'S MINISTRY

FORGIVENESS

"Then Peter came to Jesus and asked, 'Lord, how many times shall I forgive my brother who sins against me? Up to seven times?' Jesus answered, 'I tell you, not just seven times, but seventy-seven times!'" Matthew 18:21-22

I am thankful to serve women through bible studies. Often the topic of the inability to forgive comes up and there are some common statements 1. But, I have a right to be angry, hurt (their story is often so heart breaking we can almost always understand). 2. I have forgiven them but I can't forget it (umm, no! Holding on tightly usually means true forgiveness has not really been given).

Most will say they know that Christ commands them to forgive, but it's just so hard. Here's the thing, it may be hard. In fact, it may be the hardest thing we have ever done. However, if we stay close to Him, if we continue to pray for the ability to forgive, in His timing we will see God's great plan unfold. In Romans 8:28, His word tells us, *"That all things work together for the good of those who love the Lord and are called according to His purpose."*

I am convinced that our God uses every life experience we have to change and mold us, no matter how painful it may be. It is when we really allow ourselves to reflect on how He used that situation for His Glory that our hearts will soften and forgiveness will flow freely.

PRAYER TARGET:
Those struggling to forgive.

PERSONAL PRAYER FOR KNOXVILLE:
Lord, I know the pain inflicted by those we love can often cut deepest. Lord, I pray that those struggling to forgive, will turn to You alone for help and they will find Your mercy and grace. Lord, please deliver them from the weight that unforgiveness bears that may they receive their freedom and peace in You. In Jesus' Name, I pray. Amen.

WEEK FORTY ONE: FRIDAY

AUTHOR: DASHA LUNDY
FAMILY STRUCTURE: SINGLE
OCCUPATION: COMMUNITY LEADER

KNOW YOUR VALUE

"And let endurance have its perfect result and do a thorough work, so that you may be perfect and completely developed [in your faith], lacking in nothing." James 1:4

Life is truly a journey. It is full of good days, "blah" days, and bad days. There are days that we feel like we can conquer the world and then they are days that we feel incapable of doing anything. In this crazy place, which feels like an emotional rollercoaster with the unexpected twist and turns, there is a glimmer hope. We just have to filter through the unknown.

As I walk this life of uncertainty, I have asked God plenty of questions… "Why are You punishing me," or "Why do you have me in this particular place?" Another of my questions is, "God, You told me that You will do this and You are not doing it. Where are you?"

After I slow down on my frustration and focus on Him alone, He whispers, "I am developing your faith in Me."

As you walk your journey, don't allow the distractions to allow to you get frustrated at God. Stay focused. He has a great plan for your life. He requires you to have Faith. As Hebrews 11:6 states, "Without faith, it is impossible to please God." Remember that He will provide a way out, so let your endurance perfect you and prepare you for a great work. You are valuable to Him! He has not forsaken you! You will lack nothing! Know your value!

PRAYER TARGET:
Christian men and women who forget that their identity is in Christ alone.

PERSONAL PRAYER FOR KNOXVILLE:
Lord, continue to humble us. Allow us to see from Your perspective. Give us strategies that will help transform our great city. Help us come together so we can do execute those strategies. In Jesus' Name… Amen.

AUTHOR: SUE WRIGHT
FAMILY STRUCTURE: SINGLE
OCCUPATION: RETIRED

BEING ACCEPTED BY THE FAMILY

> **"Upon You have I relied and been sustained from my birth; You are He who took me from my mother's womb and You have been my benefactor from that day. My praise is continually of You." Psalm 71:6**
> **"Yet to all who did receive Him, to those who believed in His name, He gave the right to become children of God." John 1:12-13**
> **"Show family affection to one another with brotherly love. Outdo one another in showing honor." Romans 12:10**

"I had a loving and comfortable life growing up and was told I was adopted when I was about seven. For some reason, only until recently have I felt the need to know about my heritage, good or bad." This was my statement for requesting my adoption records.

Those records changed my curious thoughts to amazing praise. The records showed me God knew me before I was formed in the womb. I have my birth mother's name but not a father's name because she did not know who the father was. That union, though, has given me good genes and health.

Records say, "She did not seem concerned about giving up the baby because it was all she could do to look after the two she had." Given her circumstances, I can't imagine I would been as loved and cared for as I was with the family that chose me to be their daughter.

Although sinful like the rest of us, mama and daddy knew how to give me good gifts including the most important one. They guided me to know Jesus and believe in His name, and through that process I was chosen again as I became the adopted child of God.

Rules were important in my family. Whether called rules by my earthly family or commandments by God, they were given for my own well-being and I accepted them as such. Growing up, I often found that disobeying them brought discipline. The beautiful thing is, whatever the circumstance, my position in the family never changed. I was and still am in the family, both the earthly family and the God-given one that God created when He adopted me as His child.

PRAYER TARGET:
Adopted adults and children

PERSONAL PRAYER FOR KNOXVILLE:
Father, reveal to the adopted children in this community Your grace, mercy, love and peace as they grow with their family. And Father, encourage parents to guide their children to Your Son and accept Him as their Savior and Lord. Amen.

WEEK FORTY TWO: TUESDAY

AUTHOR: MEGAN MURRAY
FAMILY STRUCTURE: SINGLE
OCCUPATION: STUDENT

UPON THIS ROCK I STAND

"He alone is my rock and my salvation, my fortress; I shall not be greatly shaken." Psalm 62:2

Struggling. Anxious. Depressed. Insecure.

These are words that consumed my life before I became absolutely transfixed by Jesus. I constantly sought affirmation from empty words handed out by devious men. I craved worldly, materialistic, unfulfilling attention. I built my life upon sand that fell through my fingertips. Relying on earthly things always ensured me one thing - disappointment.

But dear friends, the Lord is our Rock where our salvation stands strong. When I was eighteen, the Lord called out to me, clearly as day, "Daughter, come home."

I learned that the affirmation I deeply desired could be fulfilled by the person of Jesus. I learned that I wanted a life not without trials, but with trials that I could face with a brave and strong heart, knowing the Lord is my fortress where I find rest. I learned that my battle is not only fought but my battle is won. I learned my unhealthy relationships, hollow friendships, and desperate heart could thrive when surrendered to the Rock.

Fearless. Confident. Strong. Hopeful.

These are the words that consume my life with my pursuit of Jesus. So, I urge you with love, come Home friends. Come Home.

PRAYER TARGET:
Young women in college who may struggle with depression and insecurity.

PERSONAL PRAYER FOR KNOXVILLE:
Father, I pray for walls to be broken down and then filled by the one True King. May the women of Knoxville be absolutely vulnerable and honest with their hearts and desires and flee to Jesus in desperate times.

God, I urge You to wrap these women up so that they may feel fully known and loved by You. I pray that You would reveal Yourself to them in new and intimate ways so that they may understand Your character in ways they will understand and recognize. Call these women home, Lord. Run and embrace them with open arms, Father. I pray this expectantly, knowing that You are good and You care deeply for Your daughters. In Your precious name I pray. Amen.

WEEK FORTY TWO: WEDNESDAY

NAME: SHARON FISCHBACH
FAMILY STRUCTURE: MOTHER OF 2 MARRIED SONS AND 4 GRANDCHILDREN
OCCUPATION: RETIRED EDUCATOR

GROW UP

"Until we all attain unity of faith and of knowledge of the Son of God, to mature manhood, to the measure of the stature of the fullness of Christ, so that we may no longer be children, tossed to and fro by the waves and carried about by every wind of doctrine, by human cunning, by craftiness in deceitful schemes. Rather, speaking the truth in love, we are to grow up in every way into him who is the head, into Christ." Ephesians 4:14-15

Even though it's easy to just abide where we are spiritually, we should never be content with less than our best. To grow into maturity, we must allow His Holy Spirit to teach us and mature us through His Word, or we will never fulfill what He set us apart to do on this earth. Through two primary means, prayer and the Word, His Spirit guides us to an even deeper level. It does not happen overnight. A life of faith is not based on mountain top experiences but rather on the day-in, day-out consistency or intimacy with Him through time in His Word with opened hearts. As we read, study, and learn, we grow in knowledge of Him. He increases our faith and draws even closer. As we grow closer to Him and we respond to His Word in obedience, we become more like Him.

What kind of follower do I want to be? How am I doing with my "growth chart?" Am I more like Him this year than I was last year? Has my joy in serving increased? Do I reflect His love more today than I did last year? There are no shortcuts to growing up in Christ and we cannot achieve it on our own. Allow His Holy Spirit to teach us through His Word.

PRAYER TARGET:

Adult believers seeking to grow in wisdom and maturity, no longer children in the faith.

PERSONAL PRAYER FOR KNOXVILLE:

Father, may we each be drawn by Your Spirit into greater closeness to You, such that we devote ourselves not only to knowledge of You through Your Word, but also to obedience. May we abide daily in Your Word to become followers who grow up in every way in You. May we reach that measure of the fulness of Christ. Amen.

AUTHOR: MASON CURTNER
FAMILY STRUCTURE: MOTHER AND STEP-FATHER
OCCUPATION: CAFE EMPLOYEE

LOVE AND REBUKE

"Better is open rebuke than love that is hidden."
Proverbs 27:5

As the body of the church, we find our mutual spiritual occupation as ambassadors for Christ and the love He offers. We, through our actions and words, will either accurately display such love to the best of our ability, or openly contradict it. Here in Proverbs, Solomon teaches us that to love one another is not enough. We must show such love openly, otherwise it is useless. So useless that he says it would be better to show open hatred rather than hidden love. If the love of Christ shown by the church is the nourishment we all need to lead others to an eternal paradise with God, then how dare we hide it. How dare we refuse nourishment to the hungry for better is the poison of hatred down their throats than no food at all.

PRAYER TARGET:
The Church seeking to love openly and lead others to eternity with Him.

PERSONAL PRAYER FOR KNOXVILLE:
Father, may all those that count Christ as their personal Savior be able to accurately and openly portray His love for people as seen from the Gospels. In this modern day and time, Father, such love is either hidden or non-existent. May such love one day be able to live within our society, our country, and our church once again. I ask these things in the Name of our merciful and loving Savior, Jesus Christ. Amen.

WEEK FORTY TWO: FRIDAY

AUTHOR: VICTOR LEE
FAMILY STRUCTURE: WIFE AND 7 CHILDREN/FOSTER-ADOPT FAMILY
OCCUPATION: PASTOR OF CARE & COUNSELING

PRAYING

> **"Likewise the Spirit helps us in our weakness. For we do not know what to pray for as we ought, but the Spirit himself intercedes for us with groanings too deep for words. And he who searches hearts knows what is the mind of the Spirit, because the Spirit intercedes for the saints according to the will of God." Romans 8:26-27**

Are you ever so hurt, confounded, or confused that you don't even know how to pray? That's OK. Romans tells us that the Holy Spirit and Jesus (Romans 8:34b) are constantly at the right hand of the Father, interceding for you. That means the Trinity is always actively dealing with your life.

We should actively pray, but when we don't know what to pray, or we ask for the wrong thing, the merciful God of the universe hears the Holy Spirit and Jesus praying rightly for us! Often in my prayer life, I hear the Holy Spirit say, in essence, "Stop, I've got this." I then maintain a posture and attitude of prayer, conscious that the Trinity is *"working all things together for good"* (v. 28). And He very often speaks to me in that time. Sometimes we should just *"be still and know that I am God"* (Psalm 46:10). In the midst of the confusion, imagine the Holy Spirit and Jesus stepping in, and let the Trinity do the work. He's got us!

PRAYER TARGET:
All who seek to pray according to God's perfect will.

PERSONAL PRAYER FOR KNOXVILLE:

Father, I pray that the prayers of the people of our city will be filled not merely with personal requests, a list of 'things to fix,' but with deep, quiet reverence for God and fellowship with Him as the Holy Spirit and Jesus do the work of praying according to Your will. May Your peace overwhelm us as we are assured of You working all things together for good. Amen.

WEEK FORTY THREE: MONDAY

AUTHOR: RON BRENDEL
FAMILY STRUCTURE: WIFE AND 1 DAUGHTER
OCCUPATION: PROFESSOR OF MUSIC

SINGING YOUR TESTIMONY, EVEN IF YOU AREN'T A SINGER

"I will sing of the lovingkindness of the LORD forever; To all generations I will make known Your faithfulness with my mouth." Psalm 89:1

I am a professional singer and teacher of singing. As such, my life's work is the focus of three main concepts: breath, resonance, and articulation. In a spiritual sense, these ideas are also the life of the Christ-believer.

Breath is the image of the Holy Spirit. With breath, the singers delivers the sound. The Holy Spirit enables us to deliver the essence of Jesus to the world. The breath, the Spirit, is the presence of the Lord in real life.

Resonance is the idea of projecting sound. With the Lord's help, we project His Truth to the world, living a testimony and literally speaking the Truth of Jesus, as He gives us opportunity.

Articulation is the skill of being clearly understood. In the Christian life, we always try to beautifully display the life of Jesus to others. We must intentionally deliver not only the presence of the Lord, but also the specifics of a life of holiness. The believer is observed by the world…they both watch and listen. We articulate the Truth in Love by how we live our lives.

God help us to breathe the presence of the Lord, project His love, and articulate His Truth to the world.

PRAYER TARGET:
The creative arts factions of our region.

PERSONAL PRAYER FOR KNOXVILLE:
Gracious God, we ask You to grace our city with Your creative love. As we are created in Your image, we acknowledge that we must also be creative. Help our creativity to be based in Your image. Help us to sing our testimony to the community around us: to breathe Your presence, to project Your Truth, and to articulate that Truth in observable ways as we are watched and heard. Without Your help, we can do nothing. But with You, our lives can sing Your praises to our world, to all generations. In the Name of Jesus Christ, and for His glory alone we pray. Amen.

WEEK FORTY THREE: TUESDAY

AUTHOR: AIMEE KLENSKE
FAMILY STRUCTURE: HUSBAND AND 2 CHILDREN
OCCUPATION: STAY-AT-HOME MOM

THE BURDEN OF WORRY

> **"Be anxious for nothing, but in everything by prayer and supplication with thanksgiving let your requests be made known to God. And the peace of God which surpasses all comprehension, will guard your hearts and your minds in Christ Jesus." Philippians 4:6-7**

I am a serious worrier. I worry about my children, my husband, the health of family members, the state of this crazy world....you name it, and I can find an angle on it to worry about! Worry is a lack of faith and it is definitely my most repeated sin. In my heart, I know that God is in control and that He has my best interest at heart. But somehow, my mind runs away to scenarios that run contrary to the peace that God intends for me. One day, my mom sent me this quote from an unknown author: "Worry is a thin stream of fear trickling through the mind. If encouraged, it cuts a channel into which all other thoughts are drained."

My reaction was, "Wow! This is me!" I allow worry to take my focus off Jesus and onto the subject of my worry, so much so that soon I can think of nothing else. I become consumed, unable to be productive, and paralyzed with the burden of worry.

My mom also shared the verses above from Philippians with me. I love what it says...be anxious for *nothing* and in *everything* pray.

Then, God promises us a supernatural peace and tells us that He will guard our hearts and minds. When I follow the call of these and focus on Jesus and His promises, I always receive peace. His peace equals relief....relief from the burden of worry.   Does this verse rid me of worry forever? No, because I am human. But, I visit these verses frequently and every time I do, I reattach myself to His promises and I can feel the worry being lifted away.

PRAYER TARGET:
Everyone who is consumed with worry.

PERSONAL PRAYER FOR KNOXVILLE:
Heavenly Father, please help us to remember that You are in control no matter how out of control our lives may seem. You see the things we cannot see and always have our best interest at heart. You love us deeply and know our every need before we speak it. I pray that every person in this city would surrender their worries to You … the small worries and the overwhelming ones. Help us to be anxious for nothing but instead, give it all to You. And then God, I pray that You would fill all those that call upon You with Your supernatural peace. Guard our hearts and our minds and direct our focus to You, the One who holds us in the palm of His hand. Thank You, Lord, for loving us and for Your promises on which we can always stand. Amen

WEEK FORTY THREE: WEDNESDAY

AUTHOR: MICHAEL HOUBRE
FAMILY STRUCTURE: WIFE AND 3 CHILDREN
OCCUPATION: ATTORNEY AND HR PROFESSIONAL

WALKING THROUGH HARDSHIPS

> "Therefore we do not lose heart. Though outwardly we are wasting away, yet inwardly we are being renewed day by day. For our light and momentary troubles are achieving for us an eternal glory that far outweighs them all. So we fix our eyes not on what is seen, but on what is unseen, since what is seen is temporary, but what is unseen is eternal." 2 Corinthians 4:16-18

I don't know anyone who has escaped life's troubles. For those who live a fairly problem-free life, even the reality and pain of death affects us all eventually. On a personal level, I went through a period of extended joblessness several years ago. I understand how it feels to be "wasting away" further with each failed job application. It was one of the most difficult experiences of my life, and my family and I would not have made it through without the love and support of the Body of Christ.

As trying as that time was, I came to understand that there are aspects of the character of God that cannot be learned apart from experiencing hardship. That's not to say that I prefer those times – I certainly do not. But when I look back today at the toughest times of my life – joblessness, illness, financial hardship – I clearly see the fruits in the form of wisdom, faith, and character that would never have formed otherwise.

Our troubles are not pointless. Do not let your hardships go to waste by failing to recognize that God is walking with you through them. God will not waste them, and neither should you.

PRAYER TARGET:
Knoxville's unemployed and underemployed.

PERSONAL PRAYER FOR KNOXVILLE:
Father, I pray for the those experiencing the various hardships that come in life – the loss of a friendship or job, or the death of a family member or friend. Show them Your love, and show those around them how to love them better. Allow them to weep without shame, and help their loved ones to offer solace without judgment.

I pray especially for the unemployed and underemployed in our city. I pray that You would grant them persistence and joy during this trying time. This will not be easy, as the pressure of providing for one's self and family can be enormous, but protect them from depression and allow them to be renewed in gratitude every morning. Even more so than a job, I pray that You would show them the path to a GREAT job.

May they not lose heart. Amen.

WEEK FORTY THREE: THURSDAY

AUTHOR: MCKENZIE MITCHELL
FAMILY STRUCTURE: SINGLE
OCCUPATION: STUDENT

THINKING ON GOOD THINGS

> "Finally, brothers, whatever is true, whatever is honorable, whatever is just, whatever is pure, whatever is lovely, whatever is commendable, if there is any excellence, if there is anything worthy of praise, think about these things. What you have learned and received and heard and seen in me—practice these things, and the God of peace will be with you." Philippians 4:8-9

I have a problem. I think too much. I think upwards, backwards, forwards, diagonally, across, in zigzags. I think about what seems like EVERYTHING all the time. And I can't stop. The thoughts just come to me all the time. And for years this has been a problem. I've cried so many tears over trying to decipher what is true and what is false. And then God let this verse cozy have its way into my life.

This verse is my formula for knowing which thoughts I should dwell on and which thoughts I should cast away. So now, anytime a thought pops into my mind I try go through this checklist, "Is it true, honorable, just, pure, lovely, commendable, excellent, or worthy of praise?" If it's not, I throw the thought away. If it is, then I know it honors God and try to walk in that direction. And like the verse says, when I practice these things, the God of peace is always with me.

PRAYER TARGET:
College students that would long to focus on eternal values and not worldly chaos.

PERSONAL PRAYER FOR KNOXVILLE:

Dear God, thank You for allowing me to pray for the college students of Knoxville, TN. I pray that with everything going on in our lives (all the choices and unknown futures) You would allow us to rest in the fact that You'll always take care of us. I pray that You would guard our minds to only focus on what's true, honorable, just, pure, lovely, commendable, excellent, and worthy of praise. Thank You for giving us this verse. I pray that joy would abound in our hearts as we think on these things. In Jesus' Name I pray. Amen.

WEEK FORTY THREE: FRIDAY

AUTHOR: BRENDA HARRISON BOGARD
FAMILY STRUCTURE: HUSBAND, 2 CHILDREN, AND 4 GRANDCHILDREN
OCCUPATION: RETIRED

WORSHIPING GOD THROUGH MY ART

**"For the gifts and the calling of God are irrevocable."
Romans 11:29**

Once God places a gifting and calling on someone's life, there is no straying from the path. Gifts are used to bring honor and glory to God and one way that takes place is through art. God, the Creator, has gifted His children in many ways. Let us step forward, expose, and share our talents. Your reward will be the glorifying of God! And you will feel it!

PRAYER TARGET:
People who do not know what their creative gifts are…. especially those interested in creative arts.

PERSONAL PRAYER FOR KNOXVILLE:
Dear God, let everyone in the city that is involved in the arts use their talents for God's glory. We ask You, God, to bless our labors and fulfill the creative purposes in us today. Lord, teach me to pray with my hands. Remind me that the work of my hands belong to You. Bless all who create in the name of Christ. May their works be fulfilling. In Christ we ask. Amen.

WEEK FORTY FOUR: MONDAY

AUTHOR: JOHN FISCHBACH
FAMILY STRUCTURE: WIFE
OCCUPATION: CREATIVE DIRECTOR

THE WONDER OF IT ALL

"You should not be surprised at my saying, 'You must be born again.' The wind blows wherever it pleases. You hear its sound, but you cannot tell where it comes from or where it is going. So it is with everyone born of the Spirit. 'How can this be?' Nicodemus asked." John 3:7-9

John's Gospel, my favorite, offers three progressive glimpses of a seeker, Nicodemus. Initially, the well-respected Pharisee discreetly brings his intellectual curiosity to Jesus under cover of darkness (American painter Henry Ossawa Tanner captures this scene beautifully in *Nicodemus Visiting Jesus by Night,* a worthwhile Google search). *"How can someone be born when they are old?"* Nicodemus wonders. Encountering Jesus has staggered his understanding; this challenge to a new life defied all logic. Sleep would be hard to come by that night.

When next we see Nicodemus in John 7, a seed of spiritual understanding has begun to grow, to transfer, from his head to his heart. Newfound conviction compels him to publicly defend the controversial Jesus to his peers, even at considerable risk to his own reputation. He is no longer undercover. Inside him has begun a regenerated heartbeat.

John 19 finally reveals a radically transformed man. Together with Joseph of Arimathea, Nicodemus boldly requests the body of the crucified Christ for burial, embalming Jesus with 75 pounds of myrrh and aloe—an amount traditionally reserved only for royalty. Nicodemus has made a decision, as we all must, about who this Jesus is: Lord. Savior. King.

PRAYER TARGET:
Those who seek the One true God.

PERSONAL PRAYER FOR KNOXVILLE:
Father, we are created in Your image to know You. We sometimes seek to fill that void with poor substitutes for Your presence. We can be far more impressed with our own intellect—the very intellect You have given us. But encountering You changes everything we understand. Lord, may we come face to face with Your glory. May recognition of who You are create a Nicodemus-like reorientation of our minds to find fulfillment in You. A Nicodemus-like transformation of our hearts to beat in sync with yours. A Nicodemus-like acknowledgment of our desperate need for Your grace. Create in us a clean heart, O God, and renew a steadfast spirit within us. And we ask this in the Name of the one who gives new life, Jesus. Amen.

WEEK FORTY FOUR: TUESDAY

AUTHOR: LAUREN LINGAR
FAMILY STRUCTURE: I AM A DAUGHTER
OCCUPATION: STUDENT

FORGIVEN MUCH AND SHOWING MUCH LOVE

"I tell you, her sins – and they are many – have been forgiven, so she has shown me much love. But a person who is forgiven little shows only little love." Luke 7:47

Living in a perpetual and intense love of Jesus for His atoning work on the cross is how a believer ought to live. As we understand just how sinful we are, our love for the Savior should abound. Timothy Keller puts it this way, "The gospel is this: We are more sinful and flawed in ourselves than we ever dared believe, yet at the very same time we are more loved and accepted in Jesus Christ than we ever dared hope."

Living in light of this is what Jesus was talking about when he contrasted the prayers of the Pharisee and the tax collector (Luke 18:9-14). He commended the tax collector's prayer that said, "God, have mercy on me, a sinner" (Luke 18:13). Truthfully, we are all tax collectors, but we tend to think of ourselves the way the Pharisees did. Let us pray like the tax collector and be reminded that God is "faithful and just to forgive" (1 John 1:9). Because of this, our only response should be an overflowing of absolute love for the Savior. The gospel is not about what we can do but what Jesus has done.

Let us all respond in much love to our great Redeemer.

PRAYER TARGET:
Legalistic believers.

PERSONAL PRAYER FOR KNOXVILLE:

O, God, I thank You for sending Your beloved son to redeem us from our sin. I thank You for loving us despite our utter sinfulness and unworthiness. God, I pray that You would open our eyes to see our sin more clearly and that You would make us loathe it. I pray that while You are opening our eyes to our sin, that You would make us see Your redeeming love in a fresh, fuller, and radical way. I pray that You would let our response and our lives be a cherishing of the forgiveness that You freely give us. I pray that showing much love in response to Your indelible grace would be the hallmark of our lives. Let us never hold ourselves in high esteem but rather hold Your perfection and redeeming love in high esteem. Thank You for having mercy on us sinners. In Jesus precious and holy Name I pray. Amen.

AUTHOR: ELLIE MILLIKAN
FAMILY STRUCTURE: MOTHER, FATHER, AND 1 BROTHER
OCCUPATION: HIGH SCHOOL STUDENT

REJOICING IN ALL TIMES

"Rejoice in the Lord always I will say it again: Rejoice! Let your gentleness be evident to all. The Lord is near. Do not be anxious about anything, but in every situation, by prayer and petition, with thanksgiving, present your requests to God." Philippians 4:4-6

Last night I read a devotional from Emily Anne Roberts, which led me to my verses. She challenged me with this question: Am I restless, discontent with where I am and in need of perspective? This is the question I want to ask you today? Are you? Has school been a big burden on you? Do you feel unloved? Have you felt like you're not worth it? Have you been mean to your parents? Have you just been lazy? Have you just been mean? Have you and your spouse been getting in arguments? Has your child misbehaved a lot recently? Have you lost someone you loved? Do you feel like your whole world is falling apart? Many of these things have happened to me, especially feeling like the whole world is falling apart. If you think you and I are the only ones who feel this way, well you are wrong. Everyone has days and months where they are not content. I was having one of those a couple of weeks ago. You see, I was wishing time away, and worrying about the future. I was discontent with some of my classes and how the week was taking "forever." I had not given God as much time as I should. The week has been one of the most stressful weeks for me and I had little sleep. School and soccer had been my busyness from God. In this particular week, I was not content and I was getting jealous of people for no reason. Perhaps I was just annoyed with them. This verse was a wakeup call. I realized I needed to look at life with a new perspective. Rejoice in God! When? Always! We are called to *rejoice* in God when we lose a soccer game, break our arm, fail a test, lose a sibling, get a raise, get a spouse, or get the lead in a play. We don't have to be super happy when the bad things happen in our lives. We can rejoice by giving them to God and praising him like it says in Philippians 4 above.

So here's my last question: Where do you see yourself today? Do you see yourself like I did earlier this week? Do you see yourself not sure of Christ? Do you see yourself as this perfect person - because you're not? Do you see yourself as a dirty rotten sinner? Do you see yourself as a person who needs to grow more with Christ? or Do you see yourself as an individual who I needs to surrender his or her life to Christ?

PRAYER TARGET:
Men, women, and teens of God remembering to rejoice in everything! Remembering you are a child of God.

PERSONAL PRAYER FOR KNOXVILLE:
Dear Lord, I pray that the people in Knoxville will hear and see You. Father, I Pray for the people that are struggling with addictions or with following You completely. I pray that hearts will be changed and that people will find You. I pray for love in the city, Jesus. I pray that we have patience with each other and encourage each other. Father, don't let the enemy get in the way. I pray that fear doesn't stop us. Lord challenge the people of Knoxville and grow us as a whole. Help us to be still and know that You are God. In Your name I pray. Amen.

WEEK FORTY FOUR: THURSDAY

AUTHOR: JOHN AVANT
FAMILY STRUCTURE: WIFE, 3 MARRIED CHILDREN, AND 4 GRANDCHILDREN
OCCUPATION: LIFE ACTION MINISTRIES

SEEING WHAT WE'VE NEVER SEEN

"Call to Me and I will answer you and show you great and mighty things which you do not know." Jeremiah 33:3

Jeremiah heard this promise from God while he was imprisoned in a dungeon! I love the fact that in the Bible God's promises are made in the context of impossible situations. Today, the church in America finds itself in a very bad place. The culture has changed both within the church and most certainly without. The average church member attends about 1.2 times a month and the average lost person does not attend at all. It seems like we find ourselves in an impossible situation. And that is exactly where God loves to step in!

In the year 1995 we saw God step in at Coggin Avenue Baptist Church in Brownwood, Texas and move in such a mighty way that it spread to over 100 college campuses and churches across the country. It can happen today! Will you believe God for a mighty move of His Spirit in your church? Will you be a part of it? Will you refuse to fuss and fight over lesser things? And will You pray the prayer God gave Jeremiah and believe it for your church? He is ready to answer if we will call!

PRAYER TARGET:
Revival in The Churches everywhere.

PERSONAL PRAYER FOR KNOXVILLE:
Lord, I pray that across this city our churches will cry out to You and believe what You say. Show us, Father, great and mighty

things that we have never seen before! Do this for Your glory and the advancement of Your kingdom. In Jesus' name. Amen.

WEEK FORTY FOUR: FRIDAY

AUTHOR: LISA OSAKUE
FAMILY STRUCTURE: 1 ADULT SON, DAUGHTER IN LAW AND 1 GRANDCHILD
OCCUPATION: DISABLED

WALKING OUT ON FAITH

"A song of ascents. I lift up my eyes to the mountains—where does my help come from? My help comes from the LORD, the Maker of heaven and earth. He will not let your foot slip— he who watches over you will not slumber; indeed, he who watches over Israel will neither slumber nor sleep. The LORD watches over you— the LORD is your shade at your right hand; the sun will not harm you by day, nor the moon by night. The LORD will keep you from all harm— he will watch over your life; the LORD will watch over your coming and going both now and forevermore."
Psalm 121:1-8

I once heard a message called, "Journey to the Judge." In this message, we were challenged to realize our main goal in life is to meet the Lord. We will have bumps in our journey; we will question our faith; and we will wonder why others seem to have better families and more wealth. We will wonder why others have better bodies and better hair. And we will wonder why things that come so easy for others are so difficult for us.
In the times I question my faith; the times I wonder why I lost everything I had in Hurricane Katrina; and the times I wonder why my brothers left me so soon, I then think why I am the last of my mom's children to still be here. I wonder why I have had life-time health challenges and I wonder why I have been morbidly obese my entire life. My questions continue when I ask why I am the shortest adult in my family. It is in my many wondering that I look to God and pray for Him to give me peace and help me find joy in all the ways life has challenged me. I know all in this life is temporary. I am only here to serve and help

others as they go on their "Journey to the Judge."

PRAYER TARGET:
Those who are questioning.

PERSONAL PRAYER FOR KNOXVILLE:
Lord, let me be Your humble servant always helping others bear their burdens. Lord, let me be a ram in the bush. Let all I endure and all I go through give me wisdom to help my fellow man to grow closer to You. Lord always put me where you need me to be.

Most of all, Father, when my days are done and I come to You, I ask that all I leave behind will be peace and joy. I ask You forgive me my short comings. I hope You, Father, can say to me, "Servant, well done." Amen.

WEEK FORTY FIVE: MONDAY

AUTHOR: KATHRYN COMPEAU
FAMILY STRUCTURE: HUSBAND
OCCUPATION: MENTORING INITIATIVES COORDINATOR

STAND FIRM IN TRUTH

> "Put on the whole armor of God, that you may be able to stand against the schemes of the devil. For we do not wrestle against flesh and blood, but against the rulers, against the authorities, against the cosmic powers over this present darkness, against the spiritual forces of evil in the heavenly places. Therefore, take up the whole armor of God, that you may be able to withstand in the evil day, and having done all, to stand firm." Ephesians 6:11-13

If one reads further, the passage above goes on to explain each piece of armor that the Lord gives us to use in battle. Several years ago, the Lord opened up my eyes and my heart to studying spiritual warfare. For a long time, I didn't know much about it, and I surely didn't understand that all Satan does is distort Truth in our lives. If he is able to succeed, nothing makes him happier.

This passage is incredible because God has given us the tools, all the tools we need to *stand firm* in the face of adversity. When everything is falling apart, when lies are creeping in, we can *stand firm*. And why? Because Jesus has already won the victory! Jesus came, fully man, fully God, died on a cross, took all our sins with Him, and rose again. He paved the way. He defeated Satan that day, and as we know from the book of Revelation, He will come again and throw Satan into that fiery pit where he belongs. We know the ending of the story. It's already been given to us; therefore, there is no need to fear the Enemy and his tactics. Instead, we need to gird ourselves with the belt of truth, the breastplate of righteousness, the shoes of the Gospel of peace, the shield of faith, the helmet of salvation, and the sword of the Spirit.

PRAYER TARGET:
All people that are faced with spiritual warfare and seeking Gods armor.

PERSONAL PRAYER FOR KNOXVILLE:
Father, I pray that the people in Knoxville and surrounding areas will recognize the lies that the enemy tries to tell us, because we are so rooted in the Truth, that the lies will stick out like sore thumbs. I pray that we will encourage one another to stand firm in the face of adversity, because we know that we will face trials and difficult times. Help us to know that Jesus has won. He is our victory! I pray that we will remind one another of this TRUTH every day. May we all recognize that we do not wrestle against flesh and blood, but against the rulers, against the authorities, against the cosmic powers over this present darkness, and against the spiritual forces of evil. Amen.

WEEK FORTY FIVE: TUESDAY

AUTHOR: GRACE HARTZOG
FAMILY STRUCTURE: WIDOW
OCCUPATION: RETIRED

YOU CAN'T OUT GIVE GOD

**"They had come to hear him and to be healed of their diseases; and those troubled by evil spirits were healed".
Luke 6:18**

I have believed for many ears that all that I have belongs to God and He has given me authority to use or misuse my resources and my time. One week ago today we were blessed in the part of the country we live in to experience a phenomenal event, a total solar eclipse. I had a pair of viewing glasses and had anticipated seeing the eclipse. I have a dear brother-in-law who is an invalid. His main source of entertainment is watching the History channel or the Discovery channel. He wanted very much to see the eclipse. My sister had not been able to obtain glasses and it looked as if he would not be able to watch. I felt I should give him my glasses and watch it on tv, The day before the eclipse, I called my sister and told her to come and get my glasses. She reluctantly came and got them. The next day I was busying myself in the morning when my neighbor came and ask me if I gave my glasses away. I had confided my thoughts to her. I told her I did and that I was fine with that. She said, "Here is a pair for you. Go and watch the event." With Joy, I shared them with my neighbors and we saw a magnificent work of God. Again God proved to this 86-year-old woman that He knows and cares about even the most minute things in our life.

PRAYER TARGET:
Young families seeking to learn the way of the Lord and His glory.

446

PERSONAL PRAYER FOR KNOXVILLE:

Dear Father, You established the family in the beginning. The family is the vehicle you use to stabilize this unstable world. Father, I ask you to bring revival in families. Stir hearts that have gotten so wrapped around things of this world. I ask that you stir the hearts in the church families in our city and bring revival to our city. Bring hearts united to the cross. I thank you that you love us enough to give your best to us, your only begotten Son, our Blessed Savior, Jesus the Christ, in whose name I ask. Amen

WEEK FORTY FIVE: WEDNESDAY

AUTHOR: JOY JAMES-FOSTER
FAMILY STRUCTURE: HUSBAND AND 3 CHILDREN
OCCUPATION: EDUCATOR

FROM DECREASE TO INCREASE

"He must increase, but I must decrease." John 3:30

John 3:30 is vital to me because I feel it helped me take the emphasis off me and my situation. He reminded me that in everything I do it is about using my talents and gifts for His glory.

I was at a point in my life when I felt that God left me, but what God showed me through His Word is that it was I who left him. Although with my words I gave God the glory for allowing me to accomplish my goals, I never asked God what His goals were for my life. God showed me through the scripture above that He must increase. That meant then that I had to decrease. He gave me the charge to use my talents for His glory because He had a major purpose for me. Although He allowed me to accomplish what I thought I wanted, He was just preparing me for another work for Him. Therefore, God removed me from my plans and recalibrated my compass. Today I let Him use me for His purpose and walk a changed path.

PRAYER TARGET:
All who feel forgotten, that they will learn to focus on Him.

PERSONAL PRAYER FOR KNOXVILLE:
Father, our purpose on Earth is to bring others to Christ. I pray that everyone will allow God to increase and let ourselves decrease. Dear Lord, when people see us, allow them to see the love of Jesus Christ. Take away the layers of the outer man in order that others can see You in us. Dear God, let us decrease in

order that others can see You in us. Dear God, let us decrease in order that You may increase. It is not about us. The goal is not to make us look good for our own applause, but to ensure that our efforts cause others to follow and seek after You. In Jesus' Holy Name. Amen

WEEK FORTY FIVE: THURSDAY

AUTHOR: KATHERINE DUTT
FAMILY STRUCTURE: HUSBAND AND 1 SON
OCCUPATION: HOMEMAKER

TEARS OF SORROW

"You keep track of all my sorrows. You have collected all my tears in your bottle. You have recorded each one in your book." Psalm 56:8

I am the last and youngest child in my family. Being the youngest, I have experienced quitea bit of loss in my life. My oldest brother was eleven years older than me and I lost him when he was only 48 years old in 2002. In 2007, I lost my beloved mother to multiple myeloma cancer. In 2015, my father passed away from Alzheimer's disease. My mother was my best friend.

When my mother passed away, I received a gift from my Ladies Bible Study teacher. She came to my house and brought me a bouquet of beautiful flowers and an ornate, etched, glass bottle. She shared the verse, Psalm 56:8 with me at that time. I can remember reading the verse and thinking to myself how amazing that my Lord, the God of the universe, cared so much for me that he collected all the tears I had shed for all of my lost loved ones. I was totally bowled over that the Lord loves and cares about us so much, even the small details in our everyday life. I found so much comfort in the verse above and I pray you will too.

PRAYER TARGET:
All who are experiencing sorrow or loss.

PERSONAL PRAYER FOR KNOXVILLE:

Precious Lord, I pray for protection and unity at this time in our lives in Knoxville. Father, I ask that we as Christ followers will come together in worshipping You and sharing the gospel with our brothers and sisters in Knoxville. May Your name be glorified through it all. Amen.

WEEK FORTY FIVE: FRIDAY

AUTHOR: KAREN ALEXANDER DOYEL
FAMILY STRUCTURE: HUSBAND, 3 MARRIED SONS, AND 5 GRANDCHILDREN
OCCUPATION: MINISTRY MULTIPLIER, INSPIRATIONAL SPEAKER,
CONFERENCE AND BIBLE LEADER

TAKE HEART

> **"Praise be to the God and Father of our Lord Jesus Christ, the Father of compassion and the God of all comfort, who comforts us in all our troubles, so that we can comfort those in any trouble with the comfort we ourselves have received from God. For just as the sufferings of Christ flow over into our lives, so also through Christ our comfort overflows." 2 Corinthians 1:3-5**

I struggled to get my rain jacket over my shoulders and the aching bones still tingling from yesterday's chemo double dose. I was grateful that even though I hurt, I was actually driving, going to the store, and doing it on my own two feet! As I checked out my groceries, exhausted from the "huge outing" that I have been on, a woman behind me quietly says: "Ma'am, do you have cancer?" Slightly smiling as if to say "How'd you guess with this bald head and head wrap," I politely said, "Yes I do." She followed up with a heartfelt, "I sure hope your prognosis is good". It was then I remembered and said "Medical prognosis not so good, but my eternal prognosis is FABULOUS!"

Each place I speak, I hear heartbreaking stories. What does God want you and me to do as we listen to the trials in the lives of the people we meet? How are we impacting the people He puts in our lives? Jesus clearly tells us in John 16:33 "I have told you these things, so that in me you may have. peace. In this world you will have trouble. But take heart! I have overcome the world."

As Christians in the city of Knoxville we must make a decision to act, pray, serve, and to show the reason to "Take Heart!" There are more needs than those who are willing to answer the call to comfort with the comfort you may have received. We must tell about the God of comfort and we must show them the Overcomer of this world. I personally know Him. He gives me strength for the journey, guidance for the trials, and comfort for my hurts.

PRAYER TARGET:
Hurting people.

PERSONAL PRAYER FOR KNOXVILLE:
My sweet Heavenly Father, I come to You now on behalf of our city. You know the hurts that we are experiencing. I am asking for You to show Yourself as a Comforter to our city. Let us rise up and proclaim who You are to those around us who cannot take heart because they do not know You. Our hope is firm in You. Help us share that hope with this city. Give us boldness. Give us a love that reaches beyond ourselves and touches the lives of the people we encounter every day. Open our eyes to see those You put in our lives each day that need You. Give us the willingness to reach out and touch the lives of those hurting around us. Father, draw them to You and let them see our Jesus. Jesus bring salvation to this city and bring glory to Yourself. Let us comfort with the comfort we have received from You. Bind the enemy from this place and be high and lifted up in the city of Knoxville for Your Kingdoms sake.
In the Powerful Name of Jesus I Pray for the City of Knoxville and surrounding areas. Amen

WEEK FORTY SIX: MONDAY

AUTHOR: DELORES PUGH
FAMILY STRUCTURE: HUSBAND AND 2 ADULT DAUGHTERS
OCCUPATION: RETIRED, HOUSEWIFE

THE LORD'S PRAYER

> **"Our Father which art in heaven, Hallowed be thy name. Thy kingdom come, Thy will be done in earth as it is in heaven. Give us this day our daily bread.And forgive us our debts, as we forgive our debtors.And lead us not into temptation, but deliver us from evil:For Thine is the kingdom, and the power, and the glory, forever. Amen."**
> **Matthew 6:9-13**

The Lord's Prayer has been an important part of my life since early childhood. It always was a prayer in our home and in the Baptist church in which I grew up. I had it memorized before I knew the ABCs or could spell my name! As I grew older, the Lord's Prayer (often referred to as the *Model Prayer*) grew with me – and God became focused and real in my everyday walk and relationship with Him. And I understood more clearly the Prayer's petitions that focus on God, His will and His glory, and our human needs. (The Prayer was so important to me that it was sung at my wedding 50 years ago.)

The Lord's Prayer helped me grow spiritually and more and more in love with my Father in Heaven. All prayers, if consistent and sincere, will do the same. And they will not go unheard. So, let us pray.

PRAYER TARGET:
The diverse groups of people in the city of Knoxville and surrounding areas.

PERSONAL PRAYER FOR KNOXVILLE:

It is my prayer, God, that You who created us all will be recognized by everyone as their Heavenly Father; that You will be the center of all families and households;
the leader of schools and businesses; and the head of our governments. I pray that forgiveness, love, and unity will replace divisiveness, hate, hurt, and harm. I pray that Knoxville and surrounding areas will truly be a God-fearing cities, and that the cities response will be a leading example for others to witness and want to follow. May each Knoxville and surrounding areas resident choose Jesus as Best Friend, and be happy in the Lord always. Amen and Amen.

WEEK FORTY SIX: TUESDAY

AUTHOR: ANDREW OSAKUE
FAMILY STRUCTURE: WIFE AND 1 DAUGHTER
OCCUPATION: PASTOR

FIND YOUR STRENGTH IN THE LORD

"Then they cried to the LORD in their trouble and He brought them out of their distresses." Psalm 107:28

They (Amalekites) had attacked Ziklag and burned it, and had taken captive the women and everyone else in it, both young and old. They killed none of them, but carried them off as they went on their way. When David and his men reached Ziklag, they found it (destroyed by fire and their wives and sons and daughters taken captive.) So David and his men wept aloud until they had no strength left to weep. David was greatly distressed because the men were talking of stoning him; each one was bitter in spirit because of his sons and daughters. But David found strength in the Lord his God. Then David said to Abiathar the priest, the son of Ahimelek, 'Bring me the ephod.' Abiathar brought it to him." 1 Samuel 30:1-4, 6-7

In this passage, David and his men had just arrived in Ziklag and expected a warm embrace from their families. Instead, they found the city burned and their families carried away by the enemy. The hearts of the men were shattered as they thought of never seeing their families again. All of the men wept profusely and cried so long and hard that there were no more tears left to give. A total of six hundred men were involved in this scenario. Their tears led to bitterness and they decided they would stone David for what the enemy had done. David was faced with a critical decision at this moment. He could allow his emotions to make him *bitter* or allow the Lord to make him *better*. David experienced the same devastation as these men but chose to find his strength in the Lord. Rather than picking up stones, he picked up the "phone" and called the priest to receive a word from God.

Beloved, I do not know exactly what is happening in your life at this very moment, yet I can assure you that bitterness and stones will not accomplish God's will in your life. In the midst of hurt and pain, David found his strength in the Lord, which led him to seek the presence of God. David did not entertain the bitterness of these men for one moment. The second half of the story says that David was able to lead these same men to take back their families and all the enemy had stolen! The people around you do not need to see you as a person who is good at throwing stones. They need to see you finding strength in the Lord and ushering others into His presence. In the presence of the Lord is the fullness of joy - all bitterness must flee in the name of Jesus. Yes, it will hurt so badly at times that we will cry until there is nothing left. But just like David, we do not cry to *quit*. We cry to *keep going*!

PRAYER TARGET:
The bitter and hurting to find strength in the Lord.

PERSONAL PRAYER FOR KNOXVILLE:
Father, I pray You will help those of us dealing with painful situations to find our strength in You. Let us not blame people for what the enemy has done. Instead, Father, give us strength to call on You and usher those who are hurting into Your presence. Let no one fall short of the grace of God and allow no bitter root to grow up to cause trouble and defile many. I pray everyone walking in bitterness and hurt will surrender themselves completely to You. I pray the Holy Spirit will be the lifter of our heads and give us compassion for those hurting among us. Might Your compassion move us into supernatural action toward those among us in need of Your presence. Amen.

AUTHOR: CANDA EILERTSON
FAMILY STRUCTURE: HUSBAND AND 2 SONS
OCCUPATION: HIGH SCHOOL SUBSTITUTE TEACHER AND AT-HOME MOM

IN NEED OF A GODLY GUARD

> "LORD, set up a guard for my mouth; Keep watch at the door of my lips." Psalm 141:3
> "We destroy arguments and every lofty opinion raised against the knowledge of God and take every thought captive to obey Christ, being ready to punish every disobedience, when your obedience is complete."
> 2 Corinthians 10:5-6

A challenge of being a Sanguine/Melancholy personality type is that I find myself saying the first and sometimes sassy thing that comes to mind. Then, I agonize over whose feelings I've hurt with my words.

Over the course of my faith journey, I have learned that we as humans act on our belief systems, whatever they are. As a Christian, when I'm faced with my own failures, I have an opportunity to recognize faulty patterns of my own belief systems. Then, I have to ask myself, "What specifically can I do through Christ to change so that I'm honoring God and others?" Since God made each of us unique (Psalm 139), I know that, through Him, I don't have to be enslaved by my personality propensities. According to the scripture above in 2 Corinthians I find that I must allow God to guard my words. That means I should first be taking every thought captive to obey Christ.

I can trust Jesus Christ to always glorify and honor God. By allowing God to work in me through the Holy Spirit, I am left at peace in my mind, in my heart, and in my attitudes and actions. Only with God as my guard, can I trust that every one of my words will count for His Kingdom.

PRAYER TARGET:
Minds and mouths in need of a Godly guard.

PERSONAL PRAYER FOR KNOXVILLE:
Lord, let our words honor You. Embolden our witness, so our words have meaning. When we defend Your Word, Your truth, let us do it respectfully. When we are under attack from the enemy, let us lean on each other and on You as a united church, as Jesus longs for us to be. (John 17:11). Give us strength and courage to remain in You in an environment that is increasingly at enmity with You and those who are ambassadors for You. Thank You for Your sacrificial love for us and for Your desire for a lost world to come to know You. You alone are Worthy! Help us to live to reflect that we believe this! In Jesus Name, Amen

WEEK FORTY SIX: THURSDAY

AUTHOR: EMMETTE THOMPSON
FAMILY STRUCTURE: WIFE AND 2 ADULT CHILDREN
OCCUPATION: EXECUTIVE DIRECTOR

HOPE...A KEY INGREDIENT FOR DAILY LIFE

"Let Your mercy, O LORD, be upon us, just as we hope in You." Psalm 33:22

Each and every day, we wake up and life begins with a new start. Sometimes we know in great detail what lies ahead from our calendars and our previously directed plans. But on some days we are simply not prepared for what lies ahead...and that can be troubling. Each of us is after all on a "Life Journey Path," and sometimes the pitfalls of that path can be burdensome. I feel that is where HOPE comes into play. I personally have adopted the following definition of HOPE that I cling to: The *confident expectation of good.* It doesn't mean we are entitled to anything...we just trust with blind faith that good will prevail.

PRAYER TARGET:
The forlorn and weary...and need true HOPE.

PERSONAL PRAYER FOR KNOXVILLE:
Dear Heavenly Father, may our feet never hit the floor each morning without us acknowledging Your gift of another day. We thank You for all that You bless us with and for how You meet our needs. We humbly appeal for Your Will to be done each and every day. God...please bring revival back to our country in a way that only You can so that You will be given the praise, credit, and glory for making it happen. We truly thank You for who You are and for Your provision and loving grace to all mankind. Please help us to be a beacon of HOPE for all we encounter...as we journey through Life. Amen

WEEK FORTY SIX: FRIDAY

AUTHOR: JOYCE K. KENT
FAMILY STRUCTURE: HUSBAND AND 1 ADULT DAUGHTER
OCCUPATION: RETIRED

HOW TO PRAY

"For be it from me that I should sin against God by failing to pray for you." 1 Samuel 12:23

How to ask God for very important things, such as to delivering someone from a critical illness, became an issue in my life when I prayed that a friend's husband would not die. I failed to say, "If it be Thy will." His wife simply prayed for God's will to be done. The good news is, the man did survive.

It seemed appropriate after the emergency was over to discuss if I prayed incorrectly since the way I prayed did not match the way my friend prayed. According to my study in the Word, I believe that God answered my prayer as well as hers. We are told that our prayers can be short but they must be faith-filled. God knows our hearts; therefore, if we pray sincerely, I do believe we can ask for anything.

Praying is one of the most spiritual thing we can do as believers. God hears every prayer. This is affirmed in 1 John 5:14 where we are told, "This is the confidence we have in approaching God: that if we ask anything according to His will, He hears us."

PRAYER TARGET:
Senior citizens.

PERSONAL PRAYER FOR KNOXVILLE:

Father, I pray that everyone will look to You for all things, large and small. Let us not hesitate to ask You for our needs. Help us to not be concerned about Your answer but trust You to solve our problems in the way that will glorify You. We are Yours, Lord. Lead us to depend on You. Amen.

WEEK FORTY SEVEN: MONDAY

AUTHOR: DAVID TREMPE
FAMILY STRUCTURE: WIFE AND 7 CHILDREN
OCCUPATION: PASTOR AND CHAPLAIN

THE PRIEST OF GOD

"Children are a heritage from the LORD, offspring a reward from him. Like arrows in the hands of a warrior are children born in one's youth. Blessed is the man whose quiver is full of them. They will not be put to shame when they contend with their opponents in court." Psalm 127:3-5

If I'm being honest with myself I don't like what I'm becoming in this age of effortless technological advancements. It's easier for me to spend more time on Facebook than I do putting my face into Gods book. Many Facebook posts seem to spotlight pictures of marriage, family, and friends and most have spent more time posing for a selfie than they spent in prayer last month. Many parents get angry with their kids playing video games all day and not going outside - yet most adults spend more time addicted to the latest news on another person's Facebook page just trying to help satisfy the chasm of isolation in their own soul.

We want.... we desire.... and we are built for covenant community. We need one another to be transparent, raw and real. We, like Adam and Eve, don't believe God's instruction is best for us. We always pursue the one thing God has asked us to avoid. We think we know exactly what we want. Unfortunately, we don't! Jeremiah 17:9 says, "The heart is deceitful above all things and beyond cure. Who can understand it?"

The majority of our conversations are about everything in the universe except that which matters most. The fires that burns those around others, oddly enough, seem to warm us. We use their pain as a barometer to feel better about our circumstances. Therefore, the question must be asked, "Where is your treasure? Where do you invest the majority of your heart, mind, and emotions?"

The answer to that question is brutal, because if it's anything else but Christ and His kingdom- you may want to re-navigate your vessel! We are taught to get an education, get a great job, a house, a family, etc... but Dads, we MUST lead in war and worship. The number one goal for our children is knowing Jesus Christ. We are subject to His kingdom not our individual wants and desires. Our lives are a journey of faith. As God's ambassadors, we don't need to be perfect but we do need to be honest. To God alone be the glory and to us be His loving good.

PRAYER TARGET:
Men seeking companionship within Gods community and not in the conveniences of this world.

PERSONAL PRAYER FOR KNOXVILLE:
Lord, You alone have displayed for us the beauty of true family. You have adopted us by Your Blood into Your family. Teach every man to be the priest of his family, to cover his bride and his children with the Love of God. Teach us as men to leave something in our children instead of something for our children. May each of our children have a double portion of all the grace and joy that You have given to us. Amen.

WEEK FORTY SEVEN: TUESDAY

AUTHOR: ANGIE PODGORSKI
FAMILY STRUCTURE: HUSBAND, 3 DAUGHTERS, AND 2 GRANDCHILDREN
OCCUPATION: BIBLE STUDY FELLOWSHIP TEACHING LEADER

HOLD ON TO THE HOPE

"Let us hold on unswervingly to the hope we profess, for He who promised is faithful." Hebrews 10:23

The threat of storms is a constant reality in our world today, whether it is a severe thunderstorm, snowstorm, hail storm, or tropical storm with hurricane force winds. Imagine being out to sea with the wind and waves crashing all around you. An umbrella and rain jacket would not serve much purpose as your boat was being tossed around! Just as storms in nature occur all around us, so do storms often touch our personal lives.... storms of doubt, disappointment, discouragement, disease and even disaster. What do we do when the storms of life rage around us? Do we live in fear or do we look to Jesus in faith? Do we cling to our umbrellas & hope for the best? Or do we cling to Jesus, the *Hope*, and rest in His mighty power? Jesus will either calm the storm or He will calm us until the storm passes. He has the power to do both! Cultural hope is a boatload of 'wishful thinking' that is subject to ever changing people and circumstances. In contrast, Christian hope rests on Jesus Christ & His Word, which never changes.

Where have you placed your hope? In yourself, your dreams, your finances.... or in Christ alone? Hebrews 6:19 says, "*We have this hope as an anchor for the soul, firm and secure!*" When the storms in life come, we can hold on unswervingly to the hope we profess, because Jesus is forever faithful in all His ways!

PRAYER TARGET:
Those who need a good dose of hope in our city!

PERSONAL PRAYER FOR KNOXVILLE:
Father, You are the God of hope! Your Word declares, "No one who hopes in You will ever be put to shame." Thank You for sending Your Son, Jesus Christ, who is the Living Hope we can hold on to in the midst of the storms in life. I pray for those in our city who need a good dose of hope. May we all turn to Jesus and be filled with all joy and peace as we trust Him. May we overflow with HOPE by the power of the Holy Spirit and shine brightly for You in Knoxville and the world! Amen.

WEEK FORTY SEVEN: WEDNESDAY

AUTHOR: JASON CAUDILL
FAMILY STRUCTURE: WIFE
OCCUPATION: ASSOCIATE PROFESSOR OF BUSINESS

OUR WORK AND OUR FOCUS

> "Make it your ambition to lead a quiet life: You should mind your own business and work with your hands, just as we told you, so that your daily life may win the respect of outsiders and so that you will not be dependent on anybody." 1 Thessalonians 4:11-12

My wife wrote this verse down for me after reading it in one of her devotionals and I keep that notecard sitting on my desk. We live in a time when the greatest attention is devoted to the loudest voices rather than the wisest. In our work lives almost all of us are faced with the feeling that whatever we do today we need to do more tomorrow. This loudness, this busyness, this constant state of stress and worry is not what God intends for us. We are meant to live quietly, to work not for men but for the Lord, and to be an example to those around us of what it looks like to follow God. Whatever our profession, whatever our role in life, we can all benefit from peace and focus, and things that run counter to much of the world around us.

PRAYER TARGET:
The workforce, to be able to live godly and be a good light for the Lord.

PERSONAL PRAYER FOR KNOXVILLE:
Lord, we pray that You will give us Your guidance in our daily work and our service to those around us. Help us to maintain our focus where it belongs. Help us to live that quiet life, to

serve you, our families, and our community in ways that will reflect You and the promise that You give to us. Lead us, guide us, and bless us in all that we do. Bless our city, Lord, with peace. Draw us together and draw us closer to you. It is in Jesus' name we pray to You, Father, Amen.

AUTHOR: VICKIE TRANUM
FAMILY STRUCTURE: HUSBAND AND 2 ADULT TWIN DAUGHTERS
OCCUPATION: EXECUTIVE ASSISTANT

GRATEFUL HEARTS

"The Lord is my strength and my shield; in Him my heart trusts, and I am helped; my heart exults, and with my song I give thanks to Him." Psalm 28:7

Ever feel like things are just too good? You're just waiting for the next "shoe to drop," so to speak? Right now I'm in a season of rest. My girls are married to godly young men and have jobs of purpose and meaning. My parents are in good health. My marriage of almost thirty-nine years is in a good place. My husband and I are employed and healthy. I feel enormously blessed. So, why is there this hesitancy in my Spirit that calamity is just waiting and ready to knock at my door?

We live in a world full of hurt and hurting people, so to be exempt from that sometimes feels unnatural. But, scripture teaches us that we are to give thanks in everything. (Philippians 4) Don't only reach out to God when you are hurting or struggling. Remember to praise Him when all is well in your world. The blessings are from Him and it's just plain rude to not say, *"Thank You!"*

PRAYER TARGET:
Women of Knoxville and surrounding areas to be aware of His continual blessings!

PERSONAL PRAYER FOR KNOXVILLE:
Father, thank You! Your blessings are so underserved, yet You pour them out in abundance. Help us to remember to take

time to say, "Thank you!" As women – moms, daughters, sisters, grandmas, wives, and working women – we get so
focused on serving those around us, we often forget to stop and look at all the blessings You pour out so freely upon us. Help us to take time to recognize that it all comes from You, Father. James 1:17 tells us that, "Every good gift and every perfect gift is from above, coming down from the Father of lights…" So, today we take time to say, "Thank You!" Thank you for our families, our jobs, our very life itself. For without You, we are nothing but a vapor in the wind. May we be grateful women, sharing Your Grace with all those with whom we come in contact. We pray this in the sweet name of Jesus, the Giver of all Gifts, and Savior of our souls. Amen!

WEEK FORTY SEVEN: FRIDAY

AUTHOR: CHRISTOPHER BATTLE
FAMILY STRUCTURE: WIFE AND 19 CHILDREN
OCCUPATION: PASTOR

DESPICABLE WORSHIP

> "Stop bringing meaningless offerings. Your incense is detestable to me. New Moons, Sabbaths and convocations—I cannot bear yourworthless assemblies. Your New Moon feasts and your appointedfestivals. I hate with all my being. They have become a burden to me; I am weary of bearing them. When you spread out your hands in prayer, I hide my eyes from you; even when you offer many prayers, I am not listening. Your hands are full of blood! Washand make yourselves clean. Take your evil deeds out of my sight;stop doing wrong. Learn to do right; seek justice. Defend the oppressed. Take up the cause of the fatherless; plead thecase of the widow." Isaiah 1:13-17

The prophets of Israel were troubled by the lack of mercy and justice exercised by the nation. Amos and Micah cried against the continued mistreatment of the less fortunate. Like his contemporaries Isaiah critiqued and railed against the exploitation of the powerless and the absence of compassion for the needy. Instead of caring for the widow, the orphan and the stranger, the people of God were mistreating and ignoring them. They would take the coat of the homeless man and use it for a cushion in church. They would take the last dime from the beggar and put it in the offering plate. Somehow, they had come to believe that they could worship God in the Sanctuary and abandon the needy and the dispossessed who stood beneath the shadows of their steeples. They did not see the connection between their worship and their treatment of others. They had fooled themselves into believing that they could sing, pray, pay their tithes, attend Sunday School classes, and forsake the "least of these." They had become so consumed with their personal salvation that they became unconcerned with the plight of the immigrant, refugees, and those not like them. They wrongly assumed that God would not see those whom they overlooked.

God's response to their insensitivity to the widows, orphans, and those treated unjustly was severe. He told them their rituals mean nothing to Him. Their sacrifices and offerings were leaving a stench in His nostrils. He would not stomach their thoughtlessness, selfishness, and inattention to His people. He wanted to bless them but they had become a burden to Him. Even their prayers were no longer heard. He saw their hands as having the blood of the innocent upon them. His words, *"You make Me sick,"* were profound! But God offers hope. The prophet says that if you as a nation, a people of God and faith, will loosen the bonds of oppression, release the yoke from the poor, treat the stranger as a brother and do justice, then the Glory of the Lord will return to you to lead and guide you, to strengthen, and prosper you.

PRAYER TARGET:
The Church that would reach out beyond the pews to a world that is in need of love.

PERSONAL PRAYER FOR KNOXVILLE:
Help us Father to be a church where worship is a verb. Move upon us with Your Spirit that the quality of our worship would be judged by the way we treat the least among us and less by the size of our budgets and buildings. Amen.

WEEK FORTY EIGHT: MONDAY

AUTHOR: BEVERLY WALTON
FAMILY STRICTURE: HUSBAND, 2 ADULT CHILDREN, AND 5 GRANDSONS
OCCUPATION: HOUSEWIFE AND HOMEBOUND MINISTRY

NO LONELY SOULS

> "Praise be to the God and Father of our Lord Jesus Christ, the Father of compassion and the God of all comfort, who comforts us in all our troubles, so that we can comfort those in any trouble with the comfort we ourselves have received from God." 2 Corinthians 1:3-4

Loneliness is a noun. Love is a verb. Put them together and you have a ministry to homebound people.

Many older people are isolated because of health issues or mobility limitations. Some are far from family or are in care facilities. Bringing a little cheer and encouragement in the name of Jesus to one of these precious souls is as simple as a short visit, a phone call, or sending a note or card. Mostly it is listening – sometimes to the same thing repeated many times over. Sometimes it is just holding a hand and reminding them of God's love. Always it is praying for and with them.

Priceless rewards come to those who invest a little time and effort in developing a relationship with someone who is confined by circumstances and hungry for Christian fellowship.

PRAYER TARGET:
All citizens to show love to the homebound.

PERSONAL PRAYER FOR KNOXVILLE:
Dear God, may we be sensitive and reach out to those around us who are lonely and hurting. Let us be the hands and feet of Jesus

on this earth to minister to those who are hungry for a caring presence in their lives. Let us remember, Father, that whatsoever we do to the least of these we do unto Him. In Your precious Name. Amen.

WEEK FORTY EIGHT: TUESDAY

AUTHOR: MIRIAM ROSS
FAMILY STRUCTURE: WIDOW, 2 ADULT CHILDREN, AND 3 GRANDCHILDREN
OCCUPATION: RETIRED TEACHER

DROWNING

"When you go through deep waters, and great trouble, I will be with you." Psalm 43:2

Have you ever felt like you were swimming upstream and simply couldn't keep going? Not another stroke? Not another kick? Not another breath? You hadn't given up; you had given out! I have experienced this and I was bone weary! I was a caregiver and I personally know exhaustion.

Over a period of twenty-seven years, I watched my strong, athletic husband's body deteriorate. I loved him so much and wanted to "fix" things, but I couldn't fix his broken body. To add to my misery, caring friends asked, "How are things going?" to which I would always reply with a smile, "We are doing okay!" Behind that smile were streams of tears flowing deep into the private hiding place that only God could see. He saw every tear and He knew my burden.
This was the time that I had to get down on my knees and whisper, "I need You, Lord! I can't do this alone."

His reply was always, "Don't worry. I have you tucked under My wing!" (Psalm 91:4) That is His promise in His Word. He tells us He will walk with us and never leave us alone. I learned that is what He does! When the waters seem too deep, God picks us up and breathes strength into our weary bodies. It is always wise to remember: He chose us to be His hands and feet right where we are. The promise to give us the stamina to do it is also there. He equips us with everything to do the task that we have. If you are a caregiver, when you feel like you are "drowning" in life, remember that Your Lifeguard walks on water. Call to Him and let Him carry you through the swift waters.

PRAYER TARGET:
Caregivers that feel weary.

PERSONAL PRAYER FOR KNOXVILLE:
Precious Lord, make us aware of this beautiful place You have chosen for each of us. Help us to be grateful and not greedy. Make us aware that all over Knoxville there are those who are lonely and in need of a kind word, handshake, or even a hug. Open our eyes, Lord, to become more aware of those that You have placed in our paths for a reason. Make every day a day that we listen to Your voice and take heed. Bind our city together with love and respect. Help us be Your people, not just in word, but in our works. Let us be the people You created us to be. I pray in Your precious Name. Amen.

WEEK FORTY EIGHT: WEDNESDAY

AUTHOR: LEE M. RAGSDALE III
FAMILY STRUCTURE: WIFE, 2 CHILDREN, 5 GRANDCHILDREN.
OCCUPATION: DEACON, SEMI-RETIRED PERSON, AND PROFESSIONAL
VOLUNTEER.

SEEING CHRIST IN EVERYONE, TRYING TO BE CHRIST-LIKE WITH EVERYONE.

> **"And the king will answer them, 'Truly I tell you, just as you did it to one of the least of these who are members of my family, you did it to me.'" Matthew 25:40**

I remember the question so well: "So, if you are ordained as a Deacon, what will you want to do?" I just knew that my answer would knock the questioner off his or her feet and my reply would go down in history. I said, in my most pious voice, that I wanted to be up and under bridges, ministering to the forgotten ones, helping those folks who were beyond the margins of society, and serving those who had been completely forgotten and were now almost invisible.

The next question was not so easy to answer. I was asked how I planned to minister to these folks and tell what could I possibly do for them? Getting to them would not be the problem, but what would I do and what could I do when I got there was more difficult? Somehow, simply telling them that God loves them in the midst of their brokenness, their loneliness, and their suffering was just too inadequate, too clichéd, and maybe a little mean.

The answer is amazingly simple and, at the same time immensely difficult. The ministry help that they so desperately seek is a ministry of real presence. It is a ministry of acknowledgement. Seeing them acknowledgement.

Seeing them as children of God, created in His image, and being wonderfully made and wonderfully loved is important. So, now I listen to understand and to be truly present with them. I always strive to see the light of Christ in them, with the hope that they might see the Light of Christ in me as well.

PRAYER TARGET:
All who seek to serve others in the name of Christ.

PERSONAL PRAYER FOR KNOXVILLE:
Creator of us all, we thank You for all the wonders of Your creation and for all the blessings of this life. We thank You for Your neve ending love and grace and we offer ourselves to Your service.

Give us sight that we might see all our brothers and sisters as Your beloved children. Give us wisdom to recognize their sacredness and our connection to them. Give us the courage, strength and patience to be truly present to all who need us in their life, so that as we are present to them, we are also present with You.
 In Christ's Name we pray, Amen!

AUTHOR: JEFF LAWRENCE
FAMILY STRUCTURE: WIFE AND 2 CHILDREN
OCCUPATION: WORSHIP PASTOR

WHEN YOU THINK GOD IS SLEEPING

> "On that day, when evening had come, he said to them, 'Let us go across to the other side.' And leaving the crowd, they took him with them in the boat, just as he was. And other boats were with him. And a great windstorm arose, and the waves were breaking into the boat, so that the boat was already filling. But he was in the stern, asleep on the cushion. And they woke him and said to him, 'Teacher, do you not care that we are perishing?' And he awoke and rebuked the wind and said to the sea, 'Peace! Be still!' And the wind ceased, and there was a great calm. He said to them, 'Why are you so afraid? Have you still no faith?' And they were filled with great fear and said to one another, 'Who then is this, that even the wind and the sea obey him?'" Mark 4:35-41

The scene: Jesus and the disciples on board a fishing boat, at night in the middle of the Sea of Galilee. For the disciples, this windstorm was not something they were going to survive. And of course, Jesus is lying on a cushion, sound asleep. He is exhausted from a full day of ministry. With all that's happening, He's sleeping like a baby! Until, of course, the disciples wake Him to ask a poignant question: "Don't you care that we're going to die?"

"God," we may say, "where are you when I need you? Don't You know I can't pay my bills, keep this marriage together, survive this diagnosis, overcome this depression and anxiety, reconcile with my brother, or beat this addiction? Don't You see my enemies surrounding me and hear their insults? Why are You sleeping when I'm on the verge of death?" Fear replaces faith, even when God is so close you can hear Him breathe and feel His heartbeat. Then Jesus, speaks: "Silence! Be Still!" or literally, "Be still, and stay still." Nature always responds immediately with a great calm. The fear of the disciples refers to timidity and lack of confidence in God. But even so, Jesus transformed the great storm into a great calm with a single breath.

If you find yourself faced with a windstorm, remember: God is in the boat. But even more so, when He melts the storm away with a word, concede your flesh and ambitions for a place of humility, subjection, and submissiveness before the magnitude of who He is!

PRAYER TARGET:
People to trust God in the storm.

PERSONAL PRAYER FOR KNOXVILLE:
Thank You, Jesus, for Your promise to be with me, even in the middle of a storm. Give me wisdom to know Your voice and direction, trust to always know You have me no matter how I feel, and courage to overcome fear. God, eclipse my tendency to fear and replace it with a bold faith. Amen

WEEK FORTY EIGHT: FRIDAY

AUTHOR: TRACY WOODS
FAMILY STRUCTURE: HUSBAND AND SON
OCCUPATION: HOMEMAKER

YOU WILL BE COMFORTED

**"Blessed are those who mourn for they will be comforted."
Matthew 5:4**

The day my daddy died was one of the saddest days of my life. But, it didn't start out that way.

Before I rushed to the other side of town, not knowing the day would end in death, God sent the most beautiful sunrise I have ever seen. I took pictures and shared them with several friends. One told me that she had just taught a lesson to her Sunday School class of eight-year-old boys. She told them was how God speaks to us through His creation. She then invited me to watch the sky the next time I saw a rainbow. Even the stars, or a sunrise or sunset, would be God saying, "Hey there. I'm here and I care for you so much."

God showed me time and again through the next days that He does love and care for me. He did it through the wonderful, and sometimes surprising, people He put in my path.

The death of a precious loved one is so hard. But you do not have to go through it alone. God has already put the people in place who will help you. Dear friends helped me through those awful "stages." Surprisingly, for me, it was different friends for different stages. Some held my hand, some wiped my tears, but more importantly, all listened. And through them, I was comforted.

God loves you, He will comfort you. He will send exactly who and what you need at the moment you need it. He also wants to use you to comfort others. When that time comes, He will give you the strength and courage to go to them!

PRAYER TARGET:
Those who mourn.

PERSONAL PRAYER FOR KNOXVILLE:
Dear Heavenly Father, the death of a loved one is something we all must face. Your Word tells us that those who mourn will be comforted. Thank You for those You send to be that comfort and for being our strength when we are called upon to comfort others. In Your Son's precious Name. Amen.

WEEK FORTY NINE: MONDAY

AUTHOR: FRANCES BORUFF
FAMILY STRUCTURE: HUSBAND, 3 MARRIED SONS, AND 5 GRANDCHILDREN
OCCUPATION: RETIRED

BLESSINGS, BLESSING BOOK, AND HIS PEACE

"Be anxious for nothing, but in everything by prayer and supplication with thanksgiving, let your request be known to God and the peace of God, which surpasses all understanding, will guard your hearts and minds through Christ." Philippians 4:6-7

"You have breast cancer!" The word, cancer, is one of the most dreaded words that can be said to a person. It was the word that was given to me. CANCER! I had just retired and had my remaining life all planned to do what I wanted to do. In hindsight, I found myself asking, "Are there too many I's in the sentence about my plans for me?" Had I asked God about His plans for my life? The doctor prescribed six weeks of radiation. I noticed on day one of my treatment that many ladies were in the waiting room to receive chemotherapy. When I saw this, I thought to myself, "Not me. I am just going to have radiation. I'll just read my book because I am not as sick as they are."

The Lord spoke to me that night as I was doing my devotion and led me to the above scripture. I was reminded by Him that this was not about me but what Christ could do through me for His glory; therefore, on my next visit I began to pray silently for each woman in that room. I also prayed for the radiation personnel as they ministered to me. As time progressed through the daily treatments and meetings, we all connected and began to share our personal stories. It was during one of our "story-telling times," that I confessed my selfishness and arrogance and shared what I had learned through my Bible study – *that we are all wonderfully made in His image and that in all things, through supplication with thanksgiving, we will find that He will give us a peace that passes all understanding.*

PRAYER TARGET:
People experiencing cancer and its treatment.

PERSONAL PRAYER FOR KNOXVILLE:
Precious Jesus, thank You for the enormous blessings that You send my way. Thank You for the opportunity to serve others in Your Name. For those in our city who are suffering with cancer, be with them and give them comfort and peace during this battle. Be with them on their journey, and where it is Your will, bring about healing to their bodies. Touch also their families and give them peace. Father, I pray for all cancer patients that are awaiting results. Give them comfort and strength. For the patients who are having procedures, place Your Hand on them. Give wisdom and caring to the doctors and health professionals as they work with each patient. Lord, You are the great Healer. Wrap each person in Your loving arms and draw them close to You. Amen.

WEEK FORTY NINE: TUESDAY

AUTHOR: LINDA CAMPBELL
FAMILY STRUCTURE: WIDOWED
OCCUPATION: RETIRED

RESPECT

"Rise in the presence of the aged, show respect for the elderly and revere your God. I am the Lord." Leviticus 19:32

The word respect is defined as *a feeling of deep admiration for someone or something elicited by their abilities, qualities, or achievements.*

I had many lessons on respect while I was growing up, but I always go back to my earliest memory. At the age of five years I had a lesson on respect that formed a life-long foundation for me on the subject. It was Christmas time and my mother had given me one dollar for shopping (this was when one could purchase a small gift for twenty-five cents!). I'm sure that I mentioned purchasing something for myself, but my mother quickly told me I had to buy something for "Grandma" first. Grandma was eighty years old and my only living grandparent. This was just the beginning of my parents teaching me to respect people, property, and most of all God.

PRAYER TARGET:
Young parents teaching respect to their families.

PERSONAL PRAYER FOR KNOXVILLE:
Father, teach us all to have respect for one another to the degree that property will be protected, violence will be eliminated, illegal use of drugs disappears, and gangs are no longer in existence. In the Bible, Father, You tell us to love the family, be humble, not be selfish, to show integrity, and set a good

example. Help each of us to examine our lives and see if we are following Your guidelines, and passing the lessons on to others. Keep Your Biblical lessons before us always and gently tap us on the shoulder to remind us through Your Spirit to obey and respect. In Your Name. Amen.

WEEK FORTY NINE: WEDNESDAY

AUTHOR: LISA CATE
FAMILY STRUCTURE: HUSBAND AND 1 TEENAGE SON
OCCUPATION: PROPERTY LESSOR

A MOTHER'S FIGHT

"Finally, brothers and sisters, draw your strength and might from God. Put on the full armor of God to protect yourselves from the devil and his evil schemes. We're not waging war against enemies of flesh and blood alone. No, this fight is against tyrants, against authorities, against supernatural powers and demon princes that slither in the darkness of this world, and against wicked spiritual armies that lurk about in heavenly places." Ephesians 6:10-12
"Jesus said, 'Father, forgive them, for they do not know what they are doing.'" Luke 23:34

Mess with my son and prepare to hear this mama bear roar. Our son is a beautiful brown-skinned teen we adore. We experienced the hurt of our lives recently when we learned that several kids were racially bullying him. Our reaction was immediate: first - get it stopped. Next - seek justice. That this could happen at all was a slap in the face. There was no sense of remorse by the perpetrators. That was a second slap in the face. The third slap occurred when there was no compassion from their authority figure when confronted with the issue. Our son isn't the first, nor will he be the last, to endure the pain of racism or bullying. Searching the Word, receiving wise counsel, and prayer have helped us understand two crucial things I hope will *help* you.

    • Understand that when our enemy, Satan, uses people to tear us down, our battle is not really with those people. It is with him.

    • Second, a wise man reminded us of Jesus' words on the cross: "Father, forgive them, for they do not know what they are doing."

87

And there it is. If we are truly followers of the Lord Jesus, we must forgive. And forgive. And forgive.

PRAYER TARGET:
Parents of children who are victims of racism or bullying.

PERSONAL PRAYER FOR KNOXVILLE:
Father in Heaven, thank You for letting us sit at Your feet. We can only enter Your holy presence because of the grace and mercy shown to us through Jesus. Father, You are all knowing, all powerful, and all sufficient. We praise You, our most holy and perfect King.

We confess our own inadequacies as parents. We don't always respond as we should. Father, please help us overcome our heartbreak, anger, evil thoughts. Lord, please remind us who our real enemy is, and help us remember that vengeance is Yours, Lord, not ours. You understand our sorrow for our children better than anyone, Father. We need look only to the cross to know that. And yet You forgave then and You forgive now. And so, Father, we ask You to help us forgive those who have hurt our children. Help us to pray for their repentance and salvation, even as we pray for our own children's healing. And Father, we pray that our children may be overcomers, indeed, in the Name of our Lord Jesus Christ. Amen.

WEEK FORTY NINE: THURSDAY

AUTHOR: PAUL HARRIS
FAMILY STRUCTURE: WIFE, 2 ADULT CHILDREN, AND 3 GRANDCHILDREN
OCCUPATION: TECHNICAL SALES SUPPORT

THE BEST THING ABOUT TODAY

"But in those days, after that tribulation, the sun will be darkened, and the moon will not give its light, and the stars will be falling from heaven, and the powers in the heavens will be shaken. And then they will see the Son of Man coming in clouds with great power and glory. And then he will send out the angels and gather his elect from the four winds, from the ends of the earth to the ends of heaven. From the fig tree learn its lesson: as soon as its branch becomes tender and puts out its leaves, you know that summer is near. So also, when you see these things taking place, you know that he is near, at the very gates. Truly, I say to you, this generation will not pass away until all these things take place. Heaven and earth will pass away, but my words will not pass away. But concerning that day or that hour, no one knows, not even the angels in heaven, nor the Son, but only the Father." Mark 13:24-32

Some days at first light are, well, just not stellar. It can be tough for me to drag those feet over the side of the bed to let gravity drag them to the cold hard floor so that I can hit the ground running, let alone crawl to the shower. Sometimes it's the memory of past disappointments and failures. Or maybe it's the dread of what could possibly go wrong in the next sixteen to eighteen hours of wakefulness. I often think, is there not something that I can mentally run to every morning that can make every day something to be savored and anticipated with glee?

I'm not guaranteed tomorrow and thank God I'm not destined to plod through this life forever! I've been promised an eternity in the presence of my heavenly Father. It's going to be glorious and it's going to come at some finite point in time. The best part is, it's going to come a day sooner today than it was going to come yesterday. Yes, I'm closer to eternity today than I've ever been before! Bring on today so that I can wake up tomorrow, should He tarry, one day closer to experiencing His glory than I was yesterday.

PRAYER TARGET:

Those anxious about the future.

PERSONAL PRAYER FOR KNOXVILLE:

Dear Father, may every person in this city wake up in hopeful anticipation of the coming Savior. Even in the midst of hurt, disappointments, and anxiety, my prayer to You, God, is to daily make us aware of Your sovereignty and the majesty of Your glory. Constantly remind us, Lord, that salvation is made available to us through the blood shed on our behalf by Your Son, Jesus the Christ. Amen.

WEEK FORTY NINE: FRIDAY

AUTHOR: DARYL ARNOLD
FAMILY STRUCTURE: WIFE AND 4 CHILDREN
OCCUPATION: PASTOR

BEAUTY OUT OF BROKENNESS

"For you created my inmost being; you knit me together in my mother's womb. I praise you because I am fearfully and wonderfully made; your works are wonderful, I know that full well. My frame was not hidden from you when I was made in the secret place, when I was woven together in the depths of the earth." Psalm 139:13-15

The Lord has given me the ability to minister to His people all over the World, from the mountains of Lebanon to the dry lands of Nigeria. But one of the greatest opportunities that I have had was to minster on reconciliation at the St. Patrick's Day Prayer Breakfast in Ireland. The beauty and grandeur of the country is absolutely breathtaking.

My host family took me to see the St. Patrick's Cathedral. It was the most gorgeous and awe provoking places of worship that I had ever seen. The ancient stone, the imported marble, the hand-carved pews and the oil portraits were almost too much to comprehend at one time. The most significant and valuable furnishing, however, in the entire edifice was by far the stained glass windows. The guide told us that the windows were worth multiples of millions of dollars. What I thought was amazing was not just the price of the windows but the process that was used to make them. You see, stained glass windows start out as simple slabs of ordinary, inexpensive pieces of glass. They are then broken into many different pieces, stained and covered with different colors, and then randomly, yet thoughtfully, put back together by the Master Glazier. Finally, they are hung in the direction of the sun so that the *light* might reveal the beauty of its process.

What a wonderful expression of the handy work of God concerning His children! He finds us broken and shattered by the weight of this World, yet He refuses to discard us and throw us away. Instead, He picks us up one piece at a time, puts us back together again, and stains us with the blood of His Son. But that's not all! He shines the *light* of His Word through us so the all might see how He can produce *beauty* out of *brokenness.* Today, my challenge is for you to see yourself out of the eyes of the Father and not out the eyes of people, and view your current problems or those passed in the same way. You are fearfully and wonderfully made by your God.

PRAYER TARGET:
Those learning about their identity in Christ.

PERSONAL PRAYER FOR KNOXVILLE:
Father, in the Name of Jesus, we praise You for making us in Your own image. We bless You for taking all of our insecurities, our low self-esteem and inadequacies, and making something great out of them. Thank You for not abandoning us when we failed You and not forsaking us when we forsook You. Help us to stand in Kingdom confidence as we walk out our callings in the Earth. Remind us that we are Overcomers by the Blood of the Lamb and by the Word of our testimony. In Jesus' Name, Amen.

WEEK FIFTY: MONDAY

AUTHOR: CHRISTI WATSON
FAMILY STRUCTURE: HUSBAND AND 2 CHILDREN
OCCUPATION: DIRECTOR OF THEATRE ARTS

AVOIDING THE POISON OF CYNICISM

**"Do everything without grumbling or arguing, so that you may become blameless and pure, children of God without fault in a warped and crooked generation. Then you will shine among them like stars in the sky as you hold firmly to the word of life. And then I will be able to boast on the day of Christ that I did not run or labor in vain."
Philippians 2: 14-16**

Giving into cynicism is a colossal relief, like allowing sleep to take over when you are freezing to death; but, to accept this relief is to trade a beating heart for a bitter one. Before you know it, the enemy has incapacitated you by tainting everything in your life with the flavor of sour hope and self-pity. Here is how God's sprit has taught me to proceed when cynicism sneaks up.

    1. *Don't be naive.* God isn't. The Creator of the universe thoughtfully crafted Adam and Eve, offered them everything except what would destroy them, then watched as they chose destruction. If Adam and Eve in Eden couldn't manage to walk with God 100% of the time, no one can. Do not expect people, even God's people, to keep it together.

    2. *Don't be a Pharisee.* Ironically, cynicism makes you a pharisee, believing that you are above the faults of "those people." When we think that way we are missing the many ways we must grow in order to be most useful to God.

    3. *Be the change.* We don't have time to be cynical when we can be the change that someone's soul is counting on.

PRAYER TARGET:
Those dealing with disappointment.

PERSONAL PRAYER FOR KNOXVILLE:
Dear Father, I pray that those who have been hurt and disappointed by the church would not give in to cynicism but that they would choose forgiveness. I pray that You would empower them to "do everything without grumbling or arguing (cynicism)" so that they may "shine like stars in the universe." May they not abandon Your Church but be the change the Church needs. Amen.

WEEK FIFTY: TUESDAY

AUTHOR: JEAN JEFFORDS
FAMILY STRUCTURE: HUSBAND, 2 SONS, ONE DAUGHTER-IN-LAW,
3 GRANDCHILDREN
OCCUPATION: HOMEMAKER AND STEPHEN MINISTRY LEADER

THE TREASURE

"Trust in the Lord forever for in God the Lord, we have an everlasting Rock." Isaiah 26:4

Christmas! Oh, what special childhood memories! After decorating our twelve-foot tree and wrapping gifts, I remember desperately trying to catch a glimpse of that " treasure" inside. Surely Christmas could only mean joy!

Of course, over time, I realized that life was not pain- free. Even during a time when I was extremely close to God and involved in ministry, I experienced a horrible crisis! The future looked bleak, and Christmastime was hardly joyful! How could this be? I came to realize that it was not God's fault but sin in this world. By His grace, and over time, I could move forward and set new goals- and let God use past hurts to strengthen and encourage others. Jeremiah 31:3 became one of my favorite promises. *"I have loved you with an everlasting love; therefore, I will continue My faithfulness to you."* I learned that the process of wholeness could not take place without brokenness. During my darkest times, I began catching a glimpse of the real "Treasure" in a deeper way. That "Treasure" continues to become more visible every year as I get to know Him better.

Glory to God in the highest for His Son, Jesus Christ- the true Treasure for everlasting life!

PRAYER TARGET:
Single mothers struggling with finding true treasure in His plan.

PERSONAL PRAYER FOR KNOXVILLE:
Dear Lord Jesus, thank you that You and only You are our Rock! Thank you that You are the same yesterday, today, and forever! Lord, we need You desperately, and thank you that You always have open arms. I lift the many single moms in this city and ask you to give them grace everyday as they care for their children and carry many responsibilities. Give them wisdom, strength, and endurance! Father, for those moms who do not know you personally, bring them to salvation so that they can live with you in eternity. Thank you, Lord, that You are our hope! In Jesus' holy name, Amen.

WEEK FIFTY: WEDNESDAY

AUTHOR: JAMIE DEWALD
FAMILY STRUCTURE: WIFE AND 2 BOYS
OCCUPATION: MINISTER AND ENTREPRENEUR

FROM DIFFICULTY TO CONTENTMENT

> "I am not saying this because I am in need, for I have learned to be content whatever the circumstances. I know what it is to be in need, and I know what it is to have plenty. I have learned the secret of being content in any and every situation, whether well fed or hungry, whether living in plenty or in want." Philippians 4:11-12

When was the last time you dealt with something that truly rocked you to your core? Are you going through a difficult situation now? I am. The last several years have been simultaneously the best and most painful years of my life. But God is good!

I have personally had over 60 staph infections in the last six years, which have destroyed my immune system and harmed my body in more ways than I can explain. Intense pain! Countless doctors have told us, "We just don't know." But I always say, "I'm so blessed."

Just like Paul said in this passage, during this difficult time in my life God has shown me "the secret of being content." When I wanted to complain, he gave me this formula, and used it to change my life: PERSPECTIVE + GRATITUDE = CONTENTMENT

God has taught me that a proper perspective can illuminate my life and change my attitude. As tragic as my journey has been, my father has reminded me that so many have it much worse. He has also blessed me with a grateful heart. I can literally choose to be grateful, and no one can stop me! It's easy to complain, but it sure is more fun to be grateful. "Thank You, God, for teaching me how to be content, even during difficult times."

PRAYER TARGET:
God's beloved children who are living in difficult times.

PERSONAL PRAYER FOR KNOXVILLE:
Father, I pray that Christians will learn the true secret of biblical contentment. It is not found in a paycheck, the perfect soul mate, having a nice home, or in perfect health. I pray that Jesus followers will understand that a blessed life, a content life, is Your desire for us all. I also pray that we will accept that You, God, may choose to allow difficulties into our lives for a season. Help us to remember that Paul learned the "secret of being content in any and every situation." God, give us a proper perspective when our hearts become selfish. Remind us how blessed we truly are. Father, show us how to live in a constant state of gratitude, rather than complain. I pray, Lord Jesus, that You will teach your humble children the true secret of being content. Amen

WEEK FIFTY: THURSDAY

AUTHOR: JAY SMITH
FAMILY STRUCTURE: WIFE AND 2 CHILDREN
OCCUPATION: PASTOR

YOUR WILL BE DONE

> **"Father, if you are willing, take this cup from me; yet not my will, but yours be done." Luke 22:42**

Have you yet come to a place in life where you are satisfied? Maybe you worked really hard to achieve a life goal, or you finally got that promotion or position that you always longed for. I have finally begun to understand the depth of Jesus' confession as He sees the cross in His coming future. This isn't something He desires and He makes that known to His father in prayer. The thing I never considered was the years of hard work and teaching that Jesus did before the cross.

Have you thought of the countless hours of hard work, crazy encounters, interesting characters, and emotional energy Jesus poured out daily? He had thousands of people following Him each day and then He had to face a cross?! Many of us would just stop at the stardom and live out the rest of our days as a "success." Our human view of success, however, is sometimes very different than God's.

I have reached a place in life where I am comfortable. I am satisfied, yet I must guard against the one great temptation every comfortable person faces. It is hard to stay comfortable; therefore, staying comfortable is something I must work on daily. Have you ever got to the place where you aren't striving to move ahead but protecting your turf of the moment? We often protect the ground we've gained and then find ourselves doing things and saying things that we never would have imagined - all in an effort to stay comfortable and keep our coveted position.

Study the life of Jesus and you will find that His life was never about Him and His position. He came in the form of a servant and didn't see His equality with God a thing to be grasped. He counted himself below others and ultimately gave up his life to reveal the Glory of God.

Friend, this is the life that He has chosen for His followers. You may be seeing a cross, but God sees the salvation of the world. You may be seeing comfort, but God may see a snare. Today instead of analyzing your circumstances will you consider trusting the Lord Jesus for the fullest life as you follow Him and invite His will and direction into your life? There is no longer a need to live according to your own passions and will but in total surrender to the God who is worthy of your trust and affection.

PRAYER TARGET:
Positional leaders that might be too comfortable in their own setting to seek His will.

PERSONAL PRAYER FOR KNOXVILLE:
Father, I pray that we as a city would see You clearer. Help us not just know about Your character but help us learn to trust Your character. I pray that we would trust You foolishly and obey You with the heart of a child. Lord, we have our ideas and schemes but we ask not our will be done, but Yours. Amen.

WEEK FIFTY: FRIDAY

AUTHOR: SHERI HARRIS
FAMILY STRUCTURE: HUSBAND, 2 ADULT CHILDREN, AND 3 GRANDCHILDREN
OCCUPATION: HOMEMAKER AND GRANDMA

SEASONS

> **"You are the light of the world. A town built on a hill cannot be hidden. Neither do people light a lamp and put it under a bowl. Instead they put it on its stand, and it gives light to everyone in the house. In the same way, let your light shine before others, that they may see your good deeds and glorify your Father in heaven." Matthew 5:14-16**

Two years ago we moved my husband's mother here from South Carolina and my parents here from Chicago. They all are well into their 80's in age and need some of the assistance available from being near immediate family. This was something they didn't have before coming here. My husband and I have not lived closer than several hours from any of our extended family since we got married, so we are now experiencing yet another new season in our lives.

I have watched with joy as my mother-in-law is excited about her new local church. Both of my parents have made so many new friends at our church, even though my mom can barely hear and my dad can barely stand. Dad has taken time to meet each of our pastoral staff for lunch and probably knows most of them better than I do. They both make an effort to connect with as many new friends as possible every Sunday with a warm handshake and a cheerful word, although health issues continue to make it a challenge to even attend most weeks.

Wow! Who is helping whom here? What an inspiration they are to me, the supposed helper. I pray that I can touch as many lives for the cause of Christ as they do! Yes, this is a difficult season as we are becoming more aware of the issues that accompany declining health of those we love. But what a privilege it is to be a participant with them during this season as they continue to shine their light in a world of darkness in spite of the challenges. May this be a worthy example for all of us to follow.

PRAYER TARGET:
All those encountering new and challenging seasons in their own life.

PERSONAL PRAYER FOR KNOXVILLE:
Father, I pray that people challenged with the experiences of a new season will find comfort, strength, and peace that can only come from You, our Heavenly Father. May they find love and compassion during this time from those around them. May they be thankful for yet another new season in their lives, not only reliving the old stories of past seasons, but also in prospering in His-story that they are now living in these latter years of life. Amen.

WEEK FIFTY ONE: MONDAY

AUTHOR: CANDY LETT
FAMILY STRUCTURE: HUSBAND, 2 ADULT CHILDREN, AND 1 GRANDDAUGHTER
OCCUPATION: RETIRED SCHOOL ADMINISTRATOR

FINISH WELL

> **"For my thoughts are not your thoughts, neither are your ways my ways, declares the Lord. For as the heavens are higher than the earth, so are my ways higher than your ways and my thoughts than your thoughts." Isaiah 55:8-9**

Did you look forward to retirement and then realize that perhaps you no longer could find purpose in life? After forty-one years of service in public education, I retired and quickly realized that my identity was not in Christ, but in my job and in the position I had held for so many years. How was I to spend the remaining years? The Holy Spirit spoke to me through the Word and reminded me that Moses began his best years at age 80, and died at 120. Now that I was free of the daily responsibilities of my vocation, I was free to serve God in a better, yet different way.

Perhaps as seniors our greatest gift to God might be our availability. These years can be a new and wonderful life filled with opportunities and perhaps even the most fruitful of our days with Christ. Allow Him to speak to you and direct your thoughts and your ways. Serve Him with joy and expectation.

PRAYER TARGET:
Senior Citizens retired or nearing retirement.

PERSONAL PRAYER FOR KNOXVILLE:
Father, thank You for Your unending grace and the blessings You pour out upon me every day. Thank You for the gift of life and for a healthy body and a sound mind. Thank You for the

knowledge and experiences of life. Draw me near to You in this season of life and allow me to serve You in a new way, seeking Your kingdom first, rather than squandering my time and my energy on the affairs of the world. Allow me to finish well so that one day I will hear those words, "Well done, thy good and faithful servant."

WEEK FIFTY ONE: TUESDAY

AUTHOR: HOLLI MCCRAY
FAMILY STRUCTURE: HUSBAND AND 1 SON
OCCUPATION: CEO

LOVE LIKE CHRIST

"A new command I give you: Love one another. As I have loved you, so you must love one another." John 13:34

This one is easy, right? Love one another. How hard can it be? Let's face it, it's tough sometimes to love everyone. We don't even know some people we are called to love and if I'm being honest, there are some that we simply don't like! What are we supposed to do with that? How about the people who aren't like us? What about the people who we don't understand? What about the ones who disappoint us and hurt us? What if we don't have feelings of love for someone anymore?

From my experience, it's easier to walk away than it is to stay, listen, learn, and love. It's scary to love like that! It's hard to put yourself out there, open up, and take the risk of rejection and failure. It's so much easier to put that in our rearview mirror and surround ourselves with others like us and stay in our comfort zone; however, Christ didn't call us to our comfort zones! He called us to love one another without arrogance and judgement; always seeking the greatest benefit for the one loved. Alone, set apart from God, this is a monumental, nearly impossible task. Through Christ, however, we are equipped to make the choice to love. Love is not an emotion; it's a decision. I thank God that He made the choice to love me! I choose to learn, grow, and fail forward every day as I make the journey to learn to love like Christ.

PRAYER TARGET:

Those seeking to really understand what it is like to love like Christ.

PERSONAL PRAYER FOR KNOXVILLE:

Lord, let us love each other like You love us. Teach us to seek You first and let our thoughts, our words and our actions toward one another be Yours. Let us not live out our human actions and reactions toward each other; but Yours Lord. Amen.

WEEK FIFTY ONE: WEDNESDAY

AUTHOR: JENNIFER HINTON
FAMILY STRUCTURE: HUSBAND, 3 CHILDREN, AND DISABLED MOTHER
OCCUPATION: HOMEMAKER AND PERSONAL TRAINER

GIVING UP DAILY

"For, who has known the mind of the Lord as to instruct him? But we have the mind of Christ." 1 Corinthians 2:16

Each day is a blank canvas to surrender your heart, mind, and spirit and to release them to Jesus. After this choice and action, *"Let the peace of Christ rule in your hearts."* (Colossians 3:15.) Give Him the reigns; give Him control. He has the best plan for the day, the best mindset for your circumstances and relationships, and the best responses to situations and conversations with other people. The scripture above says, "For, who has known the mind of the Lord as to instruct him? But we have the mind of Christ." Philippians 2:5 says, "Let this mind be in you, which was also in Christ Jesus." The word "let" indicates that having the mind of Christ partly comes through an act of your will. Use your will to make a choice to let Jesus give you His thoughts, attitudes, and words. His grace drips down saturating us when we choose Him, His totality over ourselves, and what we want. Surrender brings a sense of freedom and empowerment to experience peace, joy, and confidence in being His child and His instrument here on earth.

"Be filled with the Spirit." (Ephesians 5:18) This is a constant state of action that can either be released or squelched by you. Be aware of the enemy's lies and thoughts he sends to your mind to entice you away from the mind of Christ. Arrest thoughts and examine them to ask yourself if they are from the Holy Spirit or from Satan. When you surrender, the enemy will fight you. Satan knows he is defeated and that the power of God will operate in your life bringing victory and His accomplished work when you choose to let Jesus be in control of your being.

Surrender involves your will-power to do it and then your choice to trust God to honor your surrender and work through it. Trusting God involves faith; you can't see God, and He doesn't give us tangible written signs. The more you surrender, the more you will experience hearing from Him and following His voice.

PRAYER TARGET:
Individual believers who long to surrender to Him but don't know how.

PERSONAL PRAYER FOR KNOXVILLE:
Dear Heavenly Father, thank You for letting me wake up this morning and giving me another day to live. I ask that You help me to allow You to live in me through the Holy Spirit and control me today. I want to yield to Your ways and words today. Please help me do this in my private thought life and in my communication with others. I give You complete control and praise You for residing in me. I surrender and give up. In Jesus' Name. Amen.

WEEK FIFTY ONE: THURSDAY

AUTHOR: COURTNEY COCKE
FAMILY STRUCTURE: HUSBAND
OCCUPATION: REGISTERED NURSE

SUNRISE WITH THE SAVIOR

"Be still and know that I am God: I will be exalted among the nations, I will be exalted in the earth." Psalm 46:10

It was sunrise one early March morning: I found myself perched by the back window in my favorite chair pouring out my heart to God. I begged Him to speak to me in a way that I could understand.

I had been struggling with an inner darkness and a constant unhappiness deep within my soul. I was feeling stuck in a career that was draining me and draining my marriage and I knew I was drowning. Just as I began to weep, the sun stretched its rays out over the ridge just as a loving parent stretches out their arms when reaching for their beloved child. My mind grew still and calmness imbued my bones.

As I looked out the window, I noticed that the night's freeze was beginning to melt. My eyes were drawn to the droplets of water that jumped from my tin roof. The sun illuminated each drop transforming them into dripping prisms of glowing light. It was as if the light embodied the drops so they could permeate the earth and carry light unto darkness.

He wants us to be still and to listen and to know that He is in control of this life. There is hope in this loving light, and we must let it shine into darkness.

PRAYER TARGET:

Everyone, but especially young women who may be struggling with depression and darkness in their lives.

PERSONAL PRAYER FOR KNOXVILLE:

Father, I pray for every heart out there that struggles to find their place and stand their ground as society tries to redefine values and redefine strength. Help us to unplug from the constant chaos and distractions so that we may be still and hear You when You are speaking. Lord, I pray for You to arm Your children with spiritual discernment so that we do not bend with the winds of change. May You open our eyes to the "signs and wonders" and reveal them to us in a way we can understand. But above all, fill the people of East Tennessee with Your light and Your love so we may spread the hope of Your message in dark times. Amen.

WEEK FIFTY ONE: FRIDAY

AUTHOR: KIMBERLY SHUN WATKINS
FAMILY STRUCTURE: HUSBAND AND 1 CHILD
OCCUPATION: EXECUTIVE PASTOR

BORN FOR ADVERSITY, DESTINED TO WIN

"So do not throw away this confident trust in the Lord. Remember the great reward it brings you! Patient endurance is what you need now, so that you will continue to do God's will. Then you will receive all that he has promised." Hebrews 10:35-36

Have you ever just wanted to check out of life? Does life sometimes seem so overwhelming, you don't think you can finish your course? Do you ever wonder what your purpose on this earth is or if you even have one? David lived a life on the run for years because of King Saul's jealousy of him, his leadership, and the anointing on his life. During the time Saul was trying to kill him, David had faith that God would protect Him. Later, when David committed adultery, he asked for God's forgiveness. Anytime David sinned or someone sinned against him, he always went back to God and repented. No matter what trial he faced, he always trusted God. No matter the difficulty, David never gave up on God and God never gave up on him. No matter what David faced, he never quit God. No matter what David came against or what came against him, David never disowned God. When David got consumed or began to feel overwhelmed, he relied on his relationship with the Lord and found strength in God (1 Samuel 30:6). David's faith never wavered.

When everything else fails, and at some point in time it will, you too can find strength in the Lord. David is known today for his defeat of Goliath and later liberating an entire nation, Israel, from the Philistines. None of David's battles were his alone and none of them benefited just him. Please know that whatever you're facing today, whatever your Goliath is right now, whatever your battle is in this season, it is not yours alone and victory is yours if you don't give up. *"And let us not be weary in well doing: for in due season we shall reap, if we faint not"*(Galatians 6:9). Know that your victory has the potential to liberate an entire nation. How you handle your battle will determine how someone else conquers their battle. Stay on course. Finish your race. This battle is not yours, it belongs to God and He has already won it for you. (2 Chron. 20:15)

PRAYER TARGET:
Those who are contemplating giving up.

PERSONAL PRAYER FOR KNOXVILLE:
Father, I pray for those who feel hopeless and are in despair at this very moment. I pray that You would remind us that You love us and that You would never leave us or forsake us. Remind us that if You be for us, You're more than the whole world against us. Your Word says in times of trouble, You'll hide us. When we're feeling overwhelmed, lead us to the rock that is higher than us. Thank You, Lord for removing frustration, chaos, and distress and replacing it with Your peace that surpasses all understanding and an unspeakable joy that can only come from You. When everything around us seems to be going awry, step in and be our refuge and our strength. Help us to keep our minds stayed on You, as You've promised to keep us in perfect peace. Thank You for loving us with such an unfailing and undeniable love. Thank You, Lord, that even when the world calls us failures and misfits, You call us Your masterpiece. You see us as little pieces of You, the Master. Thank You, Lord, for increasing our faith as we continue the journey to be who You have called us to be. Thank You, Lord, for creating us to win. In Jesus' Name. Amen.

WEEK FIFTY TWO: MONDAY

AUTHOR: GERALD VANDERFORD
FAMILY STRUCTURE: WIFE AND 8 CHILDREN
OCCUPATION: MISSIONARY

FAITHFUL IN THE LITTLE THINGS

"He that is faithful in that which is least is faithful also in much: and he that is unjust in the least is unjust also in much." Luke 16:10

Faithfulness in the little things leads to faithfulness in the big things. Look at 1 Samuel 16 and 17. When Samuel came looking for the next king David was out tending the sheep. On the day that David faced Goliath he was just doing what his daddy asked him to do; running an errand to deliver some supplies and check on his brothers. When he arrived, there was a giant nobody wanted to face! David recounted to Saul about the lion and the bear proclaiming this giant would *"be as one of them, seeing he has defied the armies of the living God."* David did not just get up one morning and decide to go sign up for "giant duty." He was faithful in the little things long before he faced Goliath. On that day when the soldiers were all looking at each other and saying "not me!" (v11 and 24), David ran to the battle (v.48).

If I am faithful in the little things then when the giants of life come calling (could be giant threats or giant opportunities!) I can stand with confidence like David and say, *"This day, the Lord will deliver thee into my hand."* What are the little things in my life in which I need to be more faithful?

PRAYER TARGET:
All believers to seek faithfulness in all things, not just the big things.

PERSONAL PRAYER FOR KNOXVILLE:

Father, I ask that You would show us those areas of our lives where You want us to be faithful in the routine, in the mundane, in the chores, or in the little things that we do each day. Father, build our faith muscles through repetition in the little things so that when the giants of life come calling we will not look at each other and say, "Not me!" In confidence, Father, help us stand in faith and say, "This day, You, Lord, will deliver thee into my hand." May we all be prepared to take on the giant threats and opportunities that come along in life as we walk in faithfulness each and every day. Father, I ask in the precious Name of our Lord and Savior Jesus Christ, not from habit but for Your Kingdom. Amen.

WEEK FIFTY TWO: TUESDAY

AUTHOR: AIMEE COSEY
FAMILY STRUCTURE: HUSBAND AND 3 CHILDREN
OCCUPATION: STAY-AT-HOME MOTHER

GO AGAINST THE GRAIN SPIRITUALLY

"And be not conformed to this world: but be ye transformed by the renewing of your mind, that ye may prove what is that good, and acceptable, and perfect, will of God." Romans 12:2 "The Everlasting God, the Lord, the Creator of the ends of the earth. Does not become weary or tired. His understanding is inscrutable. He gives strength to the weary, and to him who lacks might, He increases power. Though the youths grow weary and tired, and vigorous young men stumble badly, Yet those who wait for the Lord will gain new strength; They will mount up with wings like eagles, They will run and not get tired, they will walk and not become weary." Isaiah 40:28-31

Let's inspire love and the Godly revitalization of people. How can we be of the world and the Lord Jesus Christ? The world is not asking what it can do to help bring people into the Kingdom of God...it wants to pacify everyone and make everyone feel like they belong; but we belong to heaven, so we cannot ever truly belong here. This worldly process is gaining momentum, and resulting in some people looking for religious congregations that point to their own way. If we are not in a relationship with Jesus that steps on our toes, then we may be on our way down the wrong path, not the heavenly path. If the place we worship does not push us into a deeper relationship with God and His son Jesus, we are in real trouble! If we all keep doing less and less than our parents and grandparents did in spiritual growth, then what are our grandchildren and great-grandchildren going to do and say about following a righteous path?

PRAYER TARGET:
Moms, dads, grandparents, and all fishers of men.

PERSONAL PRAYER FOR KNOXVILLE:
Lord, I pray that the body of Christ will not want to belong to this world. Help us want to follow the only holy, righteous, non-worldly, non-denominational, diverse people loving, perfect Messiah that ever was, will be, and can be. As trials come, let us know that the only way to survive the trials is to turn to the You, the Savior, to heal us and bring us into eternal life with You. Lord, help us grow in You boldly and uncomfortably. Amen.

AUTHOR: PATRICIA CAPPELLO
FAMILY STRUCTURE: SINGLE
OCCUPATION: RETIRED

DO NOT WORRY

"Do not be anxious about anything, but in everything by prayer and supplication with thanksgiving let your requests be made to God, and the peace of God, which surpasses all understanding, will guard your hearts and your minds in Christ Jesus." Philippians 4:6-8

Worry and worship do not go hand in hand. You cannot worry about the problem and God is not a worrier. He takes action! Either you worry, and forfeit His peace in the process, or give it to Him to handle. When you do that you will be left free to relax in His strong arms.

Make a list of your worries and anxieties and turn them into your prayer list. So many times we pray and then we pick the burden right back up. Learning to pray and leave the burden at the cross gives one a peace in their heart. Joy will come from letting go and trusting God.

Let's keep our hearts and minds focused on Christ so no circumstance will shatter us ! Rejoice in God's will and trust in God's peace.

PRAYER TARGET:
Women who need to lay down the burden of worry and anxiety.

PERSONAL PRAYER FOR KNOXVILLE:
Father God, help each one come to You with his or her worries and anxieties. No matter their personal circumstances – worry

for our country or fear of life in general – help us all to stop and pray. Father, help us trust in Your promised Word and lay all problems at the cross for You to bear. Give each of us the peace and joy that comes from putting our trust in You. I pray for everyone in our city and country to turn their hearts to You. Help us be one nation under You, God. Give us revival. I thank You, Father, for America and the freedom we each have to worship You in this country. May You continue to bless each of us and help us be a light for You as we walk daily in Your love. Amen.

WEEK FIFTY TWO: THURSDAY

AUTHOR: DAWN WILSON
FAMILY STRUCTURE: HUSBAND AND 2 CHILDREN
OCCUPATION: CO-OWNER AND SHOPKEEPER

CHOOSING JOY NO MATTER WHAT

> **"You make known to me the path of life; in your presence, there is fullness of joy; at your right hand are pleasures forevermore." Psalm 16:11**

It seems like the phrase "choose joy" has become a common saying lately, but this little phrase has literally shaped my life over the last several years. God first gave me these two words during an extremely heartbreaking time in the life of our family. It was a time where I did not want to choose joy, but it was my only hope in a very dark season.

For me, choosing joy means having an unbreakable spirit because of who Jesus is. He is our hope. He is our joy. He leads us to deepen our trust and faith in him through big and small daily circumstances. In the midst of our trials, hardships and crazy days, He is the peace that passes all understanding. (Phil. 4:6-9)

Every day you have a choice. You can either choose joy or not. God desires for you to live a life full of joy so that you can be light in the darkness for others who are desperately looking for something different. (Ephesians 5:8 and John 1:5) God is in the details and offers hope on hard days, you just have to look for it. A grateful heart leads to a joyful heart. Choose joy.

PRAYER TARGET:
Those that are in a dark season, seeking joy.

PERSONAL PRAYER FOR KNOXVILLE:

Lord, I pray that You will grip the heart of men and women in our city. May You teach us how to choose joy. Help us to be grateful for things that we often take for granted on a daily basis so that we can share our joy in the small things with others. God, change our hearts to be a heart after Yours. Change our minds so that we focus on what really matters. Give us the strength to dust ourselves off on hard days, to refocus on You, and to honor You with our lives. Help us to be light in the darkness, full of love for one another. You have called us out to proclaim Your excellencies. Give us the courage to do that, all the while choosing joy, so that we may draw others to You. In Jesus precious Name, Amen.

WEEK FIFTY TWO: FRIDAY

AUTHOR: MARCUS EAVES
FAMILY STRUCTURE: WIFE AND 1 CHILD
OCCUPATION: STUDENT PASTOR

REJOICING IN PERSECUTION

"Dear friends, do not be surprised at the fiery ordeal that has come on you to test you, as though something strange were happening to you. But rejoice inasmuch as you participate in the sufferings of Christ, so that you may be overjoyed when his glory is revealed. 14 If you are insulted because of the name of Christ, you are blessed, for the Spirit of glory and of God rests on you." 1 Peter 4:12-14

Being a Christian is not for the coward or the weak. Being a Christian is hard. Christianity is the most persecuted people group on the planet. In the United States, it is unlikely that a Christian will die for their faith, but there will be harassment if a believer is obedient to the life that God has designed for us to live. Being a Christian can result in losing friends, your job, being laughed at, or being called names. However, when suffering comes our way for being a Christian this should not surprise us. If the world hated Jesus then they will hate His followers.

I love that this verse tells us to "rejoice in as much as participate in the sufferings of Christ." We rejoice over so many things like when our football team wins a game or when a student makes an A on their hardest test. When we suffer for Christ we can rejoice because we are sharing in Christ's suffering. If you share your faith with someone in the park and they punch you in the face you can rejoice. I also love that this passage encourages us by letting us know if insults come our way for being a Christ follower, know that "you are blessed, for the Spirit of glory and of God rests on you."

PRAYER TARGET:
Obedient Christ followers who are being harassed for their faith.

PERSONAL PRAYER FOR KNOXVILLE:
Father, I pray that committed followers of Christ in this city will continue being bold and standing tall for their faith. Father, give us courage to live according to Your word and to be obedient to the life to which You have called us. Help remind us how foolish it is to fear man and how foolish the ways of man are. Help remind us of how good You are and how rich Your word is. Strengthen our ability to love those that persecute us as You have loved us. Amen.

PRAYKNOX

After this I looked, and behold, a great multitude that no one could number, from every nation, from all tribes and peoples and languages, standing before the throne and before the Lamb, clothed in white robes, with palm branches in their hands, and crying out with a loud voice, "Salvation belongs to our God who sits on the throne, and to the Lamb!" And all the angels were standing around the throne and around the elders and the four living creatures, and they fell on their faces before the throne and worshiped God, saying, "Amen! Blessing and glory and wisdom and thanksgiving and honor and power and might be to our God forever and ever! Amen."

Then I saw a new heaven and a new earth, for the first heaven and the first earth had passed away, and the sea was no more. And I saw the holy city, new Jerusalem, coming down out of heaven from God, prepared as a bride adorned for her husband. And I heard a loud voice from the throne saying, "Behold, the dwelling place of God is with man. He will dwell with them, and they will be his people, and God himself will be with them as their God. He will wipe away every tear from their eyes, and death shall be no more, neither shall there be mourning, nor crying, nor pain anymore, for the former things have passed away."

Now to him who is able to do far more abundantly than all that we ask or think, according to the power at work within us, to him be glory in the church and in Christ Jesus throughout all generations, forever and ever. Amen.

REVELATION 7:9-11, 21:1-4 | EPHESIANS 3:20-21

Made in the USA
Las Vegas, NV
28 January 2021

16697211R00292